DATE			
		APR 4 1990	

Personal Responsibility Counselling and Therapy:
An Integrative Approach

Richard Nelson-Jones received his M.A. and Ph.D. from Stanford University in California in 1964 and 1967, respectively. After working in New England and Canada he returned to Britain where, from 1970–82, he was Senior Lecturer in Counselling at the University of Aston in Birmingham as well as serving as a counselling psychologist in the University Health Service. After a short period as Director of the London Centre for Counselling Psychology he took up his present position as Senior Lecturer in Counselling Psychology at the Royal Melbourne Institute of Technology. He has published around 50 scientific and applied articles in British, American and Canadian journals. His books include *The Theory and Practice of Counselling Psychology (1982)* and *Practical Counselling Skills (1983)*. He is a Fellow of the British Psychological Society and was on its Governing council as well as the first Chairperson of its Counselling Psychology Section. He is also a member of the Australian Psychological Society.

Personal Responsibility Counselling and Therapy: An Integrative Approach

Richard Nelson-Jones

⊙ **HEMISPHERE PUBLISHING CORPORATION**
A subsidiary of Harper & Row, Publishers, Inc.

Cambridge   New York   Philadelphia   San Francisco   London
Mexico City   São Paulo   Singapore   Sydney   Washington

PERSONAL RESPONSIBILITY COUNSELLING AND THERAPY:
An Integrative Approach

1 2 3 4 5 6 7 8 9 0   H R U K   8 9 8 7

Library of Congress Cataloging in Publication Data

Nelson-Jones, Richard.
  Personal responsibility counselling and therapy.

  Reprint. Originally published: London ; Cambridge
[Mass.] : Harper & Row, 1984.
  Bibliography: p.
  Includes index.
  1. Counseling. 2. Psychotherapy. 3. Responsibility.
4. Happiness. I. Title. [DNLM: 1. Counseling.
2. Ethics. 3. Psychotherapy.   WM 420 N4282p 1984a]
BF637.C6N45   1987   158'.9   87-17722
ISBN 0-89116-777-3

A creative and exciting book. An important contribution to the theory and practice of psychotherapy. The author sets himself the difficult task of bridging the gap between awareness and action, between humanism and learning theory, between an existential-dynamic and a behavioral psychotherapy approach and, to his great credit, succeeds to an astonishing degree. One of those rare books which combines the clarity and technical expertise of the behaviorist with the intuition and wisdom of the humanist.

Irvin D. Yalom M.D.,
Professor of Psychiatry,
Stanford University School of Medicine,
California

To Australia, my new homeland

Foreword

Who is responsible for our personal welfare and happiness? What guidelines or values can we follow to insure our happiness? Traditional answers to these questions have been found wanting in this age of stark existential enlightenment. With the loss of external frameworks for giving life meaning and for providing patterns of 'correct' behavior, ach of us must look to ourselves and the reality of our own existence to find answers and guidance on how to make our life meaningful and fulfilling. Nelson-Jones has culled many psychological theories and philosophies that purport to provide answers about our basic nature, what happiness is and how it can be achieved, and has integrated the ideas into a framework of personal responsibility. Meaning and fulfillment in life are to be found in the acceptance of responsibility for oneself and the exercise of that responsibility in ways that enhance responsiveness, realism, relatedness, and rewarding activity, the 4 Rs of *Personal Responsibility Counselling and Therapy*. Nelson-Jones' book provides counselors and therapists with an internally consistent and comprehensive framework for helping essentially normal people achieve greater satisfaction and fulfillment in their lives. More than that, the book is a self-help manual intended to aid individuals to assume personal responsibility for finding meaning and fulfillment in their lives. Nelson-Jones' book reflects a dramatic change in how psychologists view people. After 80 years of assuming environmental determinism and focusing on unconscious and instinctual determinants of behavior, psychology is adopting a view of people as active agents who are potent causes and sources of events and who are personally responsible for their own actions. The search for laws of behavior modification and effective methods of changing people with psychological problems has focused on what to do *to* people to generate desired changes. Change has been the responsibility of the psychologist or therapist rather than of the person. In *Personal Responsibility Counselling and Therapy*, people are assumed to generate their own behavior and are seen as responsible for the quality of their own lives. Additionally, the book asserts that people are most happy and fulfilled when they actively, consciously, and with determination take that responsibility. In his review of psychological theories of help-giving, Nelson-Jones finds that, while many theories of counseling and psychotherapy do not talk explicitly about personal responsibility as the objective of counseling, all theories implicitly assume that the client is responsible for his or her own actions. He finds that each approach presents ways of enhancing the client's ability to function as a self-responsible agent. While not losing sight of personal responsibility, Nelson-Jones discusses how environmental conditions can restrain self-responsible actions, and how conditions of upbringing can diminish the person's ability and skill to assume self-reponsibility. Nelson-Jones presents a unique integration of psychological ideas around the notion of personal responsibility. He identifies the 4 Rs of personal responsibility, Responsiveness, Realism, Relatedness, and Rewarding Activity, and develops them into sets of psychological skills. He describes how counselors and therapists can foster these skills through a variety of affective, cognitive, and behavioral interventions. As is appropriate for a book on self-responsibility, Nelson-Jones emphasises self-help methods as much as methods to help another. The book is a valuable source of ideas for counselors, therapists, and all adults as we face the task of living responsibly.

Stanley R. Strong
Virginia Commonwealth University
Richmond
Virginia, U.S.A.

CONTENTS

PREFACE

The idea of developing a counselling approach using personal responsibility as a central integrating concept surfaced in 1975. I've wanted to write this book ever since. All counselling approaches are means to helping people stand on their own two feet and assume effective responsibility for their lives. Thus personal responsibility becomes an obvious integrating focus. Though the concept gets implicitly or explicitly emphasized in all existing theoretical positions, none has provided the deserved coverage. Focusing on personal responsibility is almost like focusing on one's nose. Though right in front of the face, the concept is not always easy to observe.

This book aims at integration in a number of ways. It rejects the narrow 'my theory right or wrong' approach to counselling. Theoretical concepts and practical interventions are derived from a number of different sources, including the research literature. The book does not take a one-dimensional approach to behaviour in emphasizing people's actions alone. Instead it takes a three-dimensional approach emphasizing feelings, thoughts and actions. Furthermore, the book is integrative in stressing not only people's relationship needs, but also their needs for occupational fulfilment. Additionally, training and self-therapy as well as counselling interventions get examined.

Sometimes it seems that psychology has developed back to front. Perhaps there has been too much emphasis on severe disturbance and insufficient on the needs and struggles of the majority. Much psychological theorizing and practice has developed from observing those whose psychological functioning was below rather than above average. This book has 'normal' functioning as its starting point. Furthermore, it heavily emphasizes self-therapy or what people can do for themselves.

I thank the following for their help. The reviewers of the book's first draft: Paul Brown, Alan Dabbs, Ralph Hetherington and Stanley Strong. Any shortcomings are mine rather than theirs. Above all, my editor at Harper & Row, Naomi Roth, for her willingness to back this venture.

Since the background chapters review existing approaches, some readers may wish only to scan them. I hope that you find your time with this book a rewarding experience.

Richard Nelson-Jones
London, England and
Melbourne, Australia
1984

Chapter 1

WHY FOCUS ON PERSONAL RESPONSIBILITY?

This book provides a framework for counselling, life skills training and self-help or self-therapy that uses personal responsibility as a central integrating concept. Its purpose is not to have people going around saying 'my fault' all the time, but rather to explore how they can become more effective agents in securing their own and others' happiness and fulfilment. The focus here is on the struggles and problems of ordinary people rather than on those of moderately to severely disturbed psychiatric populations. In 1969, in a widely publicized presidential address to the American Psychological Association, George Miller spoke of the need to give psychology away to nonpsychologists (Miller: 1969). The psychology of how to help people to help themselves has now reached the stage where more people should be able to learn from it.

Focusing on personal responsibility

Two vignettes: Mark and Peter

The following two vignettes illustrate the point that psychological problems, and hence issues of personal responsibility, are not just pertinent to the psychiatrically disturbed.

Mark is a senior company executive in his mid-40s. He finds it difficult to get up in the morning partly because he stayed up late watching television and then took a sleeping pill. As he goes down to breakfast he senses that there are still a considerable number of unresolved issues in his marriage. His wife gets the breakfast and there is little communication with his family. He is preoccupied with eating quickly and getting out to work. He has not considered that if he got up earlier this would take the pressure off everyone.

At work Mark drives himself and others very hard. People respect his energy and ability, but do not find him an easy colleague. Other executives feel that he is competitive and continually jockeying for position in the company, sometimes at their expense. He tries to be pleasant to junior staff and secretaries. They feel that he is critical rather than supportive. Furthermore, they have noticed his absorption with his own career and advancement. Today Mark chairs a staff meeting for his unit. Though he has asked for agenda items, he arranges that items important to him come first. Instead of a genuine exchange of ideas, almost all comments are either addressed by or to Mark.

On the way home from work he has a couple of drinks and arrives late for supper. His wife and family are quite glad to see him, apart from when he comes back really irritable or tipsy. However, they wish he would show more interest in their lives. As it is they collude with him by communicating on a superficial level and avoiding challenging his behaviour. Furthermore, they continually edit what they say to prevent upsetting him by disagreeing strongly or appearing too different from his picture of them. After supper Mark does some paperwork, watches television and again goes to bed later than he really wants. For the past year neither he nor his wife have been or are particularly interested in their sex life.

Peter works in the same office as Mark. Now let us look at a day in the life of Peter.

Peter is in his late 20s with a wife Mary and a 3-year-old daughter Jane. The morning starts with a visit from Jane who wants to snuggle into bed for fifteen minutes before Peter and Mary get up. Peter enjoys seeing his daughter and spending this time with her. Peter gets up in good time for breakfast and helps prepare it. He enjoys his breakfast. Mary is able to discuss one or two housekeeping matters with him, then he leaves for work with a warm hug and kiss for Mary and Jane.

At work Peter is a junior executive. He has a responsible job and is conscientious. He works at a steady rate. Wherever necessary, he consults with his colleagues. He is afraid to admit neither ignorance nor errors. He has the knack of bringing out the best in colleagues. They see him as collaborating rather than competing. The secretaries also feel his friendliness and respect. They like working with him. During the day he attends the staff meeting with Mark. He feels uneasy at the contrived atmosphere. Disagreeing with Mark on a point which cannot be ignored, he states his position calmly and cogently, not backing down under pressure.

Arriving home, he and his family always spend time discussing their respective days and enjoying each others' company. After putting Jane to bed and having supper, Peter helps Mary with the washing up. He looks forward to the remainder of the evening with Mary. They know that, if they wish to have sex, it will be a mutually enriching experience. They have always tried to work on problems in their marriage as they arise rather than risk letting them fester and become serious.

Although neither Mark nor Peter is psychiatrically disturbed, they differ considerably in their happiness and fulfilment. Additionally, each makes a very different impact on the psychological well-being of others, be it at home or work. Assuming that Mark has four people in his immediate family and there are thirty people for whom he has responsibility at work, there may be at least thirty-four people whose lives are being diminished through his problems. Correspondingly, Peter benefits the lives of many. Although these distinctions are overstated, Peter is enabling, encouraging, helping and strengthening others. Mark is disabling, discouraging, harming and weakening them.

If asked, both Mark and Peter would probably say they were behaving responsibly. However, there are a number of recurring choice points in each of their lives where Mark would decide one way, or with a certain emphasis, and Peter would decide the other. Thus, though both may have the self-image of behaving responsibly – and it would be a very hard thing to admit otherwise in our culture – the reality seems to be that Peter is much more effective in taking responsibility for his life than is Mark.

Defining personal responsibility

Since much of this book represents an attempt to get a fuller understanding of the concept of personal responsibility, a simple definition is not offered here. Rather some elements of the concept that recur are mentioned.

First, personal responsibility is a *process* rather than a fixed state. In fact, it is more a collection of subprocesses which, at varying times and in varying degrees, make up the overall process. Regarding this process, a useful distinction can be drawn between responsibility *to* and responsibility *for*, though they are not discrete categories. In responsibility *to*, the source of authority is more external and the emphasis is likely to be on meeting others' demands.

However, responsibility *for* is a positive concept which emphasizes internal authority and people's responsibility for making the most of their own lives. The distinction is reminiscent of that suggested by Fromm between the concepts of freedom *from* and freedom *to*, the former implying absence of negative restrictions and the latter presence of positive potential (Fromm: 1942).

Second, a key part of the process of personal responsibility is that of *choosing*. People during their waking hours are in a continuing process of choosing. Maslow wrote about the continuing process of self-actualizing. To him life was a series of two-sided choices. One side represented safety, defence, being afraid and regression: the other progression or growth. Self-actualizing involved making the daily smaller choices correctly, not just the big choices. 'To make the growth choice instead of the fear choice a dozen times a day is to move a dozen times a day towards self-actualisation' (Maslow: 1971).

Third, personal responsibility is an *inner process* in which people work from 'inside to outside'. This asserts more than that personal responsibility starts at home: also, that it is unhelpful to continually focus on others' shortcomings. The process of personal responsibility starts with people's thoughts and feelings rather than with their external actions. Furthermore, especially as people grow older, many if not most of significant barriers to effective action are internal. However, this is less likely to be the case where there is marked economic and social deprivation. Thus when talking about personal responsibility, as well as an assumption of *presence* of *desirable thoughts and feelings* there is an assumption of *absence* of *dysfunctional thoughts and feelings* which act as internal barriers to people being able to meet their physiological and psychological needs. The exact nature of these self-defeating thoughts and feelings will become clearer as the book progresses.

Fourth, the issue of *self-definition* is at the heart of the process of personal responsibility. People are not only in a continuing process of choosing: by their choices they define and create themselves; by their choices they take or avoid responsibility for *making* their lives. This idea is especially emphasized by existentialist philosophers, psychiatrists and psychologists.

Focusing on personal responsibility

There are many reasons why a focus on personal responsibility is desirable. Western societies assume, to a large degree, that people have responsibility for their own lives. A contrast may be made between the Western way of life, based on individual freedom and responsibility, and that of the Eastern bloc countries, where there is a lack of political freedom and, hence, possibly of individual responsibility. However, much of people's lives in both Eastern and Western blocs is spent on the personal rather than the public level. In both societies people have the inner struggle to gain the freedom to take responsibility for their personal relations and private lives. Most people live in a state of diminished freedom in this regard.

Another reason why a focus on personal responsibility is desirable is that problems of identity seem much more common than previously. The rate of technological change, the decline of religious belief represented in the statement 'God is dead', the increasing sophistication of communications so that people come up against different life-styles, and many other factors have led people to feel there is less structure in their lives than before. Psychological problems and theories are related to the epochs and cultures in which people live. As Yalom points out, Freudian psychology was derived against the background of sexual repression in *fin de siècle* Vienna rather than the compulsive permissiveness of much of contemporary American, especially Californian, culture (Yalom: 1980). Now not only do people have problems generated by too much structure, but problems generated by too little and by the clash of traditional with emergent and freer values (Spindler: 1963). As values outside the self collapse, there is more need to rely on the self as a source of values. One way of dealing with the lack of structure is by a flight into conformity or what might be viewed as an 'other-directed' solution. The 'inner-directed' solution is to hold fast to tradition despite external changes. Only a minority become genuinely autonomous choosers of how they live (Riesman *et al.*: 1950). There is a need for psychological theorizing about the problems of choice and identity of contemporary people for whom it is harder than it was for their forebears to go through life relying on convention – or somewhat asleep!

Three of the many areas in which people have been changing their definitions of themselves and of each other are the sexual revolution, the women's movement and gay liberation. Regarding the sexual revolution, modern methods of contraception have increased the degree of choice over what people do with their bodies. The women's movement, which aims to diminish if not abolish gender-stereotyped feeling, thinking and behaviour, has vast implications for the nature and degree of choice in the lives of both women and men. Furthermore, the implications for choice of gay liberation may be much more extensive than is currently realized given the extent of bisexuality in the population (Kinsey *et al.*: 1948; 1953)

Thus, the problems we are considering are not confined to a small proportion of society. Additionally, there are grounds for thinking that many of 'the men and women on the street' are less happy and fulfilled than they would like to be. For instance, in 1975, there were over 380,000 marriages, 140,000 petitions filed for divorce and 120,000 absolute divorce decrees in England and Wales. Furthermore, the impact of divorce is not restricted to marital partners, as evidenced by the 120,522 couples in England and Wales who were granted a decree absolute in 1975 having 202,475 children, of whom 145,096 were under 16 years old (Working Party on Marriage Guidance: 1979). Writing in 1982, Rayner estimated that there were around 150,000 marriages in Britain ending in divorce each year with almost three out of four divorcing couples having children, mostly aged under 16 (Rayner: 1982). Additionally, in the United States it is reckoned that one in five children are stepchildren, one in two marriages end in divorce and that between 40 and 60 percent of remarriages fail (Jenkins: 1983). These statistics indicate considerable marital and family unhappiness, especially since the data include neither those separated but not filing for divorce nor those who are unhappily still living together. Further indications that problems of living are widespread may be found in the high demand by suicidal and despairing people for help from organizations like the British Samaritans, the huge amounts of tranquillizers and sedatives prescribed by doctors, and the burgeoning literature and interest in stress problems. Not without reason the American psychologist Maslow used the term 'psychopathology of the average' to describe most people's level of functioning (Maslow: 1970).

Possibly in the next century psychological services will be more concerned with improving the majority than on remedying the psychological problems of the more seriously disturbed minority. This represents a move toward a psychology of health – what has been termed 'full humanness', rather than a psychology of sickness or 'human diminution' (Maslow: 1971).

An additional reason for focusing on personal responsibility is that virtually every psychological theory either explicitly or implicitly attests to its importance. Some theoretical positions, for example the existential therapies and reality therapy, use the word 'responsibility'. In other theories, personal responsibility is implicit in such terms as 'personal power', 'ego strength' and 'self-control'. However, there are differences between theories depending on which aspects of personal responsibility they focus. Another insight into the importance of personal responsibility comes from psychological research, especially that focused on the ways in which people attribute cause for events in their lives.

Clients in counselling and psychotherapy also find that personal responsibility is important. Yalom observes that one of the aspects of psychotherapy that they have found particularly useful is the discovery and assumption of personal responsibility. For instance, in one study, group therapy clients were asked to sort sixty cards reflecting 'mechanisms of change' in therapy into seven categories ranging from 'most helpful' to 'least helpful'. Of the sixty items, the item ranked fifth was 'Learning that I must take ultimate responsibility for the way I live my life no matter how much guidance and support I get from others' (Yalom: 1980). Though Yalom's finding says nothing about how effectively patients then behaved in their outside lives, it suggests the importance of learning about the assumption of personal responsibility. Another indication that clients find learning personal responsibility useful is the large literature on assertiveness (Bower and Bower: 1976; Butler: 1981). Although more from a counsellor's or therapist's viewpoint, Maslow highlights the importance of personal responsibility for clients when he writes:

> Clients are not honest much of the time. They are playing games and posing. . . .
> Looking within oneself for many of the answers implies taking responsibility. . . . In
> psychotherapy, one can see it, can feel it, can know the moment of responsibility.
> Then there is a clear notion of what it feels like. This is one of the great steps.
> Each time one takes responsibility, this is an actualising of the self (Maslow: 1971).

Yet, despite the recognized importance of the concept of personal responsibility there is little on the subject in the psychological literature. Maslow's tongue-in-cheek comment about this lack was: 'This matter of responsibility has been little studied. It doesn't turn up in textbooks, for who can investigate responsibility in white rats?' (Maslow: 1971). What literature there is tends sometimes to be vague, incomplete, and often implicit rather than explicit. This gets highlighted in the following two chapters.

A final reason for focusing on personal responsibility is that it expresses a central psychological concept in a language which means something to nonpsychologists. It is more comprehensible and likely to stimulate the interest of the layperson than such psychological terms as 'ego strength'. It is free of medical assumptions like sickness and the need for medical attention. Furthermore, it has desirable connotations of self-help rather than reliance on others for a cure. If one accepts the assertion that psychological problems are widespread, then it follows that there are unlikely to be sufficient professional psychologists and helpers to cater for all needs. Increasingly people will have to develop self-help skills. This is more likely to happen if they use psychological concepts that have meaning for them. Also, those in the helping professions may find their own behaviour easier to explore and, if necessary, to change if they conceptualize it in simple language.

Some qualifications and limitations

Perhaps it is as well to state what focusing on personal responsibility does *not* mean. First, it is not meant to engender guilt induced either by oneself or by others. There is no assumption that the world is divided into two groups, the responsible and irresponsible, and that, therefore, therapists and counsellors are basically different from their clients. Where differences exist, they tend to be ones of degree. Also, although it is often helpful to be aware of personal deficiencies, this awareness is only useful if it can lead to corrective action. A clumsy focus on personal responsibility risks leading to self-defeating emotions like depression and overanxiety. Responsibility needs to be attributed accurately and realistically. If this can be achieved, the chances of negative emotions and actions are likely to be minimized. It is vital that people do not unnecessarily erode their own and others' sense of worth. To quote Epictetus:

> It is the act of an ill-instructed man to blame others for his own bad condition;
> it is the act of one who has begun to be instructed, to lay the blame on himself;
> and of one whose instruction is completed, neither to blame another, nor himself.

Second, focusing on personal responsibility does not mean that all is satisfactory in the external world. Adverse social conditions like poor housing, unemployment, poverty, racial discrimination, malnutrition and inadequate or irrelevant education may each make it difficult for people to take effective personal responsibility for their lives. Sociological and political analyses and solutions can be helpful in many situations. However, as may be seen from the United States of America, even in wealthy countries people still have problems in living fulfilled lives. Focusing on personal responsibility should not be taken as advocating a form of privatism in which only immediate personal concerns matter. Indeed as people start taking more effective control of their feelings, thoughts and actions, this may generate surplus energy and more willingness to focus on broader social conditions in the world.

Third, focusing on personal responsibility is not a simple cure-all. Although sometimes considerable positive change can be brought about through brief therapeutic interventions, possibly especially in crises, most often significant personal change is a longer and more arduous process. Then there is the problem of continuing to change after counselling or, at the very least, managing to retain the gains made during it. This book aims not to exude a naive optimism about the possibilities of changing ourselves, clients and the world. Rather, personal responsibility counselling and therapy is based on a view of life as a continuing inner struggle in which there is almost always the potential for people to be their own worst enemies, and that includes counsellors and therapists too!

An integrative approach

A trend toward integrative approaches

In an issue of the journal *Behaviour Therapy* which featured the topic of integration, Goldfried observed that the hope of finding some consensus across the psychotherapies could be traced back some fifty years (Goldfried: 1982). In the same issue Garfield mentioned that most therapists sincerely tried to incorporate aspects of different therapies which they believed allowed them to meet the needs of their clients more efficiently. He wrote: 'Such individuals are usually viewed as eclectics, although more recently the more dignified terms, convergence or integration, have been used' (Garfield: 1982). Eclecticism can, of course, mean many different things. In one study of American clinical psychologists it was found that there were 32 different theoretical combinations used by 145 eclectic psychologists blended in a number of 'individually unique' ways (Garfield and Kurtz: 1977). Especially in the last twenty-five years there appears to have been a considerable trend for psychologists and counsellors to adopt approaches that draw on more than one theoretical position.

Two of the main stimuli causing counsellors and therapists to reexamine their practice have been the behavioural 'revolution' of the 1960s and the cognitive 'revolution' of the 1970s. The start of the impact of behavioural counselling and therapy can be attributed to the publication in 1958 of Wolpe's *Psychotherapy by Reciprocal Inhibition* (Wolpe: 1958). Some evidence of this impact can be seen from a 1974 survey of theoretical orientations among a sample of American clinical psychologists in which almost 55 percent of those surveyed labelled themselves as eclectics (Garfield and Kurtz: 1974). When asked the two theoretical orientations most characteristic of their eclectic views, the three most common combinations they gave were psychoanalytic and learning theory (i.e. behavioural), neo-Freudian and learning theory, and neo-Freudian and Rogerian. The most common reason they adopted eclecticism was that they used 'whatever theory or method seems best for the client' (Garfield and Kurtz: 1977). There was a large decline between surveys reported in 1961 and 1974 in the proportion of clinical psychologists adhering to psychoanalytic and related orientations. It is notable that psychoanalytic orientations featured in each of the three leading eclectic combinations, indicating reservations about the use of psychoanalysis when faced with the demands of clinical practice. In actual fact, even in the 1960s, behavioural counselling and therapy was itself a hybrid relying for a good deal of its effectiveness on nonspecific therapeutic effects. These effects were described by Wolpe as 'presumably the emotional impact on the patient of the therapist, a trusted and supposedly wise and competent person to whom he entrusts himself' (Wolpe: 1969).

Results from studies of counsellors' and therapists' theoretical orientations are complicated by the fact that their stated theoretical orientations may not be telling the whole story. They may be doing other things as well. Furthermore, these extras may account for much of their effectiveness. Yalom writes: 'Formal texts, journal articles, and lectures portray therapy as precise and systematic. . . .Yet I believe deeply that, when no one is looking, the therapist throws in the "real thing" ' (Yalom: 1980). He sees some of these 'throw ins' or 'off-the-record extras' as hard to define qualities such as 'compassion', 'presence', caring, extending oneself, touching the patient at a profound level, or – that most elusive one of all – 'wisdom'.

Cognitive approaches to counselling and therapy approaches focusing on clients' thinking existed before the 1970s. For example, Ellis' seminal book *Reason and Emotion in Psychotherapy* was published in 1962 (Ellis: 1962). All counselling and therapeutic approaches try to alter the ways in which clients think.

However, especially since 1970, attempts have become popular to integrate cognitive with behavioural approaches forming a new hybrid cognitive-behaviourism. Meichenbaum and Beck are at the forefront of this integration. In the Prologue of his *Cognitive-Behavior Modification*, Meichenbaum writes of how for the previous ten years he had been trying to bridge the gap between the clinical concerns of cognitive-semantic therapists and the technology of behaviour therapy (Meichenbaum: 1977). This bridging appears to have two strands: adding cognitive techniques and explaining existing behavioural techniques in cognitive terms. Beck found psychoanalysis an inadequate framework. He had been practising psychoanalysis for many years 'before I was struck by the fact that a patient's cognitions had an enormous impact on his feelings and behavior' (Beck: 1976). While emphasizing the importance of patients' internal communications, he also uses a variety of behavioural techniques.

There are, of course, many other combinations of therapeutic approaches. For example, gestalt therapy involves elements of Rogerian reflection and Moreno's psychodrama. Furthermore, gestalt techniques are sometimes combined with transactional analysis (James and Jongeward: 1971). The list of combinations could go on and on. There are really two main points. First, many practising counsellors and therapists find single theoretical positions an inadequate base. Second, there have already been a number of attempts to try to bridge the gap between theoretical positions. Perhaps the most prominent recent attempt is the effort to merge cognitive and behavioural therapies. Although much of this integrative work is valuable, the varying combinations seem insufficiently comprehensive for what Lazarus terms 'treating the whole person' while 'talking the client's language' (Lazarus: 1981). Additionally, they tend not to possess a sharp enough focus on the concept of personal responsibility. Hence they insufficiently emphasize what clients and people can do for themselves.

Outline of the book

Chapters 2 and 3 review some existing theoretical positions. They show how the concept of personal responsibility occurs in the different positions and illustrate some of its meanings. Chapter 2 reviews the concept of personal responsibility in the humanistic and existential approaches. These include: the person-centred approach, where there is an increasing emphasis on personal power; gestalt therapy, with its focus on getting people to move from environmental to self-support; transactional analysis, which offers some interesting insights into personal responsibility in social relations; reality therapy, where responsibility involves facing the realities of existence so that basic needs of love and worth can be met; and integrity therapy, with its focus on honesty, responsibility and involvement. The existential approaches heavily emphasize the concept of personal responsibility and attention is paid here to the work of two leading exponents, Frankl and Yalom. Chapter 3 examines the concept of personal responsibility in cognitive and behavioural approaches and their varying combinations. Consequently, the chapter starts with an examination of rational-emotive therapy, with its emphasis on faulty thinking. It then examines personal responsibility in traditional behavioural theory before looking at such hybrid approaches as Beck's cognitive approach and Meichenbaum's cognitive-behaviour modification.

Chapters 4 and 5 present some of the main propositions of a theoretical model using personal responsibility as a central integrating concept. In their leading text on personality theory, Hall and Lindzey state that a theory is an unsubstantiated hypothesis or a speculation concerning reality which is not yet definitely known to be so. Also, that when the theory is confirmed it becomes fact (Hall and Lindzey: 1970). Theories of counselling and therapy are intellectual models designed to explain and to predict human behaviour. To be practical they must not only state their basic assumptions and explain how people acquire psychological problems, but also how these problems are being sustained and how people can be helped or help themselves to change. Chapter 4 presents and discusses propositions concerning basic assumptions of the theory. Also, it discusses how personal responsibility resources and deficits are acquired. Chapter 5 covers propositions concerned with how resources and deficits are sustained and how change may be brought about.

An integrated theoretical framework lays the groundwork for an integrated approach to practice. A possible distinction between eclectic and integrative approaches to counselling and therapy is that, whereas the former may imply decisions based on random or loose application of the different theoretical elements involved, the latter has the connotation that the theoretical and practical links are more consistent and better thought through.

The practice section of the book comprises five chapters. Chapter 6 discusses such issues as the goals of personal responsibility counselling and therapy, some assumptions for its practice and the responsibility of the counsellor. Since the goals of personal responsibility counselling and therapy involve the whole person across a number of different, yet interrelated, areas of functioning, the remaining chapters reflect this breadth. Each chapter starts with a section on why a focus on this particular area of functioning is important. Then interventions are presented for counselling, life skills training and self-therapy. Chapter 7 deals with the responsiveness dimension of personal responsibility. It emphasizes helping people take responsibility for awareness of, experiencing and expressing their feelings. Chapter 8, on thinking, inner speech and language, emphasizes ways in which people can be helped to help themselves by learning to discipline and take more effective control over their thinking. Chapter 9 focuses on the psychological skills of personal relationships. Particular emphasis is placed on people learning to define and communicate themselves authentically. There is also a focus on learning to avoid or minimize damaging others and allowing oneself to be damaged by them. Chapter 10 focuses on helping people assume personal responsibility for finding meaning in the way they allocate their time. The area of rewarding activity involves the need to experience feelings accurately, think effectively and possess relationship skills.

Chapter 2

BACKGROUND: HUMANISTIC AND EXISTENTIAL APPROACHES

The next two chapters are essentially background chapters to explore the notion of personal responsibility in some existing theoretical positions. Since the major influences in personal responsibility counselling and therapy come from the humanistic, existential, cognitive and behavioural positions these approaches are reviewed. Though the categorizations and hence the chapter divisions are not precise, this chapter focuses on personal responsibility in humanistic and existential approaches whereas the following chapter focuses on personal responsibility in cognitive, behavioural, and cognitive-behavioural approaches.

Person-centred counselling and therapy

A major strand running throughout the writings of Carl Rogers, the founder of client-centred or person-centred counselling and therapy, has been a concern with personal responsibility. In 1942 he introduced his 'nondirective' approach in the following way: 'The aim is not to solve one particular problem, but to assist the individual to *grow*, so that he can cope with the present problem and with later problems in a better integrated fashion. If he can gain enough integration to handle one problem in more independent, more responsible, less confused, better-organized ways, then he will also handle new problems in that manner' (Rogers: 1942). Much later, in 1977, he wrote of the politics of the client-centred approach as 'the facilitation of self-ownership by the client and the strategies by which this can be achieved; the placing of the locus of decision-making and the responsibility for the effects of these decisions' (Rogers: 1977). Though Rogers may not always have used the term, issues of directiveness versus nondirectiveness, counsellor versus client power and control, and of personal versus external power are fundamentally issues of personal responsibility.

Rogers' beliefs about people's capacity for personal responsibility rests upon two basic assumptions. The first is that of the actualizing tendency which he regards as the 'foundation on which the person-centred approach is built' (Rogers: 1977). The actualizing tendency is an active process representing the inherent tendency of the organism to develop its capacities in the direction of maintaining, enhancing and reproducing itself. It is a natural tendency toward complete development. The second is that the human being is basically a trustworthy organism capable of self-understanding and of accurately evaluating external circumstances, of making constructive choices and of acting on these choices. Personal responsibility therefore rests on the foundation of being in touch with the 'organismic' or bodily valuing process inherent in the concept of the actualizing tendency.

Unfortunately people learn to become distant from their own valuing process. Rogers especially emphasizes the acquisition of conditions of worth when young people's own experiencing of their behaviour is at variance with the evaluations of significant others. They become afraid of having their need for positive regard from others thwarted. Thus what the child may enjoy, the parent may disapprove. The concept of conditions of worth means that the individual now has a second valuing process, based on the internalization of other people's evaluations. This impedes the first or organismic valuing process which truly reflects the actualizing tendency. Furthermore, people have a false awareness in regard to this second valuing process. They lack awareness of its derivative rather than intrinsic nature (Rogers: 1951; 1959). All people have conceptions of themselves. However, when these self-conceptions are based on conditions of worth rather than their own valuing processes then people become vulnerable to threat and anxiety in face of discrepant information. They may sustain their difficulties by denying and distorting such threatening information. Both positive and negative information may be denied and distorted so long as it is at variance with one or more self-conceptions.

Rogers evolved what he originally termed his 'nondirective' approach to counselling and psychotherapy in opposition to what he perceived as Freudian authoritarianism, behavioural determinism and problem-focused guidance. Person-centred counselling is a process in which clients are facilitated in assuming the responsibility for making decisions in terms of their own personal meanings and evaluations. Rather than directly 'attack' conditions of worth with challenges and interpretations, Rogers aims to provide a growth-inducing emotional climate. Here clients are given the safety and freedom to explore themselves and to get more in touch with experiencing their *own* feelings. There are three conditions for a growth-promoting climate. The first is counsellor genuineness, realness or congruence. For the second, the counsellor conveys an attitude variously expressed as caring, prizing, acceptance or unconditional positive regard. Basically the counsellor is trying to communicate a trust in the client's actualizing tendency. This leaves with clients the responsibility for how they lead their lives. The third condition is empathic understanding, a form of emotional companionship which is a 'very special way of being with another person' (Rogers: 1975; 1980). This is characterized by sensitively and accurately understanding the client's feelings and personal meanings. Also, by communicating this understanding to the client in a way that does not suggest any attempt at external control.

Now what of the responsibility of the counsellor? The counsellor is responsible for offering the three growth-promoting conditions. At its deepest level this involves a form of *agape* or unselfish love for the client. The counsellor is also responsible for not colluding in the client's attempts to seek dependency and avoid responsibility. Rogers uses the technique of reflection or mirroring to get clients to explore their underlying feelings. A less experienced counsellor might encourage dependency: for instance, by offering solutions to problems rather than developing clients' abilities to find their own solutions.

A major strength of Rogers as a theorist is his acknowledgment that people need to experience their significant feelings if they are to take responsibility for their lives. Nevertheless the actualizing tendency is an insufficient basis on which to build a theoretical framework. Even Rogers appears to find it insufficient, since the actualizing tendency needs to be supplemented by the growth-promoting climate provided by genuineness, respect and empathy. If the actualizing tendency were strong, presumably people would be able to resist internalizing conditions of worth. Rogers' idealism in regard to the basic trustworthiness of human beings needs to be supplemented by recognizing that this 'basic' trustworthiness is most likely to emerge if people are fortunate enough to be exposed to the growth-inducing facilitative conditions.

Rogers presents a remarkably simplistic account of how people become ineffective or irresponsible. It centres on one explanation: that children, whose need for positive regard may clash with parental disapproval of their behaviour, may internalize some of these external values as if they were their own. As illustrated later, the acquisition of responsibility deficits is a much more complex process.

Regarding the practice of counselling, Rogers has made an important contribution in emphasizing and identifying some of the conditions of a growth-promoting person-to-person *relationship*. However, Rogers' three central facilitative conditions are the necessary yet insufficient conditions for personal responsibility counselling and therapy. Rogers' simplistic explanation of the genesis of people's problems has led to a unitary diagnosis: namely that of being out of touch with the valuing process inherent in the actualizing tendency. Consequently, he has restricted himself to what is essentially a single treatment approach. This is an inadequate way to approach the range of difficulties that people have in being personally responsible. Furthermore, it contains an over-emphasis on feelings and an underemphasis on effective thinking and action. At worst, clients may remain in their feelings of how hard life is for them, without being sufficiently challenged to explore what they are contributing to sustaining their difficulties. Rather than relying on the emergence of an actualizing tendency which has not proved strong enough to avert their problems, counsellors may also help clients acquire skills of self-help and of living.

Person-centred counselling provides a nurturing emotional relationship in which many may find the psychological freedom to experience their own feelings and attach their own meanings to their experiences. They may have been unable to do this if they were unfortunate in their earlier relationships. Even with people who have not been severely deprived in their earlier relationships, good person-centred counselling can provide the emotional support to facilitate making a decision or solving a problem. Despite its lack of comprehensiveness, there is much of value in the person-centred approach from the viewpoint of engendering personal responsibility.

Gestalt therapy

The notion of responsibility is pervasive throughout the work of Fritz Perls, the founder of gestalt therapy. Like Rogers, Perls heavily emphasized people's need to experience their significant feelings if they were to take responsibility for their lives. The overcoming of blocks to sensory awareness is central to gestalt therapy. Perls distinguished between two meanings of the word responsibility. One meaning is that of obligation or taking responsibility for someone else. The other meaning is that of the ability to *be* what one *is*. This kind of ability is really *response-ability* or the freedom of choice concerning how to respond to a certain situation (Perls: 1969a). Individuals, to be able to satisfy their needs – to complete or to close incomplete *Gestalten* – must be able to sense what they need. Also, to be able to manipulate themselves and their environments to obtain what is necessary. By being themselves or coming to their senses, people become mature. Maturing is regarded as the process of moving from environmental to self-support. Self-support entails taking responsibility for oneself which in turn entails response-ability.

The contact boundary is the boundary between organism and environment and it is at this boundary that psychological events take place. Perls and his colleagues considered that: 'psychology studies the operation of the contact-boundary in the organism/environment field' (Perls, Hefferline and Goodman: 1951). Such 'contact' or 'being in touch with' involves both sensory awareness and motor behaviour. Perls considered that contact boundary disturbances, manifested in poor gestalt formation and closure, were extremely widespread and observed: 'Modern man lives in a state of low-grade vitality' (Perls: 1973). There are a number of contact boundary disturbances, including introjection and projection, which both represent and sustain lowered response-ability. Introjection is the tendency to 'own' as part of the self what is actually part of the environment. Projection is the tendency to 'own' as part of the environment what actually is part of the self.

The aim of gestalt therapy is to get clients to support themselves rather than to seek environmental support. Perls wrote: 'The therapist's primary responsibility is not to let go unchallenged any statement of behavior which is not representative of the self, which is evidence of the patient's lack of self-responsibility' (Perls: 1973). The practice of gestalt therapy aims to increase response-ability by means of a range of largely experiential techniques aimed at increasing awareness. Gestalt therapy tends to be conducted in groups, or rather the gestalt therapist tends to work with individual members in front of the remainder of the group. Although therapists are not responsible for their patients' neuroses, miseries and misunderstandings, they are responsible for their reactions to their patients, their own motives and how they handle the therapeutic situation. They must not allow their patients to see themselves as passive agents in their lives. Instead they have to introduce clients to the mentality of responsibility and get them to acknowledge 'I am preventing myself. . . .', 'How do I prevent myself?' and 'From what do I prevent myself?' Therapists therefore have a responsibility to resist clients' attempts to manipulate them to collude in making them better neurotics.

There are some basic rules for gestalt groups which focus on individual responsibility. These are usually described at the outset (Levitsky and Perls: 1970). These rules include: encouraging members to focus on what is happening to them in the here-and-now; sending communications directly to the receiver and, if necessary, using the receiver's name at the beginning of each sentence; and using 'I' language implying choice, for example saying 'I won't do that' instead of 'I can't do that'.

Gestalt therapy views itself as an experiential rather than a verbal or interpretative therapy. Unwanted feelings, inhibited bodily and verbal communication, and inner conflicts were all grist for Perl's awareness mill. He demanded that people experience themselves as fully as possible in the here-and-now. This was both to understand their present manipulations and contact boundary disturbances and also to reexperience the unfinished business of past problems and traumas.

The focal awareness technique, expressed in the term 'Now I am aware', helps people to understand their now. Clients are asked to become aware of their body language, their breathing, their voice quality and their emotions as much as of any pressing thoughts. Thus they become aware of *how* they are interrupting their contact with themselves and the world. The therapist's own interventions also focus on the *how* of clients' behaviour – how they are manipulating the environment in ways that diminish personal responsibility.

Perls could be very challenging when he considered that clients were trying to evade responsibility through phoney manipulations. Sympathy alone spoils clients. Alongside sympathy there needs to be skilful frustration in which clients are frustrated in their efforts to control the therapist by neurotic manipulations. When he used his 'hot seat' technique, Perls would continually try to heighten his clients' awareness by focusing on the *how* of their avoidances. Frustration often led to the discovery that the phobic impasse about assuming responsibility did not exist in reality, but only in fantasy. Clients were preventing themselves from using their own available resources through catastrophic expectations.

The awareness technique in its most basic form is limited by its slowness in producing change. As well as skilful frustration, Perls used drama and fantasy work to speed up the therapeutic process. He was fond of using monodrama based on the shuttle technique in which clients were asked to shuttle their attention from one area to another. This often involved the use of an 'empty chair' waiting to be filled by fantasized people and parts of one's personality. Topdog-underdog dialogues, involving a conversation with one's superego, were one of the main examples of the use of the shuttle technique. This could involve both fantasy work and the empty chair, with the person changing seats as he or she played each part.

Perls considered that working with clients' dreams was an important way of increasing their awareness of their blocks and areas of responsibility avoidance. Especially if dreams were repetitive, very important existential issues for the client were likely to be involved. Dream work entailed acting out various elements in the dream. This could be facilitated by the empty chair technique to allow for dialogues between the different people, objects or parts of the self that were encountering each other.

Like Rogers, Perls saw the basis of responsibility as resting in people's capacity to be aware of and experience their bodily and sensory selves. He was keenly aware that people had both internal psychological processes, his contact boundary disturbances, and also external manipulative behaviours in their social relationships which sustained responsibility avoidance. Though Perls used empathy, he definitely did not consider it sufficient to maximally help clients to become aware of *how* they were contributing to their own distress. Instead, Perls stepped out of the client's frame of reference. He directly challenged and confronted any here-and-now behaviours illustrating responsibility avoidance. The issues of timing, client readiness and the quality of the counsellor-client relationship are crucial in such confronting. If these are not adequately taken into consideration, clients may leave therapy or be damaged by such interventions.

Perls' focus on the use of language, so that people acknowledged their own choices and agency in their actions, seems highly pertinent not only to responsibility assumption but also to the maintenance of responsibility. His emphasis on the social psychology of reponsibility avoidance, namely that people are not only avoiding responsibility but manipulating others including therapists in colluding with their avoidances, is valuable. Additionally, his challenging style seems almost to have been a precursor to the widespread present-day interest in assertion training. However, gestalt therapy is at best only a partial approach to helping people become more effective. It lacks specificity concerning what are many of the skills of effective human functioning. It has an overreliance on losing one's mind and coming to one's senses. Effective thinking can be one of the skills that free people to become more in touch with their senses. Additionally, having an active-directive-charismatic therapist who tells one how one should be more responsible is not necessarily the best way of learning to take more responsibility for oneself. With such therapists, under the guise of encouraging responsibility there is always the risk of fostering dependency.

Transactional analysis

Though Eric Berne, the founder of transactional analysis, rarely used the term responsibility, the notion of personal responsibility is implicit in much of his writing. Like Perls, Berne was very conscious of how people, in order to avoid responsibility, engaged in manipulating others.

Transactional analysis provides a language and set of concepts for understanding human behaviour and interactions. Each human being exhibits three kinds of ego states and, at any moment in a social situation, will predominantly exhibit one or other of these states. Ego states are patterns of feeling, thinking and behaviour. The three ego states are: 1. the Parent ego state, which represents parental and cultural influences; 2. the Adult ego state, which represents reality-oriented data processing; 3. the Child ego state, which represents childlike wishes and impulses. Further analyses of ego states focus on elaborating Parent and Child.

The acquisition of irresponsibility may be mainly viewed in terms of the development of scripts. Scripts are preconscious life plans by which people structure their time. They are usually based on childlike illusions which may persist throughout a lifetime (Berne: 1972). People's scripts are not only the result of parental programming, but also of decisions they made when very young – usually by the age of six – in response to parental programming. When parents make nurturing conditional on their children's submission to their directives, children may make conscious decisions to forgo some autonomy and adhere to parental wishes. The development of scripts can be more complex than the above description. Indeed children may also acquire counterscript directives, though in the end script directives always prevail.

In transactional analysis, series of ulterior or dishonest transactions are called games. From their earliest months, children learn games through significant experiences in their family life. A psychological game is 'an ongoing series of complementary ulterior transactions progressing to a well-defined, predictable outcome' (Berne: 1964). Each game has a motto by which it can be recognized: for example, 'Why Don't You? – Yes But'. Games are distinguished from other ways of structuring time by two characteristics: their ulterior quality and their payoff. Frequently these payoffs involve negative feelings or 'rackets' such as anxiety and depression.

Responsibility continues to be avoided for a number of reasons. Both scripts and games have their rewards or payoffs in terms of the individual's basic decisions about life. Furthermore, script and game behaviours are camouflaged by the illusion of autonomy whereby people do not acknowledge feelings and behaviours that come from their Child or Parent ego states, but instead believe that they come from their Adult ego state. Autonomous people, however, know what is practical and Adult and what comes from the other ego states.

Berne wrote: 'The aim of transactional analysis is *social control*, in which the Adult retains the executive in dealings with other people who may be consciously or unconsciously attempting to activate the patient's Child or Parent' (Berne: 1961). Autonomy entails the active development of personal and social control so that significant behaviour becomes a matter of free choice. This does not mean that the Adult ego state alone is active in social situations; rather it is capable of deciding when to release the Parent or Child and when to resume the executive.

Transactional analysis, which is often conducted in groups, can involve four different, but interrelated, approaches to responsibility assumption. These approaches are: structural analysis, transactional analysis, game analysis and script analysis. Each of these approaches requires the patient or client to understand the language of transactional analysis – in particular the concept of ego states. Thus learning some of the TA language is a prerequisite to responsibility assumption. Structural analysis consists of identifying and, if necessary, separating one feeling-thinking-and-behaviour pattern or ego state from another. This helps patients and clients become more aware of both the existence and the contents of their ego states. Furthermore, structural analysis may increase their awareness of each of their ego states so they gain more control over themselves in stressful situations. The purpose of script analysis is to get clients out of their scripts so that they can behave autonomously. Script analysis aims to get clients to abandon previous decisions, which were based on lack of awareness and which now block spontaneity and intimacy, with redecisions which give release from the script. A script antithesis is a therapeutic intervention which explicitly contradicts a parental directive. This process of helping clients toward responsibility assumption through redecision can be aided by getting the voice of the therapist into their heads, at least temporarily.

The practice of transactional analysis lays great emphasis on helping people assume responsibility through analysing their personal relations and other social interactions. Transactional analysis proper is the analysis of single stimulus-response transactions by means of transactional diagrams. These diagrams analyse a transaction into whether the ego states involved are complementary (people receive a response from the ego state they have addressed), crossed (they do not, in which case communication risks being broken off), or ulterior (in which the surface transaction is not the real transaction). Game analysis involves examining series of transactions to help clients toward social control or free choice of responses. Such analyses can be of games that clients either initiate or allow themselves to become part of by letting other people activate inappropriate ego states.

A few comments should be made about the responsibility of the therapist. Frequently client-therapist contracts are used. These involve the communication of an offer by the therapist in explicit terms, usually to attempt to remedy an unhappy state of affairs which should be formulated in specific and observable terms. This offer implies mutual effort. Furthermore, the contract contains a 'consideration' for the therapist's efforts: for instance, money. Therapists are responsible, too, for avoiding engaging in script and game behaviours, whether self-initiated or in collusion with the script and game behaviours of clients.

Transactional analysis provides a language and set of concepts not only so that therapists can help make others more responsible, but also so that clients may use it to understand themselves and their social interactions better. It is a language which, in its basic form, is relatively easy for the layperson to comprehend. For instance, the use of terms like Parent, Adult and Child is fairly close to the way they are used in everyday life. Also words like games and scripts are close to people's everyday experience. There are two points here. First, transactional analysis is comprehensible to laypeople because its language is relatively simple, though this is not to deny that so-called second order structural analysis and the detailed analysis of games may not be so comprehensible to the layperson. Second, because of its ease of comprehension, transactional analysis lends itself to being used by clients and others both in group therapy and also for self-help outside therapy. On the negative side there is always a risk of a therapeutic language like transactional analysis being used in misleading and superficial ways by people who insufficiently understand both it and the nature of psychological difficulties. The focus on ego states and games may turn into an intellectual rather than a therapeutic exercise. Both therapists and clients may attempt to force client experiences into predetermined categories in a way that both may be inaccurate and may block emotional rather than just intellectual understanding. The identification and analysis of ego states, scripts, transactions and games may itself become a game played for other than therapeutic reasons. Nevertheless, transactional analysis is an interesting attempt to foster personal responsibility by means of a therapeutic language accessible to laypeople.

Berne was a cynical man who, like Perls, had a sharp eye and ear for other people's phoniness. His concept of people attaining social control as the aim of transactional analysis is tantamount to saying that people need to learn to become more personally responsible in social interactions. Responsibility as awareness of feelings needs to be extended to include awareness of feelings when being manipulated. Responsibility avoidance includes not only denials and distortions that operate on one's own experiencing, but psychological games and power-plays that operate on others' experiencing. Responsibility assumption entails learning to have social control and autonomy in an environment which often is using subtle as well as overt pressure to curtail such control over one's life (Steiner: 1981). In short, a valuable learning from transactional analysis is that much of personal responsibility involves choices in social transactions which are often more complicated than they appear on the surface.

Reality therapy

The central tenet of reality therapy is personal responsibility for one's behaviour (Glasser and Zunin: 1973). Responsibility is defined as the 'ability to fulfill one's needs, and to do so *in a way that does not deprive others of the ability to fulfill their needs'* (Glasser: 1965). Human beings have two basic psychological needs: namely, to be loved and to feel that they are worth while to themselves and to others. Responsible behaviour is the means of attaining a success identity. The ability to behave responsibly must be learned. The most appropriate medical analogy for psychiatric problems is not illness, but weakness. People must help themselves rather than see themselves as passive recipients of mental health help. The teaching of responsibility is the most important task of all higher animals. Within the context of warm human involvement, parents must teach responsibility to their children. This entails: setting a good example of commitment to each other; caring enough to show their children responsible ways to behave; being prepared to discipline rather than punish them if they misbehave; and spending time listening to and discussing matters with them. Excessive viewing of television can be an obstacle to learning involvement. Involvement at school is also important in teaching responsibility. Many children fail at school because teachers deny that the child's humanity and needs for love and worth are primary. Teachers need to develop a warm involvement with children and then help them toward responsibility with a relevant curriculum that encourages them to think through issues, solve problems, make decisions and plan. They should cease focusing on rewarding children for attaining goals which may have little relevance for them (Glasser: 1969).

Reality therapy is an intense form of corrective training to enable people to fulfil their needs realistically rather than to sustain their failure identities by changing the real world into their fantasies. The therapy, which is often conducted in groups, consists of three elements. First, therapists create involved relationships with clients. Second, the clients get confronted with reality by therapists with whom they are involved; they are encouraged to evaluate whether their current behaviour is their best choice; continually stressing responsibility is viewed as artificial. Third, clients are encouraged to identify, plan and implement responsible behaviour that meets needs for love and worth.

Four qualities are necessary for successful reality therapists (Glasser: 1965): first, to be responsible in their own lives and able to meet needs in the context of reality; second, the strength and integrity to be able to stand up to clients requesting collusion in their irresponsibility; third, acceptance and understanding of people who are isolated and in pain through failure to meet their needs; fourth, the capacity to become emotionally involved with irresponsible clients and to be affected by their suffering.

Even when presented more fully in his own writings, Glasser's reality therapy lacks comprehensiveness on both theoretical and practical levels. Personal responsibility needs wider and sharper definition. The acquisition and perpetuation of irresponsibility is more complex than presented by Glasser. A wider range of interventions is needed to alter the thoughts, feelings and behaviours that constitute irresponsibility. The use of the word therapy in the title of reality therapy promises more of a richness of theoretical and practical concepts than gets delivered.

Having stated these reservations, there are a number of commendable features in reality therapy: its emphasis on personal responsibility; its acknowledgement that personal responsibility entails meeting needs within the existential parameters of reality, and that it is vital for people to acknowledge this; the notion that people are responsible for perpetuating their pain and lack of involvement – if people are to change they have to accept their own role in sustaining their predicament; the idea that personal responsibility has to be learned and, to a large extent, deficits in responsibility reflect deficits in learning; the view of therapy as an involved relationship *plus* interventions focused on training clients to be more effective in meeting their needs; and lastly, the implicit notion that people need to take a problem-solving approach to life – hence they need to develop realistic problem-solving skills.

Integrity group therapy

Integrity group therapy is a form of peer self-help therapy propounded by Hobart Mowrer, a noted American research psychologist. Mowrer, who wrote a very supportive introduction to Glasser's *Reality Therapy*, considered that integrity groups helped rediscover the notion of responsibility in psychology (Mowrer: 1964). Integrity group therapy is not primarily concerned with changing others but with self-change.

Anxiety and other negative emotions arise because people are dishonest to their own consciences; also in the way they relate to other people. For such people 'constructive change consists, not of extinction of supposedly unrealistic moral fears, but of repudiation of one's old strategies of secrecy and withdrawal, and a "return to community" ' (Mowrer: 1964). Neurotics are people who have had freedom of choice and have exercised it badly.

The notion of contracts underlies Mowrer's view of psychological distress and wellness. People are social animals who primarily live by mutual agreements or contracts. These contracts confer rights and responsibilities. One definition of integrity is 'How well our conduct conforms to our contracts, how closely our performance matches our promises' (Mowrer, Vattano *et al.* : 1975). Failure to keep contracts, commitments or agreements has negative consequences. Others are likely to disapprove, reprove, reject or possibly punish those who default on contracts. Also individuals themselves will suffer consequences such as guilt and anxiety. People can avoid these negative consequences if they are responsible in keeping contracts. Furthermore, they may gain added strength in keeping contracts and in overcoming temptation if they are open with a reference group. It is not paradoxical to emphasize personal responsibility and yet to suggest that people obtain support from a reference group. Rather, living in community is a basic human need. One of the characteristics of being socialized is a balance between controlling oneself and being controlled by others.

Since people's problems basically stem from disorders of communication and from being out of communion with their fellow humans, individual therapy is not recommended. A possible exception to this is brief individual work that quickly prepares someone for a group. Integrity groups adopt the slogan 'You alone can do it, but you can't do it alone' (Mowrer, Vattano *et al.*: 1975). They operate on three fundamental principles: *honesty, responsibility and involvement.*

Honesty is important because genuine personal responsibility and involvement with other group members is unlikely to emerge unless it is preceded by deep self-disclosure. This self-disclosure consists of admissions of dishonesty: for instance, contracts violated, promises broken, and unwise plans or 'temptations'. A reasonably deep level of self-disclosure is a prerequisite for entry into integrity groups.

Integrity groups 'encourage and reward' four aspects of *responsibility*. The first is the correction of contract violations or, if this is not deemed desirable, the revision or dissolution of contracts. When responsible people admit that they have done something wrong, restitution is the most constructive step. Second, responsibility can be future-oriented in that individuals 'confess' intentions, plans and actions contemplated. Confessing and seeking counsel helps to avoid both errors of judgement and yielding to temptation. The feedback of the group lays no obligations on people who have disclosed their intentions. Third, responsibility means dependability or 'keeping one's word'. This means either fulfilling one's contracts or, if they seem impossible or highly undesirable, going back and renegotiating the contract. The fourth meaning of responsibility involves not making excuses, which almost invariably involve blaming others (Mowrer: 1972).

The final integrity group principle, *involvement*, refers to the help, love and concern members give to others in becoming more honest, responsible and involved. One form of involvement is 'reaching out', which is a ritualistic form of embracing sharply differentiated from sexual physical contact. These physical contacts are primarily for use before and in a group. Involvement legitimizes the expression of emotions and feelings in integrity groups so long as they are honestly expressed.

All integrity group members are therapists in two senses. First, they have the responsibility of applying the principles of integrity groups to their own lives. As the Berkeley, California, street poster said: 'To make a better world, make yourself a better individual'. Second, they have the responsibility of being involved in the development of their fellow group and community members. Furthermore, all group members share leadership responsibilities: for example, chairing group sessions and participating in Intake Committees which review admission of new members. A major point of difference between integrity and other forms of group therapy is that participating in integrity groups tends to be seen as a way of life. Integrity groups aim not only to provide an initial therapeutic experience, but also a continuing support system through an integrity group network.

The same reservations about the lack of comprehensiveness in both theory and practice that were expressed about reality therapy also apply to integrity group therapy. Integrity groups are vulnerable to charges of diminishing rather than fostering responsibility by placing intense group pressure on people to 'confess'; and by creating a dependency on the group for advice on how to lead one's life. Furthermore, peer leadership rather than that of counsellors may lack some of the therapeutic skills that certain members – and indeed the group – may need.

Nevertheless, Mowrer's work is interesting from the viewpoint of developing an approach using personal responsibility as a central integrating concept. For instance, Mowrer's emphasis on honesty is relevant to the need for people both to assume the courage to define themselves authentically, and to assume responsibility for being dependable in their relations with others. Additionally, anxiety is rightly seen not exclusively as a negative emotion, but as having the potential to be a signal or a call to responsibility assumption. People should not discard rules, but learn to live up to rules that are necessary for keeping them in communion with their fellow humans. Mowrer's emphasis on honesty, responsibility and involvement needing to be a way of life is another way of saying that personal responsibility is a lifelong process. The notion of peer self-help groups is also valuable, though insufficient attention is paid to their limitations and difficulties. However, Mowrer might have focused more on how individuals could engage in self-therapy, either independent of or in conjunction with peer group therapy.

Logotherapy

Viktor Frankl's logotherapy is the first of the two approaches categorized as existential that are reviewed here. Regarding the existential approach, May writes: 'In psychology and psychiatry, the term demarcates an *attitude*, an approach to human beings, rather than a special school or group' (May: 1969). In the term logotherapy, *logos* signifies the spiritual or meaning dimension of human existence. The innate desire to give as much meaning as possible to one's life is the *will-to-meaning*. Frankl writes: 'Man is responsible for the fulfilment of the specific meaning of his personal life' (Frankl: 1967). To be fully human is to be conscious of this responsibility for finding meaning. At no point in their lives can people escape 'the mandate to choose among possibilities' (Frankl: 1969).

An existential vacuum, represented by loss of meaning in people's lives, is a widespread phenomenon of the twentieth century. However, existential frustration is in itself neither pathogenic nor pathological. This depends upon how responsibly the individual is able to handle it. Humans are continually being questioned by life within the parameters of death and destiny. They are not fully conditioned and determined, but are ultimately self-determining in that they can always decide whether to give in to conditions or stand up to them. The meaning of death is that it gives life a finite quality. This irreversibility means that people must realize the meaning in their lives as much as possible. Frankl sees people as sculptors who have only a limited time for completing their work of art, but are not sure when the deadline is. Death adds to rather than detracts from the meaning of life. Even in a Nazi concentration camp: 'Life ultimately means taking the responsibility to find the right answers to its problems and to fulfil the tasks which it constantly sets for each individual' (Frankl: 1959).

There are three kinds of values or ways of taking responsibility for finding meaning in life: first, creative values realized in creative actions or deeds; second, experiential values realized in receptivity toward the world – for example by experiencing someone in love or by surrender to the beauty of nature or art; third, attitudinal values realized in people's attitudes towards the limiting factors in their lives.

The responsibility for finding meaning in creative values generally coincides with a person's work. For example, doctors can fulfil creative values in what they bring to their work as human beings over and above their medical duties. Those whose conditions of work are so limiting as to give little scope for creative values can find creative meaning in life by giving form to leisure. The existential importance of work in people's lives can be seen most clearly in unemployment neurosis. Here the prevailing symptom is not depression, but apathy. However, unemployment neurosis is a position or decision taken by the individual, whose fate is not so unconditional as the neurotic may wish to believe it is. There are many unemployed people who, despite economic deprivation, do not give way to unemployment neurosis. They take responsibility for finding creative meaning in their lives. An appropriate approach to unemployment neurosis is existential analysis 'which shows the jobless the way to inner freedom in spite of his unfortunate situation and teaches him that consciousness of responsibility through which he can still give some content to his hard life and wrest meaning from it' (Frankl: 1969).

Whereas the realization of creative values is active, the realization of experiential values tends to be relatively passive. Experiential values are especially realizable in love, which represents coming to relationship with another as a spiritual being. In this relationship lovers are able to see the spiritual core of each other and to see and help realize each other's potential. Love, however, is neither the only nor necessarily the best way to fill life with meaning. Individuals without a loving relationship can still shape their lives in highly meaningful manners.

Attitudinal values are realized when individuals are faced with unalterable destiny. Frankl sees destiny as having a two-fold meaning: 'to be shaped where possible and to be endured where necessary' (Frankl: 1969). In some instances an existential analysis may need to make a person capable of suffering. There are situations in which people can fulfil themselves only in genuine suffering. In such situations, if they miss the opportunity for suffering, they also miss the opportunity for actualizing attitudinal values.

The logotherapist is an educator for responsibility consciousness or for the need to be aware of one's own responsibility for responding to the challenges of life by finding meaning. Frankl highlights the notion of responsibility by making people aware of their finiteness. He gets his patients to imagine themselves in situations expressed by the categorical imperative of logotherapy: 'So live as if you were living already for the second time and as if you had acted the first time as wrongly as you are about to act now!' (Frankl: 1959).

Logotherapy sees responsibleness for shaping one's future to be the essence of human existence. Only by making people aware not only of their finiteness but of the finality of their choices do they become aware of the full gravity of the responsibility that they bear throughout every moment of their lives.

Frankl attempts to get his patients to take charge of their lives or to move from the state of a *'patiens'* to that of an *'agens'.* Patients must be led to see that their existence is a constant effort to actualize values. Furthermore, the tasks to which they must respond vary from person to person and from hour to hour. The typical self-centredness of the neurotic is broken up by confronting them with and reorienting them toward the meaning of their lives. Sometimes Frankl confronts his patients with things that they find disagreeable to hear. His method is future-oriented in that logotherapy focuses on the meanings to be fulfilled by people in the future. Often Frankl is a companion to his patients in their search for meaning. He offers alternative ways of viewing situations. These explanations or interpretations are focused on seeing the meaning in events. For example, once an elderly general practitioner consulted Frankl because of severe depression. He was overcome by the loss of his much loved wife two years previously. Frankl helped him to see that there was meaning in his suffering by asking: 'What would have happened, Doctor, if you had died first, and your wife would have had to survive you?' Whereupon the doctor saw that he had spared his wife suffering by out-living her (Frankl: 1959).

Although he calls them logotherapeutic techniques, Frankl proposes two techniques, paradoxical intention and de-reflection, that seem as much concerned with psychogenic as with spiritual problems. If necessary, these techniques can be combined with other methods, for example hypnosis and relaxation. In paradoxical intention, clients are encouraged to focus on and exaggerate in their imaginations precisely that which they fear. For instance, the woman who gets anticipatory anxiety about sweating in social situations is asked to imagine herself sweating buckets whenever she meets someone who triggers her anxiety. Frankl does not regard paradoxical intention as a panacea, but as a very useful therapeutic technique. In de-reflection, clients are encouraged to focus their attention away from themselves. For instance, sleepless clients may be invited to remain sleepless in order to focus on their everyday problems. Clients need to be de-reflected from their disturbance toward the unique meaning of their lives.

Though logotherapy is at best a partial approach to psychological effectiveness, Frankl makes some useful points. First, like other existential psychologists and philosophers, he is keenly attuned to the role of death in life and of awareness of death in therapy. Second, he heavily emphasizes people's responsibility for their life choices. Third and related to this second point, he emphasizes people's need to create their lives rather than, for instance, merely get in touch with their senses. Fourth, he shares the existentialist awareness of the contingencies of fate and of suffering. Thus instead of seeing life's possibilities in a simplistic way, he acknowledges that personal responsibility may also involve difficult choices and self-discipline in relation to life's hardships. An example is that of his own concentration camp experience. Both attitudinal and behavioural choices are possible even in the most horrific circumstances. Fifth, he seems free of the blind spot many psychological theorists exhibit about the importance of work and other activity in psychological well-being.

Existential psychotherapy

The second existential approach covered here is Irvin Yalom's existential psychotherapy. Yalom views existential psychotherapy as 'a dynamic approach to therapy which focuses on concerns that are rooted in the individual's existence' (Yalom: 1980). The psychodynamics of individuals include the various conscious and unconscious forces that operate and may be in conflict within them. However, unlike Freudian psychodynamics where the conflict is with suppressed instinctual strivings, the conflict in existential dynamics flows from people's confrontation with the inescapable givens of existence. Yalom adopts the theologian Tillich's term 'ultimate concerns' for them (Tillich: 1952). Four of the main ultimate concerns are: death, freedom, isolation and meaninglessness. This review particularly emphasizes freedom.

Responsibility is related to the ultimate concern of freedom. Freedom refers to the absence of external structure, to groundlessness; responsibility is a key concept in the existential conflict between groundlessness and the human need for ground and structure. Responsibility means *authorship*. People have the inescapable responsibility of being the authors of their lives by their choices and actions. One can never not be responsible, despite the lack of universal external referents and despite one's own particular 'coefficient of adversity' in life.

Yalom makes a distinction between responsibility *awareness* and responsibility *assumption*. Whereas the former pertains to being fully conscious of one's responsibility for authorship of one's life, the latter entails acting on that awareness. Responsibility *avoidance* is a term used to describe both barriers or defences against responsibility awareness and blocks to responsibility assumption. The existential dynamic formula for responsibility avoidance is:

Awareness of ultimate concern — > Anxiety — > Defence mechanism

Death is a primordial source of anxiety and, as such, the primary fount of psychopathology. Yalom observes: 'The neurotic life style is generated by a fear of death; but insofar as it limits one's ability to live spontaneously and creatively, the defense against death is itself a partial death' (Yalom: 1980). Defence mechanisms can be of two types: the conventional mechanisms, described by Freud and others, and specific defences which serve the specific function of coping with each of the primary existential fears. Some of the more common defences that protect the individual from responsibility awareness are: compulsivity, displacement of responsibility to another, denial of responsibility, avoidance of autonomous behaviour, and disorders of wishing and deciding.

Responsibility is also related to the concept of existential guilt. People are guilty of transgressing against themselves and against their potential for living. Thus the notion of authorship implies a demand upon people to fulfil their potential. When people deny their potential they lay themselves open not only to existential guilt, but also to anxiety. This anxiety can operate both for and against personal responsibility: for, in that it is a call to lost potential; against, in that it may lead to counter-productive defences. Most existential therapists focus less on the past than on the future. Consequently, when they focus on guilt, it is not because clients have failed to take responsibility for themselves in the past but for their failure to make the choices which will realize their unique potential in the present and the future.

Responsibility *awareness* is only the first step in the process of change which needs to be expressed in responsibility *assumption*. Responsibility equals 'response' plus 'ability' which together connote the capability to respond. The *will* is the mental agency that transforms awareness and knowledge into action. Thus the will is the *responsible mover*. Therapists, regardless of orientation, must attempt to influence the will. The notion of will should not be confused with that of will power. Rather, there are really two elements to the concept of will: initiating through *wishing* and then enacting through *choice*.

There are a number of disorders of wishing. Since wishing requires feeling, the affect-blocked person has distinct difficulties in willing. For a number of clients the therapist persistently has to inquire 'What do you feel?' and 'What do you want?' Impulsivity rather than inhibition may also be a disorder of wishing. Impulsivity avoids responsible wishing by not discriminating among wishes, but acting on impulse or whim. Compulsivity is also a disorder of wishing as well as a defence against responsibility awareness. The compulsive individual acts in accordance with inner demands that are not experienced as wishes.

Choice or decision is the bridge between wishing and action. People find decisions difficult for a number of reasons. Decisions exclude the options that have not been decided upon, so there is renunciation in every decision. Fundamental and irreversible decisions may be regarded as boundary experiences in which individuals are confronted with their fundamental groundlessness. And such decisions can be lonely acts which confront people with their existential isolation. Decisions engender guilt for many people, especially if they have been unfortunate enough to have parents who squelched their spontaneity and ability to choose for themselves. Procrastination is the main way of avoiding a decision, though there are more subtle ways of avoiding this responsibility.

Readiness to accept responsibility varies considerably. Furthermore, individuals may accept responsibility on some issues and deny it on others. Therapists continuously need to be sensitive to the role patients or clients are playing in their own dilemmas. They also need to find ways of communicating this insight. Yalom groups under the heading identification and labelling a variety of techniques to make patients more aware of responsibility. For example, patients can be encouraged to own their feelings by their use of language (not 'he bugs me', but 'I let him bug me'); and to own their intentions by changing 'cannot' into 'will not'. This may be highlighted by a 'can't' bell whenever individuals use 'can't' in a way that indicates lack of awareness of their active contributions to situations. Yalom observes: 'The general principle is obvious: whenever the patient laments about his or her life situation, the therapist inquires how the patient has created this situation' (Yalom: 1980).

Focusing on a patient's narrative of external events is not nearly so potent as using material generated in the here-and-now of therapy. It is much less easy for patients to engage in defensive rationalizations. It is especially helpful to focus on aspects of behaviour that are similar to the problems that have brought people for therapy. Being aware of one's own feelings and reactions to a patient, can be a therapist's most important way of identifying patients' responsibilities for creating and sustaining their predicaments.

Patients' attitudes towards responsibility are also reenacted in their basic posture toward therapy. Outside therapy they may be unwilling to accept responsibility for altering an uncomfortable predicament. In therapy they may not take any responsibility for change. Instead they expect it to come from their therapists, if at all. Some therapists silently collude in this process. Other therapists may reflect that the patient seems to leave everything to them. Another option is to simply ask: 'Why do you come?' 'Patients may feign helplessness by saying 'Tell me what to do' even when they know very well what to do, but are too frightened to acknowledge it.

Yalom is especially keen on the potential for engendering responsibility awareness in small interactional therapy groups of eight to ten individuals. In the early stages of a group the major activities are directed toward each member becoming aware of personal responsibility. Group therapists, without necessarily being conscious of it, escort each patient through the following sequence: (a) learning how their behaviour is viewed by others; (b) learning how their behaviour makes others feel; (c) learning how their behaviour creates the opinions others have of them; and (d) learning how their behaviour influences their opinion of themselves. In other words, each step helps patients become aware that they are responsible for how others see them, treat them, regard them, and that they are also responsible for how they regard themselves. Furthermore, it is important to emphasize members' roles in the conduct of the group. If they become aware of how they can assume responsibility in the group, they may then become more aware of opportunities to assume responsibility outside it.

Heightening people's death awareness is another way of heightening awareness of responsibility for authorship of their lives. Death awareness can be approached through exploration of matters like the death of others and milestones in people's lives, such as marital separation or divorce. Interaction with the dying may have a powerful effect. Two approaches are observation of a terminal cancer group by everyday psychotherapy patients and having people with terminal cancer as members of regular psychotherapy groups.

Regarding responsibility assumption, therapy is effective in so far as it influences patients' wills. There are numerous will-influencing ventures including: interpretation and insight, confrontation, development of a caring and trusting relationship, and analysis of maladaptive behaviour. Here, however, the focus is on wish-influencing and decision-influencing ventures. Working with the affect-blocked clients is a long, slow process. This is not likely to be shortened by the use of powerful affect-engendering techniques, such as may be used in gestalt therapy and in intensive encounter group weekends. A trusting, accepting and caring patient-therapist relationship is crucial to the process of change.

Approaches to helping patients assume responsibility for their decisions can focus on either the conscious or unconscious levels of decision. It is important that therapists do not take over patients' decision-making functions. Approaches on the conscious level include asking patients repeatedly 'What are your alternatives?', providing them with different perspectives and encouraging them to own their decisions. Approaches to the unconscious level focus on helping patients to become aware of their avoidance tactics. This may involve providing interpretations or explanations of their behaviour in responsibility avoidance terms. For instance, it may entail exploring the 'payoffs' or conscious and unconscious gains from their behaviour and decisions. All behaviour involves a decision and every decision that a person makes has some benefits for that individual.

Therapists can help their patients assume responsibility by assisting them in acquiring insights that apply leverage to their wills. The following are four of the most common of such insights: 'Only I can change the world I have created';

'There is no danger in change'; 'To get what I really want, I must change'; and 'I have the power to change'.

The facilitation of responsibility assumption often poses a dilemma for therapists in terms of how active or passive to be. On the one hand passive therapists may collude with patients who are not taking responsibility for change. On the other hand active and forceful therapists risk infantilizing patients. A study Yalom and his colleagues conducted observed eighteen encounter groups, led by leaders from a wide variety of ideological schools, for a total of thirty hours over a ten-week period. They found the following. Too active or too passive group leadership correlated with poor outcome. Furthermore, the more structured group exercises the leaders used, the more competent did group members perceive them at the end of the group, but the less successful was the outcome of the group measured six months later (Lieberman, Yalom and Miles: 1973). Being a too active, vigorous and structuring guide impedes responsibility assumption.

Yalom's existential psychotherapy has been very selectively presented here with a focus on the ultimate concern of freedom, and its corollary responsibility, rather than on the other ultimate concerns of death, isolation and meaninglessness. However, the ultimate concerns are interrelated. For instance, the idea of death helps define the importance of responsibility for the authorship of life. Additionally, an underlying existential fear of nonbeing or death is viewed as the basis of psychopathology or of responsibility avoidance. Yalom's work lays great stress on defences, often unconscious, against responsibility assumption. He also stresses the importance of an individual's will, which is a combination of two processes – wishing and choosing – either or both of which can be blocked. Therapy is seen as a will-influencing venture in which the therapist helps the patient or client, often in a group setting, identify and correct assumptions and behaviour which impede the freedom of choice necessary for authorship of life. Yalom is very aware of the dangers of too active a therapist in impeding clients' efforts at responsibility assumption. Though it may be a function of his being a psychiatrist whose caseload is predominantly of moderately to severely disturbed people, what does not come over strongly enough is the need to impart to people the skills not only of assuming but also of sustaining responsible authorship of their lives. Additionally, many of the concepts of existential psychotherapy are relevant to people in general and not just to psychiatric patients. Yalom has, as yet, to explore this area fully.

Concluding comments

From the preceding survey, it is evident that the notion of personal responsibility is pervasive, if not always explicit, in humanistic and existential approaches. Also, it may be apparent that none of the above positions is sufficiently comprehensive for engendering personal responsibility in relation to patients, clients and people in general. If anything, they insufficiently emphasize helping people to develop the skills of helping themselves. Nevertheless, there are many useful concepts and practical ideas in the above approaches that can be incorporated into an integrative approach focused on personal responsibility.

Despite its possible surface simplicity, personal responsibility is a complex concept. It embraces the existential notion that people are responsible for fashioning their own existences despite their finitude and the contingencies of fate; it has the connotation of needing the capacity to experience and be aware of one's significant feelings and emotions; and a sensitivity to anxiety and guilt is another facet of it. Responsibility avoidances come in all shapes and sizes. They range from operating on one's own experiencing by means of denials and distortions of unwelcome information to manipulating others to collude in one's avoidances. Responsibility assumption includes not only authenticity in relationships, but the capacity to find meaning in activity and, if necessary, in suffering.

Chapter 3

BACKGROUND: COGNITIVE, BEHAVIOURAL AND COGNITIVE-BEHAVIOURAL APPROACHES

This chapter continues the exploration of the implicit and explicit uses of the concept of personal responsibility across a number of different counselling and therapeutic approaches.

Rational-emotive therapy

Although Albert Ellis, the originator of rational-emotive therapy, rarely uses the word responsibility, he is very concerned to help his clients toward freedom of choice on the basis of rational thinking. Rationality consists of thinking in ways which contribute to the chosen goals of survival and happiness. Irrationality consists of thinking in ways which block or interfere with attaining these goals. The rational person is self-responsible in using reason in pursuit of chosen short-range and long-range hedonism.

In rational-emotive theory and practice personal responsibility is synonymous with rationality. People have strong innate or biological as well as acquired tendencies to be irrational. By innate Ellis means that the organism has a natural easy predisposition to behave in certain ways and has difficulty modifying or eliminating such behaviour. The facts that people seem so easily conditioned into dysfunctional thinking and behaviour and also that this is so hard to modify are evidence of an innate tendency to irrationality (Ellis: 1977a). People's failure to think rationally and face reality almost always leads them to manifest the feelings and behaviours of emotional disturbance.

In an early paper entitled 'Rational psychotherapy' Ellis proposed three fundamental hypotheses (Ellis: 1958). First, thinking and emoting are closely related. Second, thinking and emoting are so closely related that they accompany each other, act in a circular cause-and-effect relationship, and in certain (though hardly all) respects are essentially the same thing: one's thinking becomes one's emotion and one's emoting becomes one's thought. Third, both thinking and emoting tend to take the form of self-talk or internalized sentences. For all practical purposes, the sentences that people keep saying to themselves are or become their thoughts and emotions. Thus people's self-statements are capable of both generating and modifying their emotions. Appropriate emotions are emphasized – emotions are appropriate when they are accompanied by rational or sane beliefs. Such beliefs are functional in that they enhance the possibility of effective action in pursuit of hedonistic goals (Ellis: 1973a).

Relatively little is said about the acquisition of irrational or irresponsible thinking. Irrational ideas, which once might have been appropriate in view of the helpless state of the child, are acquired for a number of reasons. These include: the inability of children to think clearly; their dependence on the planning and thinking of others; and the indoctrination of irrational beliefs by parents and the media (Ellis and Harper: 1961).

Rational-emotive therapy is much more a theory about how irresponsible thinking is sustained than about how initially it was acquired. People reindoctrinate themselves with irrational thinking and faulty self-statements. This is how they perpetuate self-defeating emotions and behaviour. Rational-emotive therapy operates within an ABC framework: A is the activating event, consisting of the existence of a fact, or event, or the behaviour or attitude of another person; B consists of the beliefs or self-verbalizations of the individual about A; C is the consequence or reaction of the individual, be it happiness or emotional disturbance, which erroneously may be presumed to follow directly from A.

Human beings, for good or ill, largely control their own destinies through the innate, acquired and continuously reindoctrinated beliefs they hold or, in ABC terms, what happens at B. People's beliefs can be either rational and functional (rB) or irrational and self-defeating (iB). Although he sometimes lists eleven or twelve (Ellis: 1962; 1977b), every disturbed feeling is closely linked to one of the following three irrational beliefs: 1. 'I *must* do well and must win approval for all my performances, or else I rate as a rotten person'. 2. 'You *must* act kindly and considerately and justly toward me or else you are a louse'. 3. 'The conditions under which I live *must* remain good and easy, so that I get practically everything I want without too much effort and discomfort, or else the world turns damnable, and life hardly seems worth living' (Ellis: 1977b).

Ellis propounds a theory of responsibility avoidance based on people reindoctrinating themselves with irrational beliefs. One of his irrational beliefs is 'The idea that you will find it easier to avoid facing many of life's difficulties and self-reponsibilities than to undertake some rewarding forms of self-discipline' (Ellis:

1977b). There is a strong notion of the importance of responsibility awareness. People are responsible for the rational fashioning of their existences despite how unfairly other people and the world may be treating them.

Characteristics of irrational beliefs include: demandingness, self-rating, awfulizing and attribution errors. A demanding person makes the mistake of treating preferences and choices as demands and commands. These demands may be in relation to self, others or the environment. Implicitly or explicitly they almost invariably contain words like 'must', 'ought' or 'should'. 'Perfectionism' and 'intolerance' are other words describing this characteristic (Ellis: 1973b). Self-rating involves going from a functional rating of specific characteristics to an overgeneralized evaluation of self-worth. The favoured solution to the problem of personal worth is to be truly self-accepting rather than self-evaluating (Ellis: 1973a). Awfulness is allied to demandingness: if I, someone or something is not the way that I demand that they should or must be, then this is awful and catastrophic. This kind of thinking leads to heightened emotionality of the sort that impedes rationality (Ellis: 1977a). Attribution errors, involving falsely blaming oneself or others, frequently contribute to emotional disturbance (Ellis: 1977c).

Ellis aims to achieve the minimization of clients' self-defeating outlooks and their acquisition of a more realistic and tolerant philosophy of life by mercilessly attacking the characteristic methods of responsibility avoidance which are reflected in their belief systems. Thus the major objective of helping clients toward responsibility assumption is to substitute rational and functional for irrational and dysfunctional beliefs. The ABC framework gets expanded into an ABCDE framework for counselling practice. D stands for debating or disputing irrational beliefs; E stands for the effects of successfully disputing these beliefs. The effects include rational beliefs, appropriate emotions and desirable behaviours. Furthermore, E can include acquiring a new philosophy that enables the client 'semi-automatically to think about yourself, others, and the world in a more sensible way in future' (Ellis: 1977a).

Rational-emotive therapy employs individual, group or combined individual and group therapy formats. Ellis sees it as a cognitive-emotive-behaviouristic method of psychotherapy. The cognitive emphasis involves an active-didactic approach to helping individuals detect and dispute their demandingness. Emotional-evocative therapy may include role-playing situations involving irrational beliefs. Behavioural methods include homework, using imaginative techniques and self-reward (Ellis: 1973b). RET frequently uses interview aids such as self-help homework sheets, directed reading and getting clients to listen to cassette recordings of their interviews.

It is valuable to distinguish between the content of rational-emotive therapy and Ellis' therapeutic style which is stridently didactic and somewhat exhibitionistic. Concerning this distinction Meichenbaum writes: 'Perhaps this point could be most simply underscored by having the reader conjure-up the image of Carl Rogers conducting RET' (Meichenbaum: 1977). The remarks here refer much more to the content of Ellis' therapy than to his style.

As a method of increasing responsibility assumption by focusing on thinking, rational-emotive therapy has limitations. It mainly focuses on only one type of thinking – that of identifying, disputing and changing self-evaluative standards. Additionally, Ellis' twelve major irrational beliefs may be a strait-jacket for different clients' problems. Clients may feel on occasion that their difficulties are being reformulated into irrational beliefs which fit someone else's theory rather than their problems.

Like transactional analysis, rational-emotive therapy provides both therapists and clients with a relatively simple language with which to understand feelings, thinking and behaviour. It provides, too, an easily comprehensible model that clients can apply to their difficulties outside as well as inside therapy. Consequently, it stands some chance of helping its clients *stay* responsible. Indeed an objective is to teach clients what are tantamount to a set of self-help skills.

More than any of the theoretical positions reviewed so far, rational-emotive therapy emphasizes people's responsibility for disciplining their thinking. Ellis' style might prove overwhelming for some clients and conducive to letting him do the work for others. Nevertheless, his approach has much to offer those wishing to do their own work. Ellis mainly writes about rational-emotive therapy as a method of individual and group therapy, but the content of rational-emotive therapy might fruitfully be incorporated into training programmes that teach the skills of effective thinking to people outside traditional counselling settings. Perhaps the main problem with rational-emotive therapy is less that it is erroneous than that it is only a partial theory that claims to have greater power and applicability than is justified.

Traditional behaviourism

Traditional or radical behavioural theory rests on two main concepts: classical conditioning and operant conditioning. Classical conditioning is a form of learning in which a previously neutral stimulus assumes the capacity to elicit the response of another stimulus with which it has been paired. For instance, in one of Pavlov's fundamental experiments, food in a dog's mouth was an uncondi tioned stimulus which automatically elicited the inborn response of salivation (Pavlov: 1955). Through repeated reinforcement consisting of stimulation by a metronome followed by feeding, the metronome became a conditioned stimulus, thus being a signal for food and eliciting the conditioned response of salivation. In another classic experiment, Watson and Raynor established in an 11-month-old boy called Albert a conditioned response of fear to the stimulus of a white rat. This was achieved by linking on some trials the loud sound of striking a bar with Albert's touching the white rat (Watson and Raynor: 1920). Watson was a strict environmental determinist who viewed people largely as 'empty scrolls' who learned behaviour by being trained or retrained.

Operant conditioning involves making a reward or reinforcement contingent upon the enactment of behaviour that operates on the environment to produce consequences. Operant conditioning is most associated with the name of Skinner whose fundamental principle is that 'Behaviour is shaped and maintained by its consequences' (Skinner: 1971). Behaviour both operates on the environment to produce consequences and is controlled or contingent upon the consequences produced by that environment. A consequence is reinforcing to the degree that it increases the probability of the same response being repeated. Ferster and Skinner observe that many significant features of the shaping and maintenance of behaviour can only be explained by reference to the properties of schedules of reinforcement (Ferster and Skinner: 1957). Such schedules can either be continuous or intermittent, with there being many variations of intermittent reinforcement. Behaviour may be shaped by reinforcing successive approximations to the desired behaviour even to the extent of teaching a pigeon to bowl by breaking down and successively reinforcing the desired behaviours.

Skinner allows for the possibility of self-control. In self-control people manipulate events in their environments to control their behaviour. Self-control involves two interrelated responses. First, there is the controlling response which acts on the environment to alter the probability of the second or the controlled response. For example, an adult may engage in the controlling response of walking away to be able to control the response of anger. However, Skinner believes that in all instances a person's learning history and the environmental contingencies are ultimately responsible for behaviour. An 'inner originating and determining agent' is considered unnecessary (Skinner: 1953).

Traditional behavioural practice is based on the model of counsellors as teachers and clients as learners. It is an educational approach in which counsellors work to weaken and eliminate maladaptive behaviours and to initiate and/or strengthen adaptive behaviours. The responsibility for choosing specific and measurable behavioural goals may be shared between clients and counsellors; the responsibility for selecting methods is that of counsellors, though consent must usually be obtained from clients. The emphasis is on changing observable behaviour, but there is also an emphasis on changing feeling states, such as anxiety. This gains its validity to the extent that it leads to changes in observable behaviour. The test-anxious college student should not only feel less anxious, but be able to behave more effectively in test-taking situations.

One of the main traditional behavioural techniques is that of systematic desensitization. As presented by Wolpe (1973), this involves three elements: (a) training in deep muscular relaxation; (b) the construction of hierarchies of anxiety-evoking situations; and (c) asking the client, when relaxed, to imagine items from the anxiety-evoking hierarchies. Wolpe's explanation of the approach is that it is based on the principle of reciprocal inhibition:

> If a response antagonistic to anxiety can be made to occur in the presence of anxiety-evoking stimuli so that it is accompanied by a complete or partial suppression of the anxiety responses, the bond between these stimuli and the anxiety responses will be weakened. (Wolpe: 1958)

This is a classical conditioning explanation of systematic desensitization. Counsellors essentially work with passive clients who are conditioned rather than encouraged to take responsibility for developing the skills to cope with their anxieties. Wolpe's explanation of assertive training, in which counsellors train clients in specific behaviour by using role-play and coaching, is also that it is based on the reciprocal inhibition principle.

Reinforcement methods aim to modify behaviour by altering its consequences and, as such, reflect operant rather than classical conditioning principles. There is a range of ways in which reinforcement can be used in counselling. First, the whole process may be seen in reinforcement terms with both counsellors and clients attempting to control each other's behaviour by unintentionally and intentionally dispensing rewards, both verbal and nonverbal. Second, counsellors can work with their clients to draw up programmes to attain specific goals and then reward clients as they make progress toward achieving the goals. For instance, the counsellors may reinforce the attempts of college students attempting to increase their skills in heterosexual relations. Third, counsellors can help clients identify reinforcers and then reinforce their attempts to attain these reinforcers. Fourth, counsellors can teach clients principles of self-control. Thoresen and Mahoney (1974) indicate that there are two general self-control strategies. First, there is environmental planning or stimulus control, in which an attempt is made to control the target behaviour *prior* to its execution. Both putting food out of sight and of easy reach and using locations conducive to studying are examples of stimulus control. Second, there is behavioural programming, which involves self-administered consequences *following* the occurrence of a target response. For instance, the person who smokes five instead of fifteen cigarettes in a day may administer a consequent self-reward of phoning up a friend.

Traditional behaviourism rests on the notion of environmental control. Classical conditioning, if it were to be the only form of learning, would leave no room for the concept of personal responsibility. As it is, classical conditioning provides a valuable explanation of why some specific behaviours, such as phobias, restrict the range of choice of certain people and hence their capacity for personal responsibility. However, just because specific maladaptive behaviours may have been acquired through classical conditioning it does not follow that classical conditioning is the only way of unlearning or altering them. An important distinction in counselling is that between how behaviours were acquired and how they are sustained.

Whereas classical conditioning is a position of no responsibility, operant conditioning appears to be a position of diminished responsibility. Skinner seems to be saying that, while it is important for people to acquire self-control, ultimately past and present environmental learning contingencies, rather than the people themselves, are responsible for their behaviour. It seems inconsistent simultaneously to advocate self-control and environmental determinism. As Bandura writes: 'To contend, as environmental determinists often do, that people are controlled by external forces and then to advocate that they redesign society by applying psychotechnology undermines the basic premise of the argument' (Bandura: 1977a). Not only people but environments have causes. In other words, people may be simultaneously both acting to control their environments and being controlled by their environments.

Traditional behaviourism has a number of strengths in terms of developing a theoretical model using personal responsibility as an integrating concept. It incorporates a welcome emphasis on specificity of goals and methods. Its learning approach indicates that deficits in responsibility can largely be viewed as *learned* difficulties which lays open the possibility of their being corrected through the acquisition of *learned* skills. Furthermore, there is considerable evidence that traditional behavioural techniques can be effective with many clients (Wolpe: 1973).

Traditional behavioural methods have come under attack from cognitive theorists and practitioners on at least two counts. First, the theory on which they are based inadequately takes into account cognitive mediating variables. Thus, even when a technique like systematic desensitization is applied in a traditional way it is indadequately explained in terms of reciprocal inhibition or classical conditioning. Second, behavioural techniques such as systematic desensitization and assertive training can be more powerful if systematic attempts are made to change cognitions as well as overt behaviours (Meichenbaum: 1977). Traditional behavioural practice leaves less room for client responsibility both during and after treatment than a cognitive-behavioural approach that incorporates cognitive as well as behavioural self-help skills. The practice of traditional behaviourism has often been less mechanistic than the theory would indicate. One reason for this is that some clients and therapists resist an approach which they consider to be de-humanizing.

Cognitive-behaviourism: Beck's cognitive therapy

The first of the two cognitive-behavioural approaches reviewed here is that of Beck and his colleagues. Beck defines cognitive therapy as 'an active, directive, time-limited, structured approach used to treat a variety of psychiatric disorders (for example, depression, anxiety, phobias, pain problems, etc.). It is based on the underlying theoretical rationale that people's affect and behaviour are largely determined by the ways in which they structure the world' (Beck *et al.*: 1979). Cognitive therapy has been especially applied by Beck to the treatment of depression.

Cognitive therapy emphasizes the role of internal communications. It is not only stimuli from the environment that determine how people act and feel. Rather there is a range of intervening thoughts or ideation between external events and particular emotional responses. So-called 'over-reactions' involving unrealistic or exaggerated anger, anxiety or sadness are based on people's peculiar appraisal of events. In his clinical work, Beck found that patients were not reporting certain kinds of intervening thoughts. It was necessary to train patients to observe their stream of unreported thoughts. He gave them the instruction: 'Whenever you experience an unpleasant feeling or sensation, try to recall what thoughts you had been having prior to this feeling' (Beck: 1976).

Beck discovered that many of these previously unreported thoughts appeared to emerge automatically and extremely rapidly. Unless patients were instructed to focus on them, these *automatic thoughts* would pass by almost unnoticed. Either patients were not fully conscious of them or it did not occur to them that these thoughts warranted special scrutiny. Nevertheless, they played a significant role in hampering responsibility assumption: for example, they were more prominent in severe disturbance such as a bad depression. Characteristics of these automatic thoughts included the following: they were specific; they were discrete and occurred in a kind of shorthand; they were autonomous, in that patients made no effort to initiate them; they were regarded by patients as plausible, although they might seem far-fetched to others; they were idiosyncratic; and they generally involved more distortion of reality than other types of thinking. These internal signals in linguistic or visual form were keys to the inner workings of emotional disorders.

The content of people's internal signals or automatic thoughts is shaped by their rules. People possess mental rule books to guide their actions and to evaluate themselves and others. These rules are absorbed to a large extent through observation of others and through personal experience. Once detected, the rules, and the evaluative inferences drawn from them, can help explain seemingly illogical behaviour and irrational emotional responses.

The cognitive model of depression focuses on three concepts to explain the psychological manifestations of depression (Beck et al.: 1979). First, there is the *cognitive triad* revolving round patients' negative views of themselves, their tendency to experience their ongoing experiences in a negative way, and their negative view of the future. Given this negative view of self, the lack of responsibility involved in a tendency to increased dependency becomes understandable. Second, there is the concept of *schemas*. The term 'schema' designates relatively stable cognitive patterns that form the basis for how an individual will interpret or structure different experiences. In severe depressions patients' thinking may be completely dominated by idiosyncratic schema and they may be completely preoccupied by persistent and repetitive thoughts.

The third concept is that of *cognitive errors* involving faulty information processing. Depressed people are inclined to think in relatively primitive ways involving making broad and global judgements about events in their lives. Cognitive errors derived from depressogenic assumptions or rules include: 1. overgeneralization, based on the rule 'If it's true in one case, it applies to any case which is even slightly similar'; 2. selective abstraction, 'The only events that matter are failures, deprivation, etc.'; 3. excessive responsibility, 'I am responsible for all bad things, failures etc.'; 4. predicting without sufficient evidence, 'If it has always been true in the past, then it's always going to be true'; 5. self-references, 'I am the centre of everyone's attention – especially my bad performances'; 6. catastrophizing, 'Always think of the worst. It's most likely to happen to you'; and 7. dichotomous thinking, 'Everything is either one extreme or another (black or white; good or bad)'.

Regarding excessive responsibility, mothers more than fathers are prone to feel guilty about the presumed problems and deficiencies of their children, whereas men are more inclined to hold themselves responsible for setbacks in their vocations. Furthermore, in male case histories, the most common stressor precipitating suicide attempts was related to their performance at work or school. Suicide attempts among females were often preceded by friction in or disruption of their personal relationships (Beck *et al.*: 1979).

The cognitive model of predisposition to depression is that early experiences provide people with the basis for forming negative concepts about themselves, the future and the external world. Although these negative concepts or 'schemas' may be latent, they can be activated by experiences similar to those which originally contributed to the negative attitudes. An example is that of a marital disruption activating a sense of loss associated with the death of a parent in childhood.

The cognitive therapist applies specific techniques within the context of a relationship characterized by warmth, empathy and genuineness. It is important that patients understand the nature and rationale of cognitive treatment. Both initially and throughout therapy, the therapist repeatedly focuses on the connection between feeling and thinking. For instance, if the patient says 'I feel terrible', the cognitive therapist asks 'What are you thinking about?' The cognitive therapist aims to define target problems and develop in the patient specific skills to handle them. These skills consist of learning (a) to assess personally relevant situations realistically, including not distorting available data about these situations; (b) generating alternative explanations about the outcome of interactions; and (c) testing maladaptive assumptions by behaving differently and thereby engaging in empirical investigation of the assumptions.

Behavioural techniques are often used early on to counteract depressed people's withdrawal and to get them more involved in life. These techniques include the drawing up of activity schedules, identifying activities which give a sense of mastery and/or a sense of pleasure, graded task assignment in which patients are encouraged to perform successively more difficult tasks, cognitive rehearsal in which patients are asked to imagine and work through each successive step in the sequence leading to completion of a task, and assertive training and role-playing. The targets of the behavioural techniques include passivity, avoidance, lack of gratification, and inability to express appropriate emotions such as sadness and anger. The idea of using behavioural techniques early on is that by observing changes in their own behaviour patients may both derive an improvement in mood and be more ready to examine their negative self-conceptions.

In introducing cognitive techniques, the therapist tries to communicate that patient and therapist are scientific collaborators who will 'investigate' the content of the patient's thinking. Therapists then teach patients the skills of observing and recording their cognitions. This is partly achieved by defining cognition and automatic thoughts; partly by demonstrating with examples the influence of cognitions on affect and behaviour. Furthermore, patients may be encouraged to read an introductory booklet entitled *Coping with Depression* (Beck and Greenberg: 1974). Therapists then assign specific projects designed to help patients detect automatic thoughts. These include: identifying and recording automatic thoughts right after they occur; setting aside fifteen minutes each evening to record any upsetting cognitions and to replay the events that led to the cognitions; working to understand the cognitions involved in specific environmental events associated with depressed feelings, for instance difficulty between 7am and 9am; and recording upsetting cognitions that have a common theme. Therapists may also confront patients with one of their upsetting events with the purpose of arousing and identifying depressive cognitions.

Therapists encourage patients to examine the reality of their automatic thoughts and images against the criteria of reasonable standards used by non-depressed people in making judgements. Reattribution and alternative conceptualization are among the techniques used to help patients gain greater objectivity. *Reattribution*, sometimes called 'de-responsibilitizing', is useful for patients who engage in excessive self-blame. Patients are encouraged to make an appropriate assignment of responsibility by: (a) reviewing the 'facts' of the events that led to the self-criticism and applying the laws of logic to them; (b) exploring whether they have a double-standard in applying different criteria when assigning responsibility to themselves and to other people; and (c) challenging their beliefs that they are totally responsible for any adverse occurrences.

Alternative conceptualization, otherwise known as the search for alternative solutions, involves the active investigation of other interpretations of and/or solutions to the patient's problems. Sometimes patients are requested as a written assignment not only to record upsetting events, feelings and cognitions, but also to list other possible interpretations of the events. Additionally, patients may be encouraged to wear wrist counters and to check off their negative automatic thoughts as they occur. Homework is an integral part of cognitive therapy. This is likely to include: filling in a daily record of dysfunctional thoughts; using the wrist counter for as long as useful; and also using activity schedules for as long as useful.

Beck's cognitive therapy is an integrative approach heavily focused on responsibility as effective thinking. Though he uses behavioural techniques, these are viewed as attempts to alter cognitions rather than in conditioning terms. Because he works mainly with depressed patients, he is extremely sensitive to issues of misattribution of responsibility. Beck talks of depressed people possessing a cognitive triad of negative views about self, current events and the future. He also lists a number of cognitive errors based on depressogenic assumptions. It is noticeable, especially in light of his psychoanalytic background, that he omits the area of defence mechanisms and self-protective thinking. Cognitive therapy has a number of positive points for developing the theory and practice of personal responsibility counselling and therapy. It is a problem-solving skills approach to therapy. The role of therapists is to offer an easily comprehensible rationale for treatment; then to teach patients, within the context of a therapeutic relationship, the skills of implementing the approach. From the start therapists collaborate with patients both to identify and also to devise strategies for dealing with target symptoms. Therapists build on their patients' experiences both when presenting the rationale and also when illustrating its practical application. The problem-solving approach, the therapeutic collaboration, the presentation of a treatment rationale comprehensible to the patient, and the willingness right from the start to illustrate the position in terms of the patient's experiencing of life all combine to convey the message that patients have some chance of learning to control their depressive reactions for themselves. This helps mobilize their resources to take greater responsibility for their lives at the start of, during and after therapy. The ultimate aim of cognitive therapy is self-therapy. However, because it is a time-limited approach, it may be insufficient to meet the needs of some people, especially if they possess marked behavioural as well as cognitive deficits.

Cognitive-behaviourism: Meichenbaum's cognitive-behaviour modification

The second cognitive-behavioural approach reviewed here is that of Meichenbaum. He considers that behaviour therapy techniques 'as originally conceptualized and implemented, have overemphasized the importance of environmental events (antecedents and consequences) and, therefore, underemphasized and often overlooked how a client perceives and evaluates these events' (Meichenbaum: 1977). Although behaviour therapy techniques may modify what people say to themselves, these procedures are likely to be more effective when augmented with appropriate self-instructional packages. His cognitive-behaviour modification focuses on regulating behaviour by means of self-instructions, either independent of or in conjunction with traditional behavioural techniques.

Meichenbaum has been influenced by the work of Luria and others on the relationship between language, thought and behaviour in children. Luria (1961) proposed three stages by which voluntary motor behaviours come under verbal control. First, the child's behaviour is directed by the speech of others. Second, it is directed by the child's own overt speech. Third, the child's inner or covert speech becomes an effective regulator of behaviour. For example, late adolescents or adults learning to drive cars may first be guided by their instructors' guidance, then by self-instructions, until, with practice, the verbalizations disappear as the behavioural sequences become automatic. In other words, private speech is initially facilitative and then drops out with the development of task proficiency.

Meichenbaum uses the term 'internal dialogue' to describe this private speech. He does not equate inner speech with thought. This speech is one aspect of the thinking process. The word 'dialogue' is preferred to 'monologue': private speech is a process of both listening and talking to oneself in a self-communication system. His belief in the importance of inner speech comes from research in three areas: interpersonal instructions, often in regard to problem-solving tasks; cognitive factors in stress responses; and the effects of instructional sets on physiological reactions.

Inner speech has two important functions: influencing clients' behaviours and influencing their cognitive structures. The concept of cognitive structures relates to clients' belief systems. Some of these beliefs (or cognitive structures) are implicit whereas other beliefs are explicit. Changing behaviour entails a mediational process involving the recognition of either internal or external maladaptive behaviours. This recognition in turn must elicit inner speech different from that engaged in prior to therapy. The altered private speech must then elicit coping behaviours, assuming that they are in the client's behavioural repertoire. If not, explicit teaching of coping behaviours may be required.

Meichenbaum and Genest: (1981) observe a consistent theme across reviews of cognitive-behaviour modification (CBM) with children who have self-control problems; although the approaches offer encouragement, evidence for the generalization of such treatment across settings and over time is equivocal. They are therefore interested in the potential of teaching metacognitive skills as compared to concrete, task-specific statements. They consider that the teaching of such skills as checking, planning, questioning, testing oneself and monitoring one's problem-solving should enhance the effectiveness of cognitive-behaviour modification procedures.

Meichenbaum and Genest refer to both CBM therapy and CBM training. In fact CBM appears as training in self-help skills. CBM with adults involves three phases: conceptualization of the problem; 'trying on' the conceptualization; and modifying cognitions and producing new behaviours. During the conceptualization phase, therapists work with clients to redefine their problems in terms that are acceptable to both. Therapists help clients to observe and realize the irrational, self-defeating and self-fulfilling aspects of their cognitions (self-statements and images). They may also be given homework assignments involving self-observation. This phase is basically laying the groundwork for clients to accept the cognitive-behavioural rationale for their problems presented in the second phase. The second phase of therapy consolidates the 'translation' process in which clients' problems are reconceptualized in ways that make the logic of the treatment plan clearer.

The third phase, that of changing cognitions and behaviours, can be approached in a variety of ways depending on the nature of the problem and the particular emphasis of the cognitive-behavioural therapist – viz. focusing on inner speech or on cognitive structures. Therapists may intervene at the point of altering specific behaviours to affect cognitions or at the point of altering cognitions so that the client can generate and implement new behaviours or 'conduct *in vivo* personal experiments'.

Meichenbaum's cognitive-behavioural practice heavily emphasizes training clients in appropriate inner speech. This self-instructional training is the main common element across all the different client populations with which he works. He finds group as effective as individual treatment: stress innoculation training is an example of how he attempts to make clients more responsible for their emotions and behaviour through working with them on the ways in which they are talking to themselves: it is a coping skills approach to the handling of stress. Meichenbaum regards stress as residing neither in the situation nor in the person, but in the transaction between the individual and the situation. He writes: 'The general principles of stress-innoculation training involve teaching or encouraging individuals to consider what lies ahead; to split stressful events into manageable doses; to think of ways to handle each mini-stress; and to practise coping skills' (Meichenbaum: 1983). Individuals may be asked to play back in slow motion the thoughts, images and feelings that preceded, accompanied and followed the stressful situation. This helps them gain insight into their own contribution to and responsibility for their stress level, and also provides material which they and their trainers can use to develop problem-solving strategies.

Individuals and trainers then work together to develop coping self-instructions or inner speech in each of the following areas: preparation for the stress; confronting and handling it; coping with the feelings of being overwhelmed; and reflection on how the situation was handled. For example, sample statements for coping with a fear or phobia are: (a) preparing for fear, 'No negative statements about myself; I must think rationally'; (b) confronting fear, 'One step at a time: I can handle the situation'; (c) coping with fearful feelings, 'I won't try to eliminate my fear totally, just to keep it manageable'; and (d) reflection afterwards, 'I made more out of my fear than it was worth'

A further example is coping inner speech that helps people take responsibility for handling their anger. Self-instructional statements include: (a) preparing for anger, 'Remember, stick to the issues and don't take things personally'; (b) confronting anger, 'I don't need to prove myself, and I mustn't make more out of this than I have to'; (c) coping with angry feelings, 'My anger is a signal telling me what I need to do: it's problem-solving time'; (d) reflection when the conflict is unresolved, 'Relax. It's a lot better than getting angry'; and (e) reflection when the conflict is resolved, 'My pride can get me into trouble, but I'm getting better at stopping myself getting into trouble' (Meichenbaum: 1983)

Meichenbaum also encourages clients to employ whatever coping techniques they may already possess, for instance using their social support systems. He may employ other techniques such as teaching physical and mental relaxation or communication skills. Furthermore, he may teach cognitive coping techniques: for example, problem-solving, altering appraisals and imaginal rehearsal. The goal of stress inoculation training is to teach people to become aware of the early signs of stress (thoughts, images, feelings, behaviours and physiological reactions); then to interrupt the cycle by using the coping inner speech and other skills developed in training. Sometimes, however, stress reduction requires changes in the social environment.

Ways in which inner speech can be used to add to the effectiveness of traditional behaviour therapy include the following. The effectiveness of relaxation techniques may be enhanced by clients saying to themselves words like 'relax' and 'calm' as they relax. Systematic desensitization may be based on learning coping skills rather than on a classical conditioning or mastery model; thus clients are asked to imagine anxiety-evoking scenes they are also encouraged to manage their anxiety by instructing themselves with appropriate coping statements. When therapists use modelling to inhibit an anxiety or to teach a skill, they can ensure that the model verbalizes the relevant cognitions for acquiring the target behaviour. This may involve the kinds of self-instructions described for stress-inoculation training. Assertive training is a matter of focusing not only on the desired behaviours, but on the thoughts accompanying the behaviours. This may be a matter both of learning to eliminate negative self-statements and of being able to talk oneself through a situation with task-relevant inner speech.

Implicitly Meichenbaum stresses the importance of responsibility as sensitivity to anxiety. Anxiety is viewed as an indicator that coping skills may either need to be developed or implemented. Above all, Meichenbaum focuses on responsibility as effective thinking. This does not just consist in disputing and changing cognitive structures or beliefs; his distinctive contribution is the emphasis he places on using the inner speech component of thinking so that people may be better able both to cope with their fears and to focus on task-oriented thoughts, feelings and behaviours.

There are a number of points to make about coping through the use of self-instruction. First, the concept of *coping* with situations is less daunting than that of having to *master* situations. This lowering of sights may have the salutary effect of making situations less anxiety-engendering and goals more attainable and hence more likely to be attained. Second, Meichenbaum goes to great lengths to ensure that clients reconceptualize their concerns in ways that allow them to share the responsibility for their treatment. Third, the end product of his treatment is a set of self-help skills that clients can use after therapy, at the very least for their presenting concern and possibly across a number of other areas. Fourth, Meichenbaum is heavily influencing clients' sense of control over their problem areas. Here belief in one's sense of control may greatly reduce the level of a stress (Meichenbaum: 1983)

Meichenbaum does not present a comprehensive theory of the development of functional and dysfunctional inner speech. He focuses more on how people maintain self-defeating attitudes and behaviour. Nevertheless, his attempts at self-instructional training with children show that his methods may have some promise of being used in preventive as well as remedial ways.

Meichenbaum's model of human functioning is too rational. Like Beck, he ignores responsibility avoidance though self-protective thinking. He seems to assume that people will be prepared first to acknowledge their problems and second to accept his reconceptualizations of them, but this is unlikely always to be the case in areas of high threat. Meichenbaum's methods may also be weak in eliciting affect from affect-blocked people. His approach seems much more geared to coping with negative feelings than with getting people to experience their feelings more fully or to express positive feelings, though self-instruction would probably lend itself to the latter goal. Possibly, the points about self-protective thinking and affect-blocked clients can be drawn together in the reservation that Meichenbaum's methods may be insufficient for people who have marked self-esteem deficits. There may be a risk of premature application of self-instructional training which does not produce the desired results and thus in turn further lowers self-esteem. A final point is that Meichenbaum's self-instructional training has much to offer the development of a theory and practice of counselling and therapy with personal responsibility as an integrating concept. The idea that people can alter their inner speech makes self-regulation more practicable than just focusing on their rules and standards.

Some further concepts: attribution and locus of control

The concepts of attribution and locus of control are derived more from research than from the practice of counselling. Attribution refers to the ways and processes by which people attribute causes and meanings to their own behaviour, to others' behaviour and to environmental events. Another way of viewing attribution is in terms of making causal inferences about behaviour and events. Attribution theorists focus on the antecedents and consequences of perceived causality. There are a number of assumptions underlying the notion of causal attribution; perhaps the most basic is that humans strive for a causal understanding of their environments in order to maximize their control over them (Heider: 1958). Other assumptions are that individuals' assignments of cause are determined in a systematic manner and that the particular cause, or causes, they attribute to given events has important consequences for their subsequent feelings and behaviour.

Seligman and his colleagues have been investigating the relationship of differing kinds of causal attributions to depression. Seligman's original learned helplessness model of depression was derived largely from animal studies. The basic hypothesis was that learning that results in one's life are uncontrollable leads to three deficits: reduced motivation, reduced ability later to learn that certain responses may produce the desired outcome, and depressed affect (Seligman: 1975). In the cognitive reformulation of the learned helplessness model, when people find that they are helpless they ask why. Their attribution of helplessness to a cause can be stable or unstable, global or specific and/or internal or external (Abramson et al.: 1978). Depression is likely to be most severe when the outcome of an event is likely to be uncontrollable and attribution of this uncontrollability is to a global, stable and internal factor. Relevant therapeutic strategies include, when the outcomes are attainable, changing the expectation from uncontrollability to controllability. For instance, when the responses are not in people's repertoires, they can be trained in appropriate skills. Also, unrealistic attributions for failure might be changed toward external, unstable specific factors and unrealistic attributions for success toward internal, stable, global factors. Seligman and his colleagues have produced some research evidence in support of their concept of depressive attributional style (Seligman et al.: 1979), though their hypotheses have not always been supported (Zuroff: 1981)

An interesting application of the concept of attribution relates to the possible influence of differences in causal attribution on achievement motivation. Weiner and Kukla (1970) have produced evidence suggesting that individuals who are high and those who are low in achievement motivation differentially attribute the causes of success and failure. High achievement motivation individuals are more likely to attribute success to effort and failure to lack of proper effort. Low achievement motivation individuals are less inclined to persist given failure. They are less likely to ascribe their failure to lack of effort and more likely to attribute it to a deficiency in ability. Dweck (1975) trained children who exhibited helplessness to correct their misattributions by taking responsibility for failure and attributing it to lack of effort. This resulted in improvement and maintenance of performance.

Attribution of cause and attribution of responsibility for what happens in one's life are virtually identical concepts. The term attribution of responsibility is favoured here. The possibility of appropriate control over one's existence seems more implicit in it. It is conceivable that, with some clients, the word attribution may mean little and the term assigning responsibility for what happens in your life may be better.

The concept of locus of control is closely related to that of attribution of responsibility. Rotter has produced an Internal-External Locus of Control Scale, known as the I-E Scale (Rotter: 1966; 1972). He hypothesizes that people differ in their generalized expectancies for internal versus external control of reinforcement. A generalized expectancy for internal control is that people perceive that reinforcement is contingent upon their own behaviour or relatively permanent characteristics. A generalized expectancy for external control is when people perceive reinforcement as having followed some action of their own without being entirely contingent upon this action. The results may be typically perceived as luck, chance, fate, under the control of powerful others or unpredictable because of the complexity of the situation (Rotter: 1966). Having made this distinction, Rotter points out that he and his colleagues were not hypothesizing a typology or a bimodal distribution (one with two main groupings). Rather they expected most people to be grouped round a central point. Furthermore, even within those scoring high on externality there appear to be a group of defensive externals. These have competitive achievement skills that might be associated with internality.

Internal locus of control resembles the notion of being aware of one's responsibility for authorship of one's life. However, the matter is not that simple. Rotter lists a number of studies which suggest that it is typical of internals to repress or forget failures or unpleasant experiences (Rotter: 1975). Responsibility awareness entails realism in regard to the parameters of existence. Some internals may not be sufficiently aware of limits on personal control. This could have the effect of making them more prone to anxiety in genuinely unpredictable circumstances and more prone to depression in adverse circumstances. Rotter points out that researchers and others should not assume a 'good guy-bad guy' dichotomy, that it is good to be internal and bad to be external. Nevertheless, some research findings support the desirability of internality as contrasted with externality (e.g. Fish and Karabenick: 1971; Rykman and Sherman: 1973). Furthermore, externality could be associated with responsibility avoidance, passivity and defensiveness.

Regarding responsibility assumption, Rotter sees teaching and encouraging generalized expectancies for problem-solving as a useful part of psychotherapy for many clients (Rotter: 1978). It is important for people to learn to solve their own problems. The most important of all problem-solving attitudes or generalized expectancies is that 'one can affect or control, at least in part, what happens to oneself' or, in other words, be reasonably accurate in attributing responsibility for what happens in one's life.

Concluding comments

Apart from perhaps radical behaviourism, all counselling approaches aim to influence the ways in which clients think. However, they differ in the specificity with which they attempt this task. The cognitive and cognitive-behavioural approaches described here are essentially trying to teach clients some skills of effective thinking. Thus implicitly, if not always explicitly, they have a major emphasis on people assuming responsibility through disciplined thinking. The goal is that of helping clients to learn to think realistically about themselves, others and their environments. Elements of such realistic thinking include possessing functional self-standards or inner rules, knowing how to instruct oneself with coping inner speech and being able accurately to attribute responsibility for what happens in one's life. Beck, in particular, showed sensitivity to the fact that people may wrongly attribute too much as well as too little responsibility to themselves. This may be a contributing factor both to creating and also to sustaining depressive tendencies.

One of the positive effects of behaviourism on psychology has been the introduction of a much greater emphasis on the learning of skills than existed previously. Cognitive behaviourism has broadened the range of skills an individual needs to include those focused on thinking as well as on observable behaviour. Indeed all skills, even movement skills, have a thinking or cognitive element in them involving choices about whether, when and how best to perform the skill. Though a complex concept, a brief definition of personal responsibility is *the process of making the choices that maximize the individual's happiness and fulfilment.* This definition is consistent with both a cognitive and a psychological skills approach to the practice of personal responsibility counselling and therapy.

Chapter 4

TOWARD A THEORY: ASSUMPTIONS AND ACQUISITION

The following two chapters present a theoretical model for counselling and therapy having personal responsibility as its central integrating concept. This theoretical model is drawn from many sources. These include the wealth of theorizing that already exists, pertinent research literature, the author's professional experience as a practitioner and trainer, his experience as a client in individual and group counselling, and introspection.

Theories of counselling and therapy need to have four main elements if they are to be stated adequately: first, a statement of the *basic assumptions* underlying the theory; second, an explanation of the way functional and dysfunctional feelings, thoughts and behaviours are *acquired;* third, an explanation of the ways in which functional and dysfunctional feelings, thoughts and behaviours are *perpetuated* or *sustained;* fourth, practical suggestions for *changing* and *modifying* feelings, thoughts and behaviour that are internally consistent with the preceding elements of the model. This structure has been used here in presenting a theoretical model. This chapter is focused on basic assumptions and acquisition and the following chapter on perpetuation and change. A leaf has been taken out of Rogers' book, or rather his first detailed presentation of his theoretical position (Rogers: 1951). Thus the model is presented in terms of a series of tentative propositions or hypotheses. Although the propositions fall short of comprehensiveness, it is hoped that they are sufficient to describe a framework for conceptualizing counselling and therapy. Each proposition is followed by a brief explanation of what is intended by it.

Basic assumptions

1. *Human existence is a process which takes place both within existential parameters and within a continually changing world*

Without wishing to advocate a simple mind-body split, it can be said that human existence takes place on both physical and psychological levels. The concern is with the latter here. Existence means standing out, emerging, becoming, being or having a place in the world. Furthermore, it involves awareness of one's being, although this awareness may not always be as full or sharp as desirable. Human existence is a process that for each individual entails a continuing development involving many changes over the course of time. Thus, existence involves progression and movement, though the progression may not always be in desired directions and the movement or change may be barely perceptible. Humans rarely, if ever, stand psychologically still.

The parameters or conditions of human existence can be broken down into two main categories: those that are universal and those that are specific to given individuals. Death or biological extinction is the ultimate condition of existence and form of nonbeing. While not having the finality of nonbeing, there are various other threats to being. These also constitute limiting conditions within which people have to affirm their existence. Fate is one such limiting condition. The notion of contingency is relevant to the concept of fate. Contingent means of uncertain origin, accidental and unpredictable. It also has connotations of irrationality. Fate can be negative or positive, but the assumption is that it is out of the control of the individual. Suffering may be viewed as a contingency which is actual rather than potential. Here suffering means unavoidable pain, whether physical or psychological, rather than self-generated suffering. The prospect of meaninglessness is another condition of existence. A further condition is that of the ultimate isolation of human beings from each other.

The conditions of individual existence include factors that are relevant to groups as well as those that only pertain to individuals. For instance, the historical period, culture and country in which people live may be seen as group conditions of existence. Also, the rate of technological change, wars and natural disasters may be seen as affecting groups as well as individuals. Ultimately all group conditions of existence have their impact on individuals. Additionally, people live circumscribed by their own particular limiting conditions. These include: race, sex, physical characteristics, physical handicaps, and predispositions that interact with the environment, for example intelligence, musical ability and artistic ability.

People's inner and outer environments are always in process of change. Inwardly they are subject to a continuous flow of what Rogers calls 'sensory and visceral sensations' only some of which are consciously experienced (Rogers: 1951). In other words people are subject to an ongoing flow of feelings which may or may not be symbolized into thoughts. Their inner environment is still changing even if their outer environment may not appear to change. However, most often the outer environment is changing as well. Mention has already been made of some of the broader forces, viz. historical and technological change. More immediately people affect and in turn are affected by other people. This is really the position that Bandura in his social learning theory calls 'reciprocal determinism' in which behaviour is viewed in terms of a continuous interaction between personal and environmental determinants (Bandura: 1977a).

2. Humans are primarily motivated by a set of biologically derived needs and fears related to survival

Although this may seem blindingly obvious, the point is made to stress humans' animal nature as an antidote to too mechanistic a view on the one hand and too much of an emphasis on 'higher' qualities on the other. The basic survival of each individual is threatened by such matters as absence of food, warmth, water and shelter. Sexual and relatedness needs are critical for the survival of the species. The biological nature of relatedness needs is clearly indicated by the strength of the pain of loneliness. As Glasser points out, humans need involvement with others (Glasser: 1975) or, as the transactional analysis people put it, 'folks need strokes'. To survive, humans also need to be active. This is not just a matter of obtaining the basic essentials of life, but of developing and maintaining their physical and mental attributes. Though activity might be a better term than work, Selye observes: 'I think we have to begin by clearly realizing that work is a biological necessity. Just as our muscles become flabby and degenerate if not used, so our brain slips into chaos and confusion unless we constantly use it for some work that seems worthwhile to us' (Selye: 1974).

To the existential psychologists, the fear of death, nonbeing or destruction is the underlying fear from which all other fears are derived. The term survival anxiety seems preferable to that of death anxiety. Survival anxiety relates both to the fear of death itself and also to the fear of not being competent to meet one's survival needs. The notion of survival anxiety is more focused than death anxiety on the continual fears of the living. The instinct to survive is so strong in individual humans that anything that seems as though it might interfere with it is likely to be perceived as a threat and reacted to with anxiety.

So far in this section humans' animal nature and the primacy of maintaining physical life and perpetuating the species have been stressed. The nature of human destructiveness and the extent to which humans possess higher order values are two issues relevant to survival. Freud posited a strong destructive instinct which was the primary component of the death instinct (Freud: 1962). Strangely enough he did not seem to make any strong statement about the connection between human aggression and the survival part of the life instinct. In other words, are humans inherently aggressive or mainly aggressive when their survival is threatened but not otherwise? Here aggression is viewed as having a survival value for the individual so long as it can be channelled into assertion rather than destructiveness. Though the potential for destructiveness is inherent in humans, whether or not and the extent to which it gets actualized are related to many considerations. These include people's level of self-esteem; the degree to which they have been observing aggressive models (Bandura and Walters: 1963); whether or not they live in a society that is based on competition rather than cooperation; and what they say to themselves about potentially anger-evoking situations (Novaco: 1977). Another consideration is that people may perform the most highly destructive acts independent of aggressive feelings toward their victims, and sometimes with great inner conflict over how they behave. The main thrust of the findings of Milgram's obedience research is that once people become involved in social hierarchies rather than acting as independent agents, a whole range of new considerations governs their behaviour (Milgram: 1974). Furthermore, a major rationale for much destructive behaviour between nations is that of defence or survival.

The capacity of humans to possess higher order values and their potential for aggression are not mutually exclusive. The quality as well as the possibility of survival is affected by humans' possessing and striving after positive values. Though his argument may be somewhat circular, Maslow asserts that what he terms 'being values' are more likely to be the preferences and choices of self-actualizing people. These values include: truth, goodness, beauty, aliveness, justice and simplicity (Maslow: 1971). Similarly Rogers asserts that qualities such as a desire for authenticity, a desire for wholeness as a human being, the wish for intimacy, caring for others and an attitude of closeness toward nature are characteristics inherent in the organism, though they may need a growth-inducing therapeutic relationship to become manifest (Rogers: 1980). Rationally, Rogers and Maslow state the real survival needs both for the human species and for individuals. However, in the main, humans interpret their survival in less elevated terms. Initially most feel that they must allay their anxieties about for higher order values to get lost in the pressures of daily life.

3. Ultimately each individual is personally responsible for his or her survival and unique fulfilment

The way this proposition is stated applies much more to adults than to children. This meaning of personal responsibility might be labelled responsibility awareness. It incorporates the existential notion that individuals are the authors, architects, builders or creators of their lives within the conditions of existence. It in no way is meant to imply that people are not interdependent nor that they do not have some responsibility for the survival and fulfilment of others.

The way in which people assume personal responsibility for their lives is through the adequacy of their choices. Although the assumption is made that the meeting of biologically derived needs relating to survival is universal, individuals are unique in their approach to meeting these needs and to finding meaning in life. In the final analysis the adequacy of a choice relates to a particular individual in a particular context.

Personal responsibility is based on the individual's having a repertoire of psychological skills. The word skill connotes proficiency, practised ability and expertness. Skills also involve choices. They are, in fact, sequences of correct choices. The process of personal responsibility involves the application of a number of different subskills of varying degrees of complexity and focus. These skills are in the interrelated areas of an individual's feeling, thinking and acting. The fact that these skills involve choices means that they fundamentally take place within the individual, though their effects may become manifest in overt behaviour. People are viewed as decision-makers engaged in a continual process of making choices that, with rare exceptions, are intended to ensure their survival and maximize their fulfilment.

4. The process of being personally responsible is a continuous struggle in face of inherent human fallibility

Although human beings have the potential for rationality, they also have tendencies toward irrational and self-defeating thinking. Put another way, their process of making responsible choices is sometimes diminished by what seem inherent predelictions toward irrationality and self-protection. Perls used to quote Einstein as having said that only two things were infinite — the universe and human stupidity — and that he was not yet completely sure about the universe (Perls: 1969b). There seem to be a number of factors contributing to this fallibility. First, the maturational process for the development of human thinking is slow and lags behind their need to be able to use reasoning to comprehend adequately the world in which they live. Second, the long dependency period involved in growing up, combined with the need for security and with slow mental development, makes it all too easy for children to internalize self-defeating beliefs from adults. Third, people have the potential to be classically conditioned to various otherwise irrational fears. Fourth, people's need to make consistent sense out of the world, and the sense of security that this engenders, may be stronger than their ability to see the world as it really is and to process information accurately. Fifth, there may be an evolutionary lag in that the human brain has difficulty in grasping the intricacies of what seems to be an increasingly complex world.

This is a rather gloomy yet realistic view of the human condition. Humans are subject to at least three sets of limiting factors: their finitude and the universal and specific conditions of their existence; their animal nature and survival needs; and their inherent fallibility and tendencies toward irrational thinking. Perhaps this may be taken as an example of European pessimism rather than American optimism, though Americans now seem to be losing some of the innocence of their vision. The picture that emerges is that much of the time life is a struggle against one's own and other people's limitations and fallibility.

5.   From early in their lives humans are in a continuous process of implementing and validating their self-conceptions. These self-conceptions imply definitions of other people

Already it has been mentioned that psychological skills can be viewed in terms of choices. The choices that people make both create and implement their self-concepts. My self-concept relates to the various ways in which I define myself both at and beneath the level of conscious awareness. In some ways it is not a unitary construct since I can be consciously defining myself in one way and yet my underlying definition of self may be rather different, and often more negative. People's self-conceptions are extremely important to them since not only are they what the person refers to as 'I' or 'me', but also they provide the maps by which individuals negotiate their worlds. If they are going to negotiate the terrain adequately they need self-concepts that, in any situation, allow them to make realistic choices based on all the significant information available. People with personal responsibility skills deficits are, almost by definition, restricted in their ability to make realistic choices because of the inadequacy of various parts of their self-concept.

Social interaction involves two or more people relating to each other on the basis of their self-conceptions. These self-conceptions may have been created in such a way as to constrict choice. Also, they may be sustaining constriction of choice. Furthermore, since my conception of me implies my conception or definition of you and since your conception of yourself implies your conception or definition of me, there is always the possibility that we will not be viewing each other accurately, but in terms of our own needs to validate our self-conceptions. Though a great simplification, there are really three possible outcomes in a two-person interaction: first, what might be called *congruence*, the state of affairs in which both parties are relating to each other on the basis of largely accurate self-conceptions incorporating a realistic picture of themselves and each other; second, *collusion* or where both parties tacitly agree not to notice an inaccurate self-conception of one or both of them. This may involve reciprocity in the sustaining of illusions along the lines of 'I will agree not to challenge your fantasy of yourself, so long as you agree not to challenge my fantasy of myself'. The third possible outcome is *contest* or where one or both parties are attempting to impose their definitions of themselves and of each other on the other. In fact, most relationships involve all three elements.

Very frequently my need to view you to meet my own ulterior needs may be stronger than my need to view you accurately. Thus much of social interaction, including parent-child relations and marriages, may be seen as having elements of contest or of 'who is successful in defining whom' in them. In fact, so widespread are people's needs to impose false definitions on themselves and on others that much of life can be seen as an arena in which contests of varying degrees of psychological deadliness are being held. For example, perfect parents require children who provide feedback which is not too discrepant with that self-conception. Where such feedback is not forthcoming, maintaining this self-definition may be more important to parents than their children's real welfare.

In people's personal and social relationships they make many of the choices that define their level of personal responsibility. These choices involve self-definition, definition of others and having the strength and courage to stand up for themselves in face of false and often subtle power plays for them not to be true to themselves. This is not simply a matter of assertion, though in many instances assertion may be appropriate. Personal responsibility goes beyond assertion in acknowledging that individuals may have to 'set their own house in order' before being ready to enter a contest involving definition of self and others.

6.   *Humans are significantly motivated by their fears and anxieties as well as by their wants*

Earlier, it was mentioned that humans are primarily motivated by a set of biologically derived fears and needs related to survival. Furthermore, it was postulated that survival anxiety, the same as and yet the converse of death anxiety, could be viewed as the underlying form of anxiety. One form of anxiety that humans share with other animals is realistic anxiety regarding threats from the external world to their physical survival or wholeness. However, humans have the capacity for thought and awareness which makes possible a range of anxieties which are not available to animals. Thus humans are amenable to anxiety through threats and dangers, real or imagined, to their psychological as well as to their physical well-being. For example, the anxiety of people who fear they may be rejected or of people who fear that they will not be competent in assessment situations reflects an underlying anxiety about their chances for and competence in relation to physical survival. The fact that much of this anxiety is unrealistic is beside the point. People's anxieties are sustained by what they believe and by their inappropriate inner speech, rather than just by the facts of situations. However, as the existentialists in particular have pointed out, anxiety can serve as a useful warning that people are alienated from their experiencing and biological centredness. Thus anxiety is a psychological signal with underlying biological significance which may be used, if rightly perceived, in the service of both biological and psychological remediation and enhancement.

Regarding their thoughts and actions people in varying degrees harbour at least three illusions. The first is the *illusion of rationality*: in the main they consider their actions to be reasonable, logical and justified. The second is the *illusion of good intentions*: in many instances intentions will be beneficial to others, but there are often times either when this is not the case or when motivation is mixed. The third is the *illusion of personal agency or autonomy*. Put another way, people can have the feeling that they are personally responsible for their behaviour and yet be unaware of the extent that fears, anxieties and unexamined internalizations of other people's values are guiding their choices. All of these illusions are part of people's self-conceptions and have the effect of restricting their access to appropriate information and hence their range of choices.

Perhaps it is possible to make a distinction between danger and threat. Danger is when people's physical survival and wholeness is imperilled. Threat, which is frequently more imagined than real, is when psychological survival and well-being is imperilled. The adequacy and realism of people's self-conceptions determines the degree to which they are vulnerable to feelings of threat; also, to making choices about their actions based on these threatening feelings. The capacity to be personally responsible entails having self-conceptions that allow choices to be made on the basis of genuine needs rather than on the basis of unrealistic anxieties and fears.

Acquiring personal responsibility

7. *Humans grow up in the context of a two-way power and influence process between themselves and the environment in which they negotiate a set of self-conceptions and, with varying degrees of success, acquire a repertoire of psychological and other skills*

As the result of interaction with the environment, the growing individual starts developing a set of self-conceptions. Some content areas of these self-conceptions in the young child include those relating to the body, social relations, family relations and definitions of self or of aspects of self as 'good' or 'naughty'. As individuals grow they negotiate further self-conceptions in such areas as their sexuality, intellectual pursuits, working life and philosophy and values. One basis for these self-conceptions is genetic endowment: for instance people's gender and the given part of attributes such as physical appearance, intelligence and artistic ability. Another basis of these self-conceptions is what people are able, not necessarily rationally, to negotiate for themselves while growing up. The word negotiate is used intentionally.

Growing up is a continual process of two-way influence. French and Raven (1968) suggest that there are five main bases of social power and influence. Each of these may be operative in varying degrees and combinations at different times of a person's life-cycle. The five bases of parental power are: 1. reward power, based on children's perceptions that parents possess the ability to mediate rewards; 2. coercive power: children perceive that parents have the ability to mediate punishments; 3. legitimate power: children perceive that parents have a legitimate right to prescribe behaviour; 4. referent power, based on children's identification with their parents; and 5. expert power: children perceive that their parents have some special knowledge or expertness. Parents may be able to operate from all five bases of power. However, children are not powerless. Even when young they may possess reward, coercive and referent power. Furthermore, children are in a two-way power and influence process with virtually all significant people in their environments, be they older relatives, brothers and sisters, other children, teachers or whoever. Children are not just passive recipients of other people's definitions of them, though sometimes they may be engulfed and overwhelmed by oppressive environments. They can be active agents trying to assert and to define themselves. Sometimes family life, like the remainder of life, resembles Thomas Szasz's aphorism: 'In the animal kingdom, the rule is eat or be eaten; in the human kingdom, define or be defined' (Szasz: 1973).

Psychological skills are sequences of choices the presence or absence of which determines the degree to which individuals are in the process of being personally responsible. Psychological skills and self-conceptions are inextricably related. If an individual has an unrealistic set of self-conceptions these both represent and are likely to lead to skills deficits. For example, an individual who has negotiated a self-conception of personal worthlesssness is likely to have numerous skills deficits. Someone who has negotiated a self-conception which restricts acknowledgement and integration of sexuality is likely to have skills deficits in experiencing feelings and in relating to others. Someone who has negotiated a self-conception of hopelessness at practical things may have skills deficits in using time to best effect.

Whereas personal responsibility can fruitfully be viewed in terms of skills resources, the converse is not irresponsibility but skills deficits. Irresponsibility has a moralistic connotation of sin, wrongdoing and blame. The notion of skills deficits has many other advantages over that of irresponsibility. Since it is more specific, it encourages particular skills deficits to be identified and targeted so that they can be remedied. Also, it removes counsellors from any global judgements of clients as people. Rather they work with clients to decide how well various behaviours contribute to their happiness and fulfilment. Furthermore, skills deficits implies that such deficiencies can be unlearned and skills resources learned instead. Although the idea of skills resources and deficits faces the risk of being mechanistic, provided that skills are broadly defined to incorporate appropriate feelings and thoughts, this need not be the case.

8. Humans are more likely to develop a personally responsible set of self-conceptions and to acquire a repertoire of psychological skills resources if they are brought up having at least one significant adult in their lives with whom they have regular contact and by whom they feel understood

Already the human instinct for survival and the notion of survival anxiety have been emphasized. It seems a truism to say that young people need security while growing up. This is not just physical but emotional security. Bowlby (1979) talks of the concept of a secure base and writes of the accumulating evidence that humans of all ages 'are happiest and able to deploy their talents to best advantage when they are confident that, standing behind them, there are one or more trusted persons who will come to their aid should difficulties arise'. He calls this provider of a secure base an attachment figure and notes that important developmental experiences occur during all the years of childhood and adolescence and not just during the earliest months or years.

Another way of approaching the concept of a secure base is that of emphasizing the growing person's need for empathic understanding. This comes preferably from one or both parents. Failing that, from at least one other important adult. In infancy empathic understanding is likely to refer to the degree of sensitivity which the mother, in particular, shows to her baby's communications and signals. Though there may be maternal ambivalence, overall she exhibits a high degree of being 'tuned in to' her child. Ainsworth and her colleagues (1978) have produced research evidence indicating that infants' exploratory behaviour is most satisfactory with mothers who rate high on the following four scales: sensitivity-insensitivity; acceptance-rejection; cooperation-interference; and accessibility-ignoring. Sensitivity, acceptance, cooperation and accessibility are each characteristics associated with empathic understanding.

Rogers is the theorist who has most emphasized the need for empathic understanding in the practice of counselling. In Chapter 2 his three conditions for a growth-producing emotional climate were mentioned: genuineness; unconditional positive regard or nonpossessive warmth; and empathic understanding. These characteristics are highly relevant to effective parenting not just with infants, but with older children and adolescents as well. Rogers (1951, 1959) writes of the conflict in children who feel that their experience is at variance with the need for positive regard from others; and of how this conflict may be resolved by denying or distorting experience and adopting the values of the parents as if they represented the real experience. The implication of this is that, unless children have people in their environments who understand them, they neither have a secure base in other people for exploring the world nor obtain the confidence to have a secure base within themselves. Rogers is right in his assumption of an inner valuing process, and in emphasizing the importance of children learning to listen to and identify their own emotions. Being perpetually misunderstood by significant others is likely to alienate children not only from others but, perhaps more importantly, from themselves. This may engender a negative view of their own worth with serious implications for their ability to acquire the psychological skills resources of personal responsibility.

The degree to which adults are able to accept themselves is associated with the degree to which they are able to accept and understand their children. This in turn is related to the degree of self-acceptance or self-esteem of the children. Figure 4.1 is a simple diagram to emphasize this point. The diagram makes a distinction between the effects on a child's self-esteem or 'psychological size' of personally responsible parents as contrasted with those with responsibility skills deficits in the area of self-acceptance.

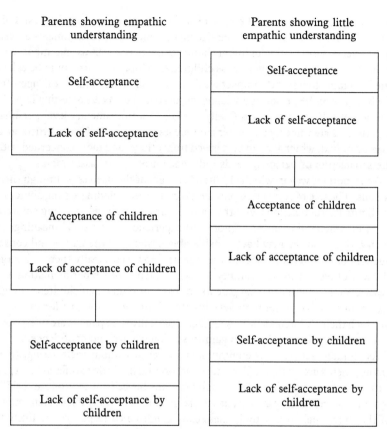

Figure 4.1 Degree of self-acceptance of parents in relation to their acceptance of their children and their children's acceptance of themselves.

9. *The processes of acquiring personally responsible self-conceptions and psychological skills resources include personal experiments, conditioning, learning from observing others and the availability of adequate information and opportunity*

This proposition refers to the subprocesses of the two-way power and influence process between growing people and their environments. These subprocesses affect thoughts and feelings as well as overt behaviour. In this section the primary focus is on the acquisition of personally responsible self-conceptions and skills resources. It is not an exhaustive account, but rather an indication of important considerations.

Personal experiments or exploratory behaviour may be initiated by the individual, by another or others, or by a combination of self and others. This process is mentioned first to emphasize that people act on environments as well as vice versa. Observation of infants indicates the pervasiveness and importance of exploratory behaviour which, as children develop, may turn out to be calculated attempts to test their impact on their environments. This is analogous to Kelly's view of the person as a scientist engaged in the process of testing hypotheses about self and the world (Kelly: 1955). At a fundamental level personal experiments are value free in that infants are less concerned with constructs such as good or bad, which tend to be derived from others, and more concerned with the satisfaction of personal needs independent of others' assessments.

An important way in which children learn about themselves is through their actions. The role of adults is to provide a secure base, including setting appropriate limits for such actions, and then also to provide an understanding environment in which children can explore and experience the personal meanings of such actions. Adults may have considerable power over the nature and consequences of children's personal experiments. However, ideally there is a large element of respect for the validity of the children's own experimentation and experiencing. This means that parents are less controlling their children through reward or coercive power than deriving their influence through referent power in which their children identify with them. Basically such parents are using their power to help their children to gain in self-knowledge and confidence.

As children act on their environments, or even without their acting, their environments act on them. Classical conditioning has little to offer as an explanation of the acquisition of personally responsible self-conceptions and skills resources since, initially at least, its effects are unrelated to any intentional actions of the individual. If anything, classically conditioned responses are likely to impair personal responsibility since they are not based on aware choice. Operant conditioning, however, is an important way in which people's feelings, thoughts and behaviours are influenced. A useful distinction is that operant conditioning may be seen as influencing rather than as shaping behaviour. This is a difference in emphasis since the shaping of behaviour implies being externally determined whereas the influencing of behaviour leaves some room for self-determination. Also, influencing behaviour implies more of a role for people's thinking processes and inner speech than shaping behaviour. Even children think about the effects the environment has had, is having and is likely to have upon them and adjust their behaviour accordingly. Furthermore, parents may not only explicitly make rewards for some of their children's behaviour contingent upon their actions, but also offer verbal explanations of why they are doing so. Additionally, they may discuss their children's reactions to their explanations. As mentioned previously, children can also be using reward power and coercive power to influence the behaviour of their parents. Consequently in family life operant conditioning operates in both directions.

Learning from observing others is an important way that personally responsible self-conceptions and psychological skills resources are acquired. The power of such learning may be enhanced if the model is attractive to the observer, if the observer is able to see the consequences of the model's behaviour, and if the model or someone else provides a verbal commentary on the model's thought processes. The observer not only sees the model's behaviour, but is likely to think about it. Indeed observational learning may be the main way in which psychological skills resources, like accurate attribution of responsibility and realistic anticipation, are acquired. It is not always the case that thought processes need to be openly shared as they tend to be in Meichenbaum's work. Indeed such sharing may be counter-productive if it is construed as preaching. Children are often very acute observers of their parents' underlying assumptions. For example, parents who attribute responsibility accurately when solving a problem may not need to 'spell it out' for the relevant thought processes to be absorbed by their children.

Children and adolescents need adequate information about the world if they are to develop personally responsible self-conceptions and psychological skills resources. For instance, keeping them in ignorance about basic facts of death and sexuality may impede their responsibility awareness and emotional responsiveness, respectively. The issue seems less whether to introduce such topics, but rather how best to do it. Furthermore, children and adolescents need the availability of adequate opportunities in line with their maturation to test out their self-conceptions and develop their psychological skills resources. For example, one way in which children and young people can find out about their abilities, likes and dislikes is through exploring themselves by means of play and leisure activities. Also, they may gain from exploring themselves in relation to the world of work. However, many people's chances of exploring themselves and developing a sense of their own competence through either play, leisure or work are restricted. This may be through no fault of their own, but, for example, through socio-economic deprivation. Thus they are unable to carry out some of the personal experiments which might help them to develop the range and depth of their self-conceptions and psychological skills resources. Additionally, people may encounter restrictions on opportunity to develop certain kinds of personal relationships, for example if attending a single-sex boarding school.

10. The processes of acquiring personal responsibility skills deficits include lack of empathic understanding, irresponsible conditioning and modelling, and lack of adequate information and opportunity

Parents and children relate to each other in terms of their self-conceptions which are of various degrees of accuracy. Furthermore, these self-conceptions involve definitions of others in relation to self. Another way of approaching this topic is to say that people create personifications of themselves and of others. My personification of me is the aggregate of my conceptions of myself, whereas my personification of you is the aggregate of my conceptions of you. If my self-conceptions are reasonably accurate, my personification of myself is reasonably accurate and I am likely to be able to process information in relation to you so that my personification of you is reasonably accurate. In other words I possess the basis for understanding you and for relating to you as you are.

Children need empathic understanding from at least one significant adult both to provide a secure base for their personal experimentation and in order to help them to learn to listen to their own thoughts, feelings and emotions. However, parents who do not understand or accept important aspects of themselves and thus have personifications of themselves involving inaccurate self-conceptions are unlikely to be perceiving their children accurately. Instead they have false personifications of their children which relate to their false personifications of themselves. The result of this is that children, instead of being *affirmed* in relation to their unique individuality and special characteristics, may be subtly or crudely *disconfirmed* by being only partially understood and incompletely responded to. The emotional message that may be received from such disconfirmation is 'I am no good' and 'I am not worthy to be valued for myself'. The upshot of this may be that personal experimentation gets distorted because it is now based on a feeling of insecurity. Furthermore, since it risks being misunderstood, sharing the results of exploratory behaviour with parents may not take place. In any event the sharing is likely to be less useful in helping children listen to and understand themselves since it is only being partially understood, if at all.

Parents are faced with the dilemma of having to set realistic limits on their children's behaviour at the same time as not perpetually giving them disconfirming experiences. Parents with accurate personifications of themselves are more likely both to allow their children the right amount of psychological space in which to develop their individuality and to become aware when their children are experiencing difficulties. Parents with inaccurate personifications of themselves are less likely to provide their children with the psychological space to develop their individuality. Very frequently they want to control their children's thoughts, feelings and behaviour by rigid prescriptions concerning the way they 'should', 'ought' or 'must' be. Since children have a need for positive regard related to their need for survival, a little of this kind of rigid conditioning can go a long way; not least since it is often enforced by withdrawal of affection in one way or another.

Here are some examples of faulty conditioning contributing to skills deficits in the area of emotional responsiveness. First, there is the Rogers example of the young child learning to deny his satisfaction at hitting his baby brother by internalizing the negative reactions of his parents in regard to this behaviour (Rogers: 1951). Here he ends up the symbolization that 'I perceive this behaviour as unsatisfying' rather than acknowledging his own satisfaction and his parents dissatisfaction. In other words the parents failed to make a distinction between *having* feelings and *handling* feelings. Whereas hitting baby brother may have been an inappropriate way of handling aggressive feelings, denying and being denied the right to have such feelings was also inappropriate and likely to lead to blockages in the child's capacity to listen to such feelings on future occasions.

The second example relates to family conflict. A man who is very unhappy with his marriage gets absorbed in his own needs for affection and hatred of his wife. He turns to his daughter for support and when he does not obtain it in an unqualified way gets very angry with her and makes out that she is letting him down. Especially if it persists, there may be at least a 'triple put-down' for the daughter. First, her father's self-absorption is depriving her of affection anyway. Second, her father's reaction to her perceived lack of support is another disconfirmation. Third, she may end up by doubting herself and her own adequacy not only as a daughter but also as a person. A possible outcome of such an experience is that the daughter learns to inhibit herself emotionally in future relationships with men.

The third example of faulty conditioning diminishing people's emotional capacity for responsiveness relates to gender conditioning. In Western cultures boys and girls are differentially conditioned as to which aspects of their feelings they can attend to and express. Bem (1974) devised a Sex-Role Inventory in which items were characterized as masculine, feminine or neutral depending on the extent that they were considered to be more desirable in American society for each sex. The twenty masculine items were: acts as leader, aggressive, ambitious, analytical, assertive, athletic, competitive, defends own beliefs, dominant, forceful, has leadership abilities, independent, individualistic, makes decisions easily, masculine, self-reliant, self-sufficient, strong personality, willing to take a stand, and willing to take risks. The twenty feminine items were: affectionate, cheerful, childlike, compassionate, does not use harsh language, eager to soothe hurt feelings, feminine, flatterable, gentle, gullible, loves children, loyal, sensitive to the needs of others, shy, soft spoken, sympathetic, tender, understanding, warm and yielding. From birth, when boys are more likely to be given blue and girls pink clothes and toys, children are gender conditioned. This considerably restricts the emotional responsiveness of most members of both sexes.

Responsibility skills deficits in the area of emotional responsiveness may also, in some instances, be attributed to classical conditioning. For example, people may have seemingly irrational fears over such things as animals or heights through having gone through an intense fear experience in the presence of such stimuli.

Conditioning can contribute to skills deficits in the way people think, or in their degree of realism, as well as in their emotional responsiveness. In fact, skills deficits in thinking and feeling tend to go together. For example, parents whose lack of self-acceptance is such that their children are likely to develop faulty standards for self-evaluation are conditioning both thoughts and feelings. Thus children may be repeatedly encouraged to achieve at school in ways that influence them to think that parental approval and affection is related to the amount of their school achievement. Consequently, achievement may engender feelings of pride and lack of achievement may lead to anxiety and depression. Often the anxiety and depression is based on anticipation of failure, for, not only do unrealistic mental rules affect feelings, they affect thoughts about the future too. Conditioning can also influence the way people attribute responsibility for their thoughts, feelings and behaviour. For example, children may quickly learn that they can avoid being disciplined if they can place the blame elsewhere for any trouble they have caused or to which they have contributed. Such placing the blame elsewhere, if successful, avoids losing parental approval.

Again, conditioning can lead children to acquire deficits both in their relationship skills and in the area of engaging in rewarding activity. For example, children who have rejecting parents are being conditioned to be wary of close human contact. Furthermore, the anxiety resulting from rejection may contribute both to poor listening skills and to shyness. An obvious example of conditioning affecting and narrowing occupational choice relates to the effect of gender conditioning on such choices – there are scarcely any women engineers, whereas women are disproportionately represented in such fields as nursing and primary school teaching.

Absence of appropriate modelling is another way by which children acquire responsibility skills deficits. For example, if either or both parents are not expressive of their emotions their children may be unable to observe how to express emotions. Parents and other adults may also be poor models for acquiring the skills of effective thinking. For instance, children may learn their parents' anxieties about various aspects of life by observing the ways in which they talk about or avoid talking about, and act in or avoid acting in various situations. And children may learn poor skills for solving family problems and resolving conflicts if they have little or no opportunity to observe people with good skills in these areas, particularly the ability to assign responsibility accurately.

Adults frequently think in overgeneralized terms with a great emphasis on how others 'should', 'ought' or 'must' be. Furthermore, they may be applying and modelling such thinking in relation to their own as well as to their children's behaviour. Effective thinking tends to be more flexible and rational. Consequently, to the extent that people model rigid and punitive standards, they model a style of thinking that contributes to their children acquiring skills deficits. Adults also model their self-protective mechanisms. For example, a child's awareness of death may be impeded by parental euphemisms and inability to handle the issue of death directly.

Children can learn poor relationship skills by only being able to observe people with skills deficits in these areas. Additionally, they may acquire difficulties in relation to how to occupy their time to best effect if they can only observe people who are not fulfilled in how they occupy their time. In the above paragraphs only a small number have been suggested of the ways in which observing models with skills deficits may contribute to children acquiring similar deficits.

Children may also grow up with considerable gaps in information about essential aspects of life. Parents are dishonest some of the time and tend to engage in impression management in relation to their children. Thus, if I am to retain my personification of myself as a parent, I want to present myself to my children in such a way that their personification of me will be in line with my own personification. For example, my personification of myself as a parent may not include letting my children become aware of my sensuality. Therefore, I do not talk about and in other ways I discourage my children from becoming aware of this aspect of me and, unless they have other sources of information, of themselves. Goffman's ideas on the presentation of self in everyday life and on the management of stigmas or of spoiled identities are highly relevant to the ways in which, to a greater or lesser degree, all parents relate to their children and, in time, all children relate to their parents (Goffman: 1959, 1963). Also, as mentioned previously, children may be prevented from developing their skills in the areas of relationships, leisure and in preparing for work through lack of adequate opportunity.

11. *When humans are in groups and hierarchies, they may acquire and exhibit responsibility skills deficits that differ from those in their one-to-one personal relationships*

This proposition takes into account the observation that being part of groups or hierarchies may sometimes facilitate the acquisition of certain behaviours. The proposition is stated in terms of acquiring negative characteristics, but groups and hierarchies can also model and condition responsible behaviour. Here, however, three areas are briefly mentioned in which group participation can facilitate giving up personal responsibility.

The first area is that of conformity. Groups sometimes put considerable pressure on individuals to conform. Here this mainly refers to peer groups made up of people of roughly the same characteristics, for example a group of classmates or workmates. The survival anxiety associated with rejection and of being wrong can be so strong that individuals give in against their better judgement. They may even misperceive situations in the direction of the group viewpoint. In a well-known series of experiments Asch (1956) placed naive individuals in situations where they were required to make judgements about such matters as the length of a line in relation to the lengths of three other lines. All the other eight or so members in the group were confederates putting pressure on the individual to make incorrect judgements. In one series of experiments, over a third of the judgements were in error. Despite there being marked individual differences in response to the majority pressure, most of the subjects reported that they longed to agree with the majority. A number of observers of American culture, for example Riesman (1950) and Spindler (1963), have noted an increased tendency there to conform to group pressure.

The second area is that of obedience. Whereas conformity involves going along with one's peers, obedience entails compliance with authority. There are considerable pressures on children to comply with authority both in the family and in the school. Later on there may be further pressures to comply with authority in the workplace. Thus many people learn a tendency to obey that involves relinquishing some if not all the responsibility for an action to an authority. This is the 'I was only obeying orders' syndrome when individuals commit acts as part of performing their roles in hierarchies that they would not commit as individuals. In Milgram's obedience research ordinary Americans of both sexes frequently were prepared to administer electric shocks to the experimental confederate, each time he made an error in a learning task. These shocks were up to and beyond an excruciating level of pain (Milgram: 1974). Milgram considered that their willingness to engage in this behaviour could not be explained by any aggressive feelings toward the subject, but by the fact that they were being firmly instructed to continue with the progressive escalation of the shocks by the legitimate authority figure of the experimenter. The most common mental adjustment those administering the shocks made was to divest themselves of responsibility for their actions by attributing all initiative to the experimenter. Milgram calls the position in which people see themselves as agents for carrying out another person's orders the agentic state. He considers this a fundamental mode of thinking for many people once they are locked into a subordinate position in a structure of authority. There are, of course, other reasons why people obey authority, for example fears of rejection, of reprisals or of loss of employment. Indeed, fear of rejection may have contributed to the subjects' behaviour in the Milgram experiments. Nevertheless, the observation retains its validity that it may be easier to commit unpleasant acts against others when acting under orders than as individuals.

The third area is that of identification with an authority. In discussing obedience, the assumption was made that the individual and the authority figure were in personal contact. However, the point here relates less to obedience to authority and more to authoritarianism. To overcome a sense of inferiority, powerlessness and isolation, individuals merge their identities with a strong leader, without there necessarily being personal contact. Thus, they may blindly follow the whims and wishes of the authority figure. Such relinquishing or avoidance of responsibility may be voluntary rather than in obedience to orders – the authority figure offers people a mechanism of escape from their feelings of deficiency. This need to have a compensatory identification with authority was a point emphasized by Fromm in relation to the spread of Nazism (Fromm: 1942)

In all three examples provided above, the external circumstances in which individuals found themselves had characteristics conducive to lack of personal responsibility. Thus they were examples of environments influencing individuals. However, even under the challenge of such adverse environments, some individuals may still acquire and develop their personal responsibility skills resources.

Chapter 5

TOWARD A THEORY: PERPETUATION AND CHANGE

This chapter is a continuation of the previous chapter. Together they present a theoretical model using personal responsibility as a central integrating concept. Most of this chapter focuses on how personal responsibility skills deficits are perpetuated or sustained. Some propositions are also presented and discussed concerning how people may be helped to overcome skills deficits and to develop skills resources.

Perpetuating personal responsibility skills deficits

12. Humans' self-conceptions and psychological skills resources and deficits mediate the quantity and quality of information that they have available for making choices

In the section on acquisition suggestions were made of ways in which children acquire psychological skills resources and deficits. However, the past cannot be relived. If people are to overcome their responsibility skills deficits, the focus must be on how their problems are being sustained in the present. Consequently, an understanding of how responsibility skills deficits are being perpetuated is vital to changing them. All but the most radical behavioural psychologists consider that people process or operate on the information they have available. At one level this may be a matter of coding and classifying it in terms of their construct and linguistic systems. At another level this processing may involve applying what Sullivan (1953) termed 'selective inattention' to some or all of the information.

People's self-conceptions, or the ways in which they view themselves, to a large extent regulate the accuracy of their information processing. People whose self-conceptions allow them to acknowledge most of the important information they receive, either from within or outside, have a more accurate base for making choices than those not so fortunate, and such people are more likely to possess the skills resources involved in realistic thinking. They allow themselves the necessary information for formulating realistic internal rules and for attributing and anticipating accurately. Additionally, people functioning at high levels of self-awareness are less likely to engage in self-protective operations than those less aware.

However, for most people, matters are not so simple. They possess areas of accuracy in their self-conceptions that allow for full awareness as well as areas of inaccuracy that make for partial or sometimes total lack of awareness. Areas of lack of awareness both represent and contribute to individuals having psychological skills deficits. If the content of the self-concept is inaccurate, the processes of living dependent upon accuracy are not working properly: people are unable to apply the necessary corrections. Here is an example. A husband acknowledges that at times he can be moody and difficult. During a domestic row he becomes aware that he has contributed to his wife's distress. Consequently he has some chance of resolving this difficulty by altering his behaviour. Another husband is equally moody and difficult, but cannot acknowledge it. A domestic row blows up. His solution is to keep blaming his wife, which does not resolve anything. Thus the original difficulty is expanded into a real problem because his attempted solution has been so inadequate. In fact, sometimes a distinction is made between difficulties and problems, the latter being difficulties in which the attempted solutions have added to and become part of the problems.

There are a number of reasons why inaccurate self-conceptions are likely to give rise to feelings of threat. In proposition 5 (see Chapter 4) it was mentioned that people's self-conceptions are what they refer to as 'I' or 'me', and that these provide the maps by which individuals negotiate the world. Especially if fundamental self-conceptions are challenged by discrepant information, people may view this as a threat to their psychological survival. People with accurate self-conceptions may have to struggle to maintain them in the face of a sometimes hostile environment. However, unlike those with inaccurate self-conceptions, they interact with the world with accurate information. The threat to those with inaccurate self-conceptions comes from challenges to what are basically dishonest positions. Furthermore, since people with inaccurate self-conceptions have less information available for making choices (see Figure 5.1), they are more prone to making ineffective choices. These may engender further discrepant feedback and hence further threat. One outcome may be a progressive lowering of self-esteem with increasing vulnerability to feelings of threat.

(a) Less responsible person

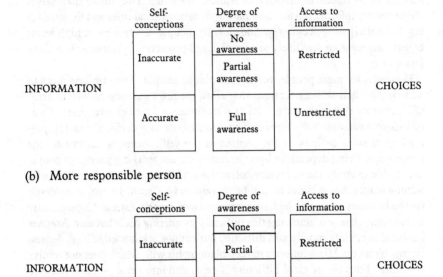

(b) More responsible person

Figure 5.1 Accuracy of self-conceptions, degree of awareness and access to information for choices of less and more responsible persons.

13. *There are a number of important thinking errors, with accompanying inner speech, which contribute to humans sustaining their distress*

The ability to think realistically is a vital skills resource. Environmental circumstances may contribute to perpetuating people's skills deficits. However, errors in thinking as well as being important deficits in themselves also contribute to other deficits, for example lack of emotional responsiveness. Ellis' rational-emotive therapy has its main focus on the way people sustain their distress. As a simple model he suggested an ABC framework in which, as mentioned in Chapter 3, A is the activating event, B is the individual's belief system, and C is the consequence of A which is mediated by what the person is thinking at B. Building on Ellis' idea, an ATC framework may help an understanding of people's contribution to their distress. Here A is still the activating event, T represents the individual's thoughts in relation to the activating event, and C represents the choices the individual makes as a result of A and T. This *activating event-thoughts-choices* framework allows for more variety of thinking error at T than Ellis' central irrational beliefs. Also, the emphasis on choices rather than consequences at C implies more of a potential on the part of the individual for personal responsibility, including choosing to alter any thinking errors at T. As emphasized by Meichenbaum, people's thinking is quite often accompanied by inner speech in the form of an internal dialogue. In the ATC framework inner speech is relevant at both T, or a person's existing thoughts, and C, where the individual may be making choices concerning either altering existing thoughts or acting.

Assuming that individuals have accurate information available, there are four main areas of thinking error involved in perpetuating distress. These thinking errors tend to be interrelated. They are briefly presented here and commented on more fully in Chapter 8. First, there are many forms of *self-protective thinking*. Denial involves totally warding off from conscious awareness something regarded as too threatening or painful. Distortion involves altering some aspects of incoming information to make it more consistent with existing self-conceptions. For instance, a student may get positive feedback about an essay but then distort it, perhaps by thinking of it as 'luck' or a mistake on the part of the teacher, in order to sustain a negative conception of self. Self-protective thinking can also involve what might be called transpersonal defences involving operating on the experiencing or behaviour of others so that they collude in providing feedback that sustains one's picture of oneself. For example, children may be pressurized, on pain of withdrawal of affection, neither to notice nor to comment on their parents' shortcomings.

Second, there are the thinking errors involved in *misattributing responsibility*. At one level this involves a diminished awareness of people's responsibility for fashioning their existences within the parameters of life. On a more everyday level, this involves inaccurately attributing responsibility in specific situations. An oft-repeated example is the tendency to blame others rather than to acknowledge one's own contribution to undesirable situations. As Beck emphasizes, misattributing can also involve taking excessive responsibility upon oneself, for instance in relation to causing negative events.

Third, there are the thinking errors involved in *unrealistically anticipating events*. These events can concern oneself, other people or the environment. One thinking error in anticipating is an inadequate sense of one's ability to cope with life. Most often this is lack of confidence. However, this inaccuracy includes over-confidence. An aspect of many people's inadequate sense of their ability to cope with life is focusing on potential risks rather than gains in situations.

Fourth, there is the area of *unrealistic internal rules* for self-evaluation. As with the previous three thinking errors a number of these rules operate below immediate awareness. Most frequently these unrealistic rules involve overgeneralizations in regard to the need to have one's own behaviour, other people's behaviour and the behaviour of the physical environment as one would ideally like it to be all the time. The sting of unrealistic internal rules tends to be in the tail. Since they are based on values absorbed from other people, including the media, adherence to them runs the risk of perpetuating the self-alienation involved in trusting other people's judgements rather than one's own. Both pride, on account of having lived up to these internalized standards, and guilt and self-disparagement, for failure to live up to them, are united by a common factor. People live in a state of false awareness in which others' rules are being treated as if they were their own.

A further point about thinking errors is that each may be couched in characteristic language. For example, the use of 'should', 'ought' and 'must' indicates that an unrealistic internal rule operates. Similarly, the use of an expression like 'I can't' instead of 'I won't' indicates misattributing responsibility.

People unaware of their thinking errors are likely to repeat feelings and behaviours based on these errors. Negative feelings and behaviours, for example depression and outbursts of anger, most often signal faulty thinking. As well as through specific thinking errors, people sustain their distress through lack of a rationale linking such unwanted feelings and behaviours to thoughts. Lack of an adequate rationale relating thoughts to influencing feelings and behaviours is arguably a meta or superordinate thinking error under which all the others belong.

14. Humans who do not have access to at least one person who is able to offer them a relationship characterized by empathic understanding are more likely than those who do to sustain responsibility skills deficits

In proposition 8 (see Chapter 4) the desirability was mentioned of children having regular contact with at least one adult by whom they feel understood. People who have already acquired responsibility skills deficits have similar needs and for similar reasons. Without such a relationship they are more prone to continue in their 'stuckness'. Here stuckness refers to individuals possessing self-defeating patterns of feeling, thinking and behaviour, and not having the degree of awareness and access to information for making realistic choices in problem areas. Without an empathically understanding relationship they are less likely to have a secure base for self-exploration and personal experiments.

People's responsibility skills deficits may not only be sustained by the absence of the positive effects of empathic understanding, but also by the presence of the negative effects of lack of empathic understanding. For example, they may still have to relate to people whose self-personifications cause them to relate to others on the basis of inaccurate personifications of them. In other words the game of 'define or be defined' continues as Person B struggles to impose a definition on Person A and Person A either leaves the relationship (which physically, if not psychologically, is difficult for children), fights for his or her own identity, or admits psychological defeat and internalizes Person B's inaccurate definition.

Another reason why people with skills deficits may continue to lack an empathically understanding relationship is that such relationships may be difficult to find. In his *Becoming Partners* Rogers (1973) gives a moving account of a woman named Irene who perceived that her mother never loved her. She was divorced from her first two husbands and alienated from herself. Irene found a loving third husband who was able to see beyond her negative feelings about herself: he related to her potential. Many people are unlikely to be so fortunate since the quality of empathic listening in our culture is low. Furthermore, people with responsibility skills deficits may isolate themselves from those who might help them; they may withdraw from seeking close relationships; or their skills deficits may put such a strain on relationships that the others involved psychologically and/or physically withdraw. Some people with responsibility skills deficits have difficulty in getting others interested in them, some in sustaining others' interest, and some in both getting and sustaining relationships in which they are likely to be empathically understood.

15. The processes of perpetuating personal responsibility skills deficits include irresponsible conditioning and modelling and lack of adequate information and opportunity

Lack of positive conditioning experiences and modelling, as well as negative or irresponsible conditioning and modelling, can contribute to personal responsibility skills deficits. Even when children have gone some way to acquiring negative self-images, parents, siblings and others may continue relating in ways that sustain rather than alleviate them. This process is not helped by the likelihood that people having acquired personal responsibility skills deficits then behave in less rewarding ways than previously, for example by being aggressive or inhibited. Frequently children are labelled as problem children or, in Satir's term, as 'identified patients' (Satir: 1967) when others' faulty conditioning has contributed to the problems. Also, the misguided conditioning implicit in others' attempted solutions helps to sustain them. A power contest may then develop which is even more threatening for parents and others than the original behaviour of the child. If the contest escalates, the conditioning involved in the parents' reactions may further add to the damage from the original faulty conditioning.

In proposition 10 (see Chapter 4) mention was made of the kinds of conditioning that were likely to contribute toward people acquiring responsibility skills deficits in the areas of emotional responsiveness, realistic thinking, personal relationships and use of time. For example, gender conditioning contributes to many of both sexes not expressing the full range of their feelings. Such is the strength of this conditioning that, even though attitudes are changing relatively quickly, the absolute rate of change is slow. Consequently most people who acquire gender-related restrictions on expressing feelings are likely to have further conditioning throughout their lives sustaining their lowered emotional responsiveness. The lack of realistic thinking example in proposition 10 concerned acquiring false standards for achievement. Again, in many families and work settings, pressures on individuals to achieve continue contributing to their alienation from themselves as persons. This is sometimes at great cost to their physical as well as emotional well-being.

Conditioning can contribute to sustaining relationship skills deficits in a number of ways. First, people who initially brought about the skills deficits may not change their behaviour. Rejecting parents may continue rejecting their children. This perpetuates underconfidence and inhibition in social contacts. Second, the culture may continue to reinforce skills deficits: for instance in certain areas of British culture the 'stiff upper lip' tradition hinders learning good intimacy skills. Third, the behaviour of people with relationship skills deficits may have a 'self-fulfilling prophecy' quality about it. For example, individuals with a fear of rejection may be clinging and possessive in close relationships and thus increase their likelihood of rejection. Such rejection may further condition them to be fearful of rejection.

The contribution of conditioning to restricting choice in the area of occupation of time is frequently continuous rather than just initial. For example, women in Western countries are likely to continue being conditioned that engineering is a male occupation; and males, that knitting is a female leisure pastime.

A major difference between the acquisition and the perpetuation of responsibility skills deficits through conditioning is that perpetuation is likely to involve internalized as well as external conditioning. Furthermore, deficits may be perpetuated on the basis of internalized conditioning alone, for example unwillingness to discuss certain topics after leaving home because they were taboo subjects in the home. Such faulty internalized conditioning was mentioned when discussing the thinking error of unrealistic internal rules.

Lack of appropriate models contributes to the perpetuation of responsibility skills deficits. Being solely around unresponsive people and thus unable to observe the behaviour of emotionally responsive people and the rewards they obtain is likely to contribute to people staying out of touch with their feelings. Inability to observe people who think effectively about their difficulties means that a valuable method of learning realistic thinking is lost. Being brought up in families where both parents have poor conflict resolution skills, means less opportunity to remedy any skills deficits in this area. Similarly, being restricted to observing people with poor work habits contributes to sustaining people's poor work habits through lack of appropriate modelling.

There is a difference between genuine lack of information and lack of information-seeking behaviour. Responsibility deficits may be sustained by both. Lack of information may range from such everyday matters as not having information about job opportunities in one's locality to broader considerations, such as lack of information with which to formulate a realistic conceptual framework for understanding one's own and others' behaviour. Lack of information-seeking behaviour may entail having neither motivation nor skills to discover available information.

There is also a difference between genuine lack of opportunity and lack of the skills of creating opportunity. Again, responsibility deficits can be sustained by both. For instance, people's intimacy skills may lack development because there may genuinely be no suitable partners in their localities. This is different from failure to create opportunity through any one or a combination of reasons, such as lack of effort or fear of intimacy.

16.   Humans tend to be part of groups and hierarchies which may also place pressure on them to sustain responsibility skills deficits
In proposition 11 (see Chapter 4) conformity, obedience and identification with a powerful authority were mentioned as three ways in which people acquire responsibility skills deficits through participation in groups and hierarchies. Group and hierarchical pressures are likely to continue after the initial acquisition of these deficits and thus sustain them. For example, individuals in a workplace are often continually placed under considerable pressure by their peers not to think for themselves but to go along with the group. People in hierarchies, such as soldiers in the army, having been initially indoctrinated to obey orders without question are frequently reindoctrinated. Furthermore, if they do dis-

obey orders even on ground of conscience, they are liable to face the most severe penalties. The army may be an extreme case of a hierarchy requiring unquestioning obedience to authority, but industrial organizations, schools and political parties may all exhibit similar characteristics.

The pressures put on individuals can be quite subtle in that the game of 'who defines whom' is often played. For instance, people who do not obey may be labelled as 'troublemakers', 'disloyal', 'having problems with authority' and 'unhelpful' despite, or sometimes because of, the fact that their observations may be valid. Though dealt with briefly here, the contribution of groups and hierarchies to making it more difficult for certain individuals to overcome responsibility skills deficits should not be underestimated. This observation applies to people in powerful positions as well as to ordinary group members and to those lower down in hierarchies. Lord Acton's dictum that 'Power tends to corrupt and absolute power corrupts absolutely', though not sufficiently acknowledging the personal responsibility of powerful individuals in their own corruption, indicates the pressures hierarchies put on those with power.

Changing and assuming personal responsibility

17. Change in direction of overcoming responsibility skills deficits is more likely to occur if individuals learn to assume responsibility for the ways in which they perpetuate their distress

In the previous sections an attempt was made to show that responsibility skills deficits are not only acquired in the first place but then go on to be perpetuated. In many instances this perpetuation continues after individuals have left the settings, for example the parental home, in which they first acquired their skills deficits. In short, individuals ofter become stuck with a set of self-conceptions and responsibility skills deficits which cause them mild to great distress, albeit not always acknowledged. Individuals come to counselling with two sets of pasts: the past in which they acquired their skills deficits, and the past in which they have been perpetuating their deficits. These pasts can overlap since individuals can be perpetuating one deficit at the same time as acquiring another. Unless there is some appropriate intervention by individuals, either on their own or in conjunction with others, pasts are likely to influence negatively their presents and futures. Although people can change the ways in which they think about their pasts, they cannot go back and relive these times. Consequently, if change is to occur, it must take place in the present and the future. The focus must be on present thoughts, feelings and behaviours that both indicate and sustain responsibility skills deficits.

Proposition 3 (see Chapter 4) stated that ultimately each individual is personally responsible for his or her own survival and unique fulfilment. Relating this proposition to overcoming skills deficits inside and outside counselling, ultimately individuals are responsible for the ways in which they perpetuate their skills deficits. From here it is a short step to saying that change in the direction of overcoming skills deficits is more likely to occur if this responsibility is acknowledged. This does not mean that external factors, such as good fortune in personal relations or work, may not also be beneficial independent of any change in the degree to which individuals acknowledge their contribution to perpetuating their own distress. Furthermore, in practice, this responsibility may be only gradually acknowledged. Such realization is part of the process of change.

Figure 5.2 attempts to illustrate what is meant by people learning to take responsibility for the ways in which they perpetuate their distress. Even as infants people had the capacity for choosing, though at first the choices were more concerned with bodily gratification than based on reasoning. Responsibility skills deficits were the result of incorrect choices made at the time of acquisition. The term incorrect choices seems more appropriate than wrong choices since it is a less value-laden term and does not have the connotations of guilt and blame. Quite apart from having little if any therapeutic value, it seems unrealistic to hold people responsible for choices they made when children. Then they were mainly dependent on adults not just for their physical survival, but also for their view of the world, and many of these incorrect choices were made at an age when their own reasoning ability had yet to mature.

In addition to incorrect choices in relation to acquisition, many of the incorrect choices in relation to perpetuation also were childhood ones. Again the notion of the incorrectness of choices as being conducive to people's fulfilment seems more appropriate than that of wrongness, which implies accountability, guilt and blame. Responsibility skills deficits were acquired and are pepetuated because individuals could not see and have not learned more appropriate choices with which to meet their needs for survival and fulfilment. Rather than blaming them, the counsellor's task is to cut into the cycle of perpetuation and help their clients to become better choosers.

For counsellors and for clients the choices that matter are those relating to the present and the future. These include choices concerning how the past is to be viewed in the present and future. Furthermore, the personal responsibility that matters relates to these present and future choices rather than to past choices, unless they are reconceptualized by present and future choices.

Column A *The Past*	Column B *The Past*	Column C *The Present and Future*
Acquisition of responsibility skills deficits	*Previous perpetuation* of responsibility skills deficits	*Current and future perpetuation* of responsibility skills deficits
Past choices	Past choices	Present and future choices
Incorrect choices	Incorrect choices	Possibility for correct choices
Groundwork laid for diminished fulfilment	Maintenance of a state of diminished fulfilment	Possibility for responsibility assumption
Faulty learning	Previous stuckness in relation to faulty learning	Possibility for change and constructive movement
No potential for change – the past has happened	No potential for change – the past has happened	Potential for further perpetuation of deficits or for change

Figure 5.2 Degree of potential for change in relation to acquiring and perpetuating personal responsibility skills deficits

Regarding Figure 5.2, both counsellors and clients and also those interested in self-help need to focus on Column C or on choices avoiding current and future perpetuation of responsibility skills deficits. With very distressed clients, counsellors may help them make progress without their having much of an awareness of their responsibility for sustaining their distress. However, counsellor skills alone are insufficient to help those wishing to attain more than a minimum level of personal responsibility. Instead, clients must become active participants in changing themselves.

Personal responsibility counselling and therapy entails a progressive unfolding to and by clients of the nature and degree of their responsibility for their own lives. Learning to take responsibility for the ways in which people perpetuate their distress is not a once-for-all process. Rather as they learn personally responsible self-conceptions and skills resources, they become aware of areas in which and ways whereby they can develop themselves still further as well as avoid the constant danger of backsliding. Additionally, as people go through life, they are challenged by different tasks, adjustments, unexpected events and suffering.

Concepts like fairness and unfairness and like justice and injustice can be dangerous to people struggling to take responsibility for perpetuation which is the prerequisite to taking responsibility for change. Frequently those with responsibility skills deficits have suffered considerably at the hands of others. Although these clients' anger, distress and pain should not be ignored, neither should it be allowed to blind them to the nature of their individual tasks in life. In such cases their assumption of personal responsibility includes the task of affirming themselves despite the effects of others' deficits. They may have to work extra hard to retrieve bad situations as best they can. Sometimes this entails acknowledging and accepting that some psychological damage may be irretrievable given the current state of knowledge. Here, however, it is still possible to choose the attitude one adopts to this realization.

18. The assumption of personal responsibility is more likely to occur if approached in the context of a relationship characterized by empathic understanding

In proposition 8 (see Chapter 4) the importance was emphasized of young people having the secure base provided by an empathically understanding relationship with a significant adult. This helps them learn self-reliance through personal experiments. In proposition 14 it was indicated that people's responsibility skills deficits could be perpetuated both by the presence of being misunderstood by others and also by the absence of an empathic relationship. The present proposition, for a number of reasons, stresses the importance of an empathic relationship in facilitating clients in changing themselves. All of these reasons are based on the assumption that, though they may be helped by their counsellors, in the final analysis clients make the choices that change themselves. First, empathic understanding helps create and strengthen the counselling relationship so that the counsellor can be more effective as a helper. The counsellor's influence base is increased so that clients are both more likely to continue in counselling and also more likely to take notice of counsellor interventions than if they did not feel understood. Furthermore, the accuracy of the counsellor's understanding means that these interventions have a good chance of being attuned to clients' needs.

Second, and perhaps much more important, empathy helps clients to do things for themselves. The accepting and understanding companionship involved in empathy helps loosen clients from their stuckness by giving them the psychological safety to lower their defences and explore more deeply characteristic methods of responsibility avoidance. Furthermore, being empathically understood may also give clients the sense that it is safe to have, share and experience their feelings; and that it is safe to have opinions. Thus, along with an exploration of avoidances, there can be an experiencing of potential and of uniqueness. Another important outcome of being in an empathic relationship is that it provides a secure base for personal experiments outside counselling. This is analogous to the nurturing environment provided for their offspring by effective parents. They give their children permission and protection as they explore the world. They also provide an understanding emotiónal climate in which children can derive their own meanings from these experiences. Empathic understanding is discussed again in the remaining chapters. It is the foundation skill of counselling for personal responsibility. Additionally, since it is vital that people are able to listen to themselves, inner empathy is the foundation skill of self-therapy.

19. Counsellors need a repertoire of skills in addition to empathic understanding if they are going to be as effective as possible in helping clients overcome their responsibility skills deficits

Personal responsibility counselling and therapy is an integrative approach in a number of ways. All its interventions are based on the assumption that the object of counselling and therapy is to help clients as much as possible to help themselves. It derives most of its interventions from a range of existing therapeutic approaches. It is integrative too in that it aims to be of help to individuals in all areas of their psychological functioning. For instance, unlike some approaches, it focuses on the ways in which people occupy their time. In other words occupational psychology, rather than being a fringe area, becomes one of the central areas of concern. The dimensions of responsiveness, realism, relatedness, rewarding activity discussed in subsequent chapters, taken together, offer a fairly comprehensive coverage of human functioning. A further way in which personal responsibility counselling and therapy is integrative is that it encompasses higher as well as lower levels of psychological functioning. Since it takes ordinary rather than severely disturbed people as its starting point, it is more likely to be concerned with eupsychology (Maslow: 1965) or the psychology of wellness than just with the remediation of deficiencies. Additionally, since its ultimate focus is self-help, time spent with a counsellor is a form of inoculation to help people prevent or contain recurrences of their skills deficits. Still another way in which it is integrative is by incorporating individual and group counselling, life skills training and self-therapy among its modes of intervention.

Personal responsibility counselling and therapy involves counsellors in assessing their clients' skills resources and deficits, then drawing from their repertoire of skills those that are most appropriate for each person. In addition to empathic understanding, counsellors may need further skills depending on the extent to which their clients' deficits are in the particular areas of responsiveness, realism, relatedness and rewarding activity. Counsellor skills include assessing and identifying skills resources and deficits, forming an effective counselling relationship, focusing on thinking, facilitating behaviour change, and working with couples and groups. Although counsellors need to be sensitive to all major areas of human functioning, they may choose to specialize in particular areas and develop particular skills related to the needs of their clienteles. For example, though all counsellors should know about sexual dysfunction and occupational choice, these may be specialty areas as well. Thus personal responsibility counselling and therapy provides a framework in which different counsellors can help clients with different patterns of skills resources and deficits. Furthermore, counselling within this framework is not necessarily a once-for-all-time event. Clients may seek assistance as and when they consider it necessary, for any deficit, and from any counsellor they consider best meets their needs.

20. Counselling and therapy should not be seen independently of living and ultimately the best form of therapy is self-therapy

It may seem obvious that counselling should not be seen independently of living, but a number of approaches to counselling practice operate from conceptual frameworks that are far removed from the ways in which people think about their lives. Both psychoanalysis and radical behaviourism fall into this category. Ordinary people may be unrealistic about the extent to which they are currently assuming responsibility for their lives. The notion of personal responsibility is one which allows counsellors and clients to relate what goes on in counselling to how they live outside. For example, the idea of helping clients in counselling to learn to take responsibility for the ways in which they perpetuate their distress has relevance to how clients approach problems in their outside lives. Clients are not led to believe either that their behaviour is controlled by external stimuli or that much of their behaviour is unconsciously motivated and related to their childhood sexual development. Everything that the personal responsibility counsellor does is geared to, as clearly as possible, translating to clients what they might do to live more effectively outside counselling. Though counsellors may be experts in changing behaviour, much of this expertise relies on creating the conditions whereby clients change their own behaviour, and on imparting to clients an understanding of how they have brought this about. This enables them to go through the process again on their own if necessary.

Clients and people in general need to learn to become their own best therapists. Earlier a distinction was made between difficulties and problems. Effective self-therapy involves the capacity to listen to oneself well enough to be able to identify difficulties as they emerge, then the capacity to work through to acceptable solutions. Furthermore, it involves maintaining skills resources that are conducive to preventing difficulties. Problems arise when attempted solutions to difficulties are unsuccessful. Thus the attempts at solving the difficulty become part of the problem. These problems are much less likely to happen to people who have learned the skills of psychological self-help, yet to date the notion of self-therapy seems to have been insufficiently developed in the psychological literature. The function of personal responsibility counselling and life skills training is to help people become more effective self-therapists.

Chapter 6

CONSIDERATIONS FOR PRACTICE

This chapter reviews some considerations that are pertinent to the practice of personal responsibility counselling and therapy. These include: goals and assessment; some assumptions for practice; and issues involved in counsellor and client responsibility inside and outside counselling.

Goals and assessment

Starting points

The practice of personal responsibility counselling and therapy is primarily focused on the needs of ordinary people rather than on those of the moderately to severely disturbed minority. *Developmental tasks, transitions* and *individual life tasks* are three relevant concepts for developing and providing psychological interventions for the less seriously disturbed majority.

Havighurst defines a *developmental task* as 'a task which arises at or about a certain period in the life of the individual, successful achievement of which leads to his happiness and to success with later tasks, while failure leads to unhappiness in the individual, disapproval by society, and difficulty with later tasks' (Havighurst: 1972). Havighurst's six major age periods with illustrative developmental tasks are: infancy and early childhood (birth–6), forming concepts and developing language; middle childhood (ages 6–12), learning an appropriate masculine or feminine social role; adolescence (ages 12–18), achieving more mature relations with both sexes; early adulthood (ages 18–30), getting started in an occupation; middle age (ages 30–60), assisting teenage children; and later maturity (age 60+), adjusting to decreasing physical strength and health.

Other writers listing developmental tasks include: Erikson (1963) with his eight ages of man and their developmental conflicts; Ginzberg and his colleagues (1951; 1972) with their periods of occupational choice; Super (1957) with his stages of vocational self-concept development; Blocher (1966) with his five major stages of human development; and Egan and Cowan (1979) with their integrative developmental map of the life cycle in the United States culture. Though these writers differ in orientations and emphases, they share the common perspective that life is a series of challenges and adjustments from birth to death.

Blocher goes so far as to label his approach 'developmental counselling' to bring it firmly within the purview of meeting the needs of ordinary people rather than being focused on mental illness. He views the purpose of such counselling as the facilitation of individuals in mastering the tasks that will equip them with the coping behaviours necessary for handling those roles and relationships involved in the next stage of development. As such, counselling may be relevant for a wide variety of people. So long as the notion of developmental tasks does not impose a strait-jacket on people to conform to the norms of their culture, it provides a useful perspective on where the needs of nonpsychiatric populations lie.

The notion of developmental tasks is one of central tendency and assumes a progression through the stages of the life cycle. The notion of *transitions* both applies to progression through life stages and acknowledges that change can be unpredictable and not necessarily in accordance with normative developmental tasks. For example, redundancy and divorce are transitions without being normative developmental tasks. Hopson and Adams define a transition as 'a discontinuity in a person's life space of which he is aware and which requires new behavioural responses' (Hopson and Adams: 1976). Possible transitions include: marriage, parenthood and divorce; leaving home for the first time; change of job or career, including positive as well as negative changes; redundancy and retirement; change of culture; and the death of a partner. It is possible in the Western world that people are undergoing more discontinuity in their lives than previously. They adjust to technological change, engage more often in short-term relationships, move about more geographically and become more independent from larger family networks and from traditional values. Sometimes transitions may precipitate crises in which people feel that their coping resources are being stretched, if not overwhelmed.

The notion of *individual tasks* represents more the existentialist idea of people having to create their lives through their daily choices. One aspect of this is helping people to confront and make the most of both the common and the unique aspects of their human potential. Here the emphasis may be less on overcoming deficits them on learning to be creative about using resources and talents. This area of counselling sometimes goes under the name of the 'growth movement'. Though the growth movement has less reputable fringe areas and activities, helping people take responsibility for actualizing their higher potentials and values is thoroughly desirable. Another aspect of the notion of individual tasks is that of learning to confront what Yalom, using Satre's term, calls one's 'coefficient of adversity'. This is also similar to Frankl's idea of the necessity of finding meaning in suffering. It involves confronting and coming to terms with the negative parameters of fate and existence as constructively as possible. Yet a further aspect of the notion of individual tasks is that of self-definition. Personal responsibility counselling and therapy lays great stress on people learning to overcome the 'shoulds', 'oughts' and 'musts' of their childhood, adolescence and later life. Also, on learning to define themselves both in their own and in others' eyes.

In sum, personal responsibility counselling and therapy mainly focuses on the challenges and tasks which form part of everybody's lives. Though some people have severe psychological problems, for instance psychotic tendencies or deeply ingrained obsessive-compulsive ruminations and rituals, they are not the target population for this approach. Such people may require additional therapeutic and medical interventions.

Goals and psychological skills

Parloff (1967) suggests that the goals of counselling and therapy can be better understood if they are divided into two categories: mediating and ultimate. A similar differentiation between goals is the distinction between specific and general goals. For instance, behaviourists focus on specific goals, whereas person-centred counsellors focus on the general goal of facilitating client self-actualizing. Thus it might be said that the behaviourists do not have a vision of ultimate goals, whereas person-centred counsellors do not see the need for specifying mediating goals. In a comprehensive approach to counselling and therapy, there seems merit in retaining both ideas. The concept of personal responsibility is viewed as an integrating link which operates both vertically (between the ultimate and mediating goals) and horizontally (among the various mediating goals). Progress toward the ultimate goal involves paying attention to mediating goals (Nelson-Jones: 1979).

The paramount objective of personal responsibility counselling and therapy is to increase people's effective conscious control over themselves and their environments so that they may best meet the four basic needs or four Rs of psychological well-being: responsiveness, realism, relatedness and rewarding activity, all of which are mediating goals. Each mediating goal is comprised of a number of psychological skills in which individuals can be seen as possessing resources and deficits. Psychological skills resources relate to making correct choices for that individual's survival and fulfilment. The term psychological skills is used broadly. Some of the skills, for example appropriate self-disclosure, come closer to the conventional idea of a skill than others, for example awareness of feelings. Nevertheless, awareness of feelings could be seen as choosing to be aware of them which might in turn be seen as a skill.

When using constructs like psychological skills resources and deficits, it is important that they are not used too simplistically. An individual may have both resources and deficits in a psychological skill area. Also, there is overlap between the psychological skills. Furthermore, some deficits may be more amenable to change than others.

Table 6.1 shows the ultimate goal, mediating goals and some illustrative psychological skills of personal responsibility counselling and therapy. The first two mediating goals, responsiveness and realism, contain the fundamental psychological skills while the second two mediating goals, relatedness and rewarding activity, are more areas of application of the fundamental skills.

Table 6.1 Ultimate goal, mediating goals and illustrative psychological skills of personal responsibility counselling and therapy.

Ultimate goal	Mediating goals and psychological skills	
	1. Responsiveness	Existential awareness
		Awareness of feelings
		Awareness of inner motivation
		Sensitivity to anxiety and to guilt
	2. Realism	Realistic conceptual and linguistic framework
		Realistic internal rules and standards
		Realistic attribution of responsibility
		Realistic anticipation
Personal responsibility (effective choosing for survival and fulfilment)		Absence of self-protective thinking
	3. Relatedness	Capacity for self-definition
		Appropriate self-disclosure
		Empathic listening
		Conflict resolution skills
		Integration of sexuality
		Social empathy
	4. Rewarding activity	Identification of interests
		Participation in activities
		Appropriate activity level

The above psychological skills of each of the four mediating goals are now briefly described in an attempt at a definition of the process of being personally responsible.

Responsiveness

Existential awareness. Awareness of the parameters of human existence such as one's finitude and the contingencies of fate. Awareness of the existential demand for authorship of one's life.

Awareness of feelings. The capacity to be aware of one's feelings and emotions. Openness to experience and inner empathy.

Awareness of inner motivation. Awareness of wishes and of one's own will. Sensitivity to anxiety and to guilt. Awareness of warning signals that are indicative of possible responsibility skills deficits.

Realism

Realistic conceptual and linguistic framework. A realistic set of concepts or working hypotheses to govern one's approach to life. These are best expressed in clear and functional language.

Realistic internal rules and standards. A personal rule-book of standards about oneself, others and the environment that are functional in terms of survival and fulfilment.

Realistic attribution of responsibility. Accurate attribution or assignment of cause and responsibility for one's own behaviour, others' behaviour and for environmental events. Avoidance of inappropriate external attribution, incorrectly assigning too much cause and responsibility outside oneself, and of inappropriate internal attribution, incorrectly assigning too much cause and responsibility to oneself.

Realistic anticipation. Accurately assessing the future in terms of the risks, gains and consequences of one's own behaviour, other people's behaviour and environmental events.

Absence of self-protective thinking. Absence of defensive thought processes and of the need to manipulate the feedback one receives from others. Honest self-evaluation.

Relatedness

Capacity for self-definition. Ability to create one's own identity and to resist, where appropriate, colluding in other people's false definitions of oneself.

Appropriate self-disclosure. Ability to talk about and to reveal oneself in ways that are appropriate to different situations. Capacity for intimacy and honesty in personal relations.

Empathic listening. Ability to listen to and to receive accurately others' communications. Capacity to convey understanding to them.

Conflict resolution skills. Ability at negotiating differences of interest in ways that are assertive rather than inhibited, dishonest or aggressive. Capacity to minimize the damage to self and others where differences of interest persist.

Integration of sexuality. Ability to experience one's sensuality and to engage in mutually enhancing sexual relations.

Social empathy. Appropriate identification with the wider community and species. A sense of fellowship with humanity expressed in deeds.

Rewarding activity

Identification of interests. Ability to listen to oneself and identify what interests oneself and not just other people.

Participation in activities. Having sufficient sense of and actual competence to participate in activities that lead to happiness and fulfilment. At worst, having the skills to make the most of bad situations.

Appropriate activity level. Understanding and, where possible, working at one's own best level of activity and stress. Looking after one's health. Achieving a good balance between work, family and recreational activities.

Assumptions for practice

Some of the assumptions for practice of personal responsibility counselling and therapy now get briefly described.

1. This is a framework rather than a narrow approach

Though personal responsibility counselling and therapy has been labelled an integrative approach, it really provides a framework for thinking about human development, counselling, life skills training and living. The fundamental assumption of the framework is that of the desirability of humans learning to assume responsibility for their lives. Derived from and related to this fundamental assumption are numerous interventions for counselling, training and self-therapy. The framework makes explicit a theme running throughout existing counselling approaches. Each of these is partial and insufficiently comprehensive to provide a broad framework for viewing all major areas of human functioning.

2. There is no assumption of mental illness

This framework is essentially nonmedical. It involves what Szasz refers to as 'a rejection of the languages of both madness and mad-doctoring' (Szasz: 1973). People are seen as having difficulties of living related to developmental tasks, transitions and life tasks. They have deficits and resources in psychological skills. The four Rs of responsiveness, realism, relatedness and rewarding activity provide a simple classification into which psychological skills resources and deficits can be categorized, bearing in mind that both mediating goals and psychological skills tend to overlap.

3. There is no concept of cure

The concept of total cure is viewed as total nonsense. People have psychological skills resources and deficits and the balance between them may be shifted to decrease the deficits and increase the resources. However, this is never an either/or matter even, for instance, at the end of counselling. Since personal responsibility is a process, its component skills are also processes. Even when an improved level of resources relative to deficits has been attained there is always the possibility of backsliding. Personal responsibility is a continuous struggle between resources and deficits within each and across all psychological skills. After counselling, people still have to go on living with their resources and deficits. Hopefully, however, they have more resources with which to work on their deficits.

4. There is no blaming

With a concept like personal responsibility as an integrating focus, there is a risk that counsellors may categorize clients as irresponsible and blame them for shortcomings. The counsellor attitude advocated here is that of acceptance of clients as persons at the same time as acknowledging their skills deficits and resources. Any assessment is likely to be done in conjunction with clients to the extent that it seems appropriate. By no means do the counsellors blame clients for any skills deficits. Rather deficits are viewed as behaviours which are perpetuating clients' distress. They need help in learning to shift the balance more in the direction of resources.

5. There is no assumption of a single counselling relationship

What is meant by a single counselling relationship is a series of interviews with one counsellor over a period of time, anywhere from a few to a hundred or more sessions. Since there is no concept of cure, there is a related assumption that a single counselling relationship is insufficient for altering the balance of psychological resources and deficits for a person's lifetime. People may use counsellors to overcome the effects of earlier emotional deprivation, to develop specific skills resources, and for handling crises, amongst other reasons. They may use different counsellors, with different skills, for different purposes, at different times. Furthermore, they may be in individual counselling, group counselling, or attending psychological skills training programmes, to mention three possibilities. Additionally, people always have the need to engage in self-therapy. This aspect of personal responsibility counselling and therapy is a continuing process that lasts until death. Though the nature of the interventions may alter, the inescapable demand is ever present for people, during their waking hours, to engage in the processes of personal responsibility.

6. There are different kinds of counselling interviews depending on clients' needs

Many theoretical positions are suited to just one kind of counselling interview. Elsewhere, it has been suggested that there are five main kinds of counselling interview (Nelson-Jones: 1983). Each of these may help clients toward responsibility assumption. First, there is the *developmental* interview. Here the major emphasis is on the development of the person rather than on specific problems or decisions. Developmental interviewing involves providing clients with a nurturing emotional relationship to remedy real or imagined deficiencies in previous relationships, especially those provided by parents. Here clients tend to need help in developing the skills resource of self-acceptance prior to having the confidence to focus on more specific skills.

Second, there is the *problem-focused* interview. Here counselling is focused on helping clients develop specific skills resources for overcoming or learning to cope better with problems in their lives. Problems that get presented to counsellors are many and varied. Illustrative examples are the communication problems of marital partners, the various learning difficulties of pupils and students, the stress problems of executives, and coming to terms with a physical disability. The behavioural approach to counselling is based on a problem-focused style of interviewing.

Third, there is the *decision-making* interview. Here the focus is on helping clients make one or more specific decisions. Much counselling in the area of rewarding activity is concerned with decisions. These include choosing: a career; the educational route to obtain qualifications; whether or not to accept redundancy or early retirement; whether or not to change jobs in mid-career; and what to do when retired. Sometimes decision-making interviewing attains a broader focus than that of a specific decision. Clients are taught the psychological skills involved of making decisions wisely, including coping with anxiety.

Fourth, there is the *crisis* interview. Here clients come feeling that their coping resources are under great strain, if not overwhelmed. They feel under enormous stress and require immediate help in getting the balance of their psychological skills shifted in the direction of resources rather than deficits. Such interviews are often characterized by heightened emotionality. Counsellors must make immediate assessments of clients' situations. Considerations include the clients' psychological skills resources and deficits, suicide risk, support system, the desirability of medication and/or hospitalization.

Fifth, there is the *supportive* interview. Here clients, though not in major crisis, nevertheless consider that extra support and understanding is necessary to help them through an awkward phase. This kind of counselling may last for only one session. Ideally, supportive interviews quickly put clients back in touch with their skills resources so that they cope without counsellors.

7. Psychological skills resources can be developed by helping contacts

Counselling interviews involve counsellors and clients in formal settings. However, counselling-type relationships and interventions may be useful in many situations that are not formal counselling interviews. A valuable distinction is that between counselling interviews and helping contacts. Helping contacts may be made by people who use counselling skills as part of different or more complex roles. For example, teachers, preachers, doctors, nurses, social workers and a host of others in the helping professions may each have opportunities to exhibit the skills of personal responsibility counselling. Furthermore, all close personal relationships people can develop others' skills resources through helping contacts. Obviously there will be other communications as well. Like counselling interviews, helping contacts can be classified as developmental, problem-focused, decision-making, crisis or supportive, albeit overlapping. Just as the process of personal responsibility applies to counsellors and others alike, so these others can use their resources not only for self-therapy but in ways that foster the skills resources of those with whom they come into contact. People do not have to be counsellors to be helpers. They do not have to be clients to be helped to help themselves.

8. The notion of stages in counselling is valuable

The notion of stages relates to the *timing* of counselling interventions in relation to the *state of readiness* of clients. With highly vulnerable clients, an early direct focus on their realism or relatedness difficulties may be inadvisable for the following reasons. First, they initially may need to discuss and discharge feelings of hurt and pain. Second, until they become less anxious and more centred in themselves, they do not have the underlying minimum level of responsiveness for working on realism and relatedness skills. Third, vulnerable clients require time to trust their counsellors. Until a good relationship is established, they may be too threatened to perceive their responsibility for sustaining their distress. Thus a developmental or person-focused style of counselling, focusing on responsiveness, may have to precede a problem-focused style of counselling, focusing on realism and relatedness skills. Additionally, to engage in rewarding activities, clients need to develop the skills of responding to themselves before they are in an adequate position to choose and carry out their desired activities. In this instance, developmental may have to precede decision-making interviewing.

9. This is primarily a developmental approach

A distinction is frequently made between remedial, preventive and developmental counselling. Remedial counselling aims to mitigate psychological pain in the moderately to severely disturbed. Developmental counselling is oriented to the developmental tasks, transitions and life tasks of the majority. Prevention can have a number of meanings: it can involve screening pupils and students to see that those in need receive remedial counselling attention; consultancy with teachers to change aspects of the environment that are contributing to pupil distress; and running training courses in psychological skills so that those responsible for others facilitate rather than debilitate their development. In fact, prevention, remediation and development are highly interrelated. For instance, remedial counselling with parents may lessen the degree to which skills deficits are visited on their children. Also, running what might be viewed as developmental parent training programmes might have a preventive outcome for children. Nevertheless, however important remedial and preventive interventions may be, personal responsibility counselling and therapy has the developmental needs of the majority as its primary focus. This extends to an interest in higher level development and not just in the problems of the average.

Responsibility and the counsellor

Pierce and Schauble (1970) observed that responsibility as a therapist variable had been almost totally neglected in the literature. After analysing a variety of therapy sessions, they developed a five-point scale to measure 'facilitative responsibility'. At level one: 'The counsellor communicates that he has no sense of responsibility for client exploration and growth. He either completely abdicates his responsibility by actively denying his own impact, by acting bored, or he takes over to the point that the client cannot use any of his own resources'. At the other extreme of the scale, level five: 'The counsellor communicates that he feels very deeply and accurately his own responsibility to help. He both leads and follows appropriately and at the same time actively facilitates the client's ability to bring his own resources to bear'. Pierce and Schauble further reported that, 'using 20 personal-social problem cases', the successful cases received significantly higher levels of facilitative responsibility than did the unsuccessful ones. In other words, counselling is more likely to be helpful where the counsellor offers empathic understanding plus additional interventions focused on helping clients to develop and use their resources.

Despite Pierce and Schauble's assertion, counsellor or therapist responsibility has been present in the literature though often, as with client responsibility, it has been more implicit than explicit. If anything, the trend is toward greater explicitness: for instance, the work of Yalom (1980) and Smail (1978), though neither of these is primarily a research book. The notion of counsellor responsibility encompasses counsellors' responsibility both for their own lives and for their counselling interviews. The following review is mainly focused on interview issues.

First, counsellors should think through their beliefs about responsibility. It is inconsistent to *talk* radical behaviourism and environmental determinism and then *act* in counselling as though clients had some freedom of choice and hence some personal responsibility for their lives. The fundamental attitude for counselling within a personal responsibility framework is that life is a continuing series of choices and it is the function of counselling to help clients make choices that are more conducive to their survival and fulfilment. This position does not deny the importance of environmental circumstances, rewards and punishments. Nor does it deny such matters as fate and genetic endowment. Rather it asserts that, even within these constraints, the demand to choose among possibilities and potentialities is inescapable. Even though people, for various reasons, may be poor choosers, they are always choosers. Thus, in counselling, they must be helped to see and alter how they perpetuate their distress through their choices.

Second, there is the issue of how much the counsellor should stay within the client's frame of reference. Almost by definition clients' frames of reference are causing them distress. The issue then becomes one of whether clients' choices are more likely to be improved if the counsellor only offers an empathic relationship or if further interventions are also used. This can be a delicate question since it involves the what, how, when and even where of the future interventions. Without getting into detail at this stage, counsellors within a personal responsibility framework are educators or trainers as well as facilitators. They accept their clients' frames of reference as their perceptions of reality. Also they are sensitive to choices which clients may be making below their current levels of awareness and which involve responsibility avoidance rather than assumption.

Chance, bad luck and bad genes may all have contributed to the *acquisition* of deficits in the psychological skills of personal responsibility. However, patients or clients must learn to take responsibility for the way these psychological skills deficits are being *perpetuated*. Sometimes clients can assume responsibility with the support of counsellors who stay primarily within their frame of reference, assuming the counsellors have good skills at this. However, Yalom's statement that: 'No therapist goes through a day of clinical work without encountering several examples of responsibility-avoiding defences' (Yalom: 1980) rings true. To be able to identify such defences involves the capacity of counsellors to relate to their own as well as to their clients' perceptions. If counsellors are accurate in their perceptions, they may have an awareness of choices within the client's underlying rather than surface frame of reference. In sum, counsellors require sensitivity to the client's frame of reference on two levels: the level of the client's surface awareness, and the level of the client's underlying choices which perpetuate responsibility avoidance and block responsibility assumption.

A third issue, and related to the issue of how much they should stay in clients' frames of reference, is that of how active, directing and controlling counsellors should be. In Chapter 2 the findings were cited of the study of eighteen ten-session encounter groups, led by therapists from a wide variety of ideological schools, in which too active or too passive group leadership correlated with poor outcome (Lieberman, Yalom and Miles: 1973). There are many considerations relating to how active counsellors should be. These include: the level of vulnerability of clients; the suicide risk; the degree of trust between client and counsellor; and whether or not a specific technique is being used. Also, it is not only the *what* of an intervention that is important but *how* it is done. Thus a challenging intervention may lose much of its sting if done in a gentle and supportive way. Another series of issues relates to the division of responsibility in deciding how the time in counselling is spent and when termination of the relationship is appropriate. As a general rule counsellors and clients work together to decide such issues. Both need to assume responsibility for their own decisions. Across most activity/passivity issues, the Lieberman, Yalom and Miles study suggests, there is much to be said for counsellors following the happy medium.

A fourth issue that counsellors need to think through is the limit of their responsibility for clients. Smail (1978) suggests that therapists are not responsible *for* their patients, but only for their own conduct toward them, and the same holds true for counsellors and their clients. Clients must learn to accept responsibility for the ways in which they perpetuate their distress. All counsellors can do is help them in this endeavour. Counsellors are personally responsible for the standard of service that they offer their clients, but they are not responsible for leading their clients' lives for them.

Blocher (1966) makes a distinction between *process* and *outcome* decisions in counselling. Decisions to do with the counselling process, for example choice of interview content and number of sessions, tend to be joint decisions between counsellors and clients. Outcome decisions, such as choice of an occupation or mate, are always the responsibility of clients. What counsellors can do is help clients confront and overcome any avoidances in making such decisions as rationally as possible. However, these decisions should never be made for the client. Nor should clients feel that counsellors have vested interests in the results of outcome decisions. Such vested interests may be subtly rather than overtly expressed. Either way they represent influence attempts. However much clients may request them, they diminish rather than increase their capacity for responsibility assumption. They indicate that counsellors have unresolved needs. Because of these, they are unable to appreciate and value the separateness of their clients.

Counsellors have to set limits on themselves and clients in a number of frequently interrelated ways. For example, not going over interview length is a limit on counsellor and client alike. Counsellors may indicate their limits regarding between-session contact. Extending this, counsellors may also have to be clear not just about the limit of their responsibility to individual clients, but also to clients as a group and to any institution that employs them. Hidden agendas may be present in counsellors' attitudes toward their workloads and jobs. For example, counsellors may be trying to prove themselves, and as a consequence, they take on far too much work. Egan and Cowan (1979) write of the 'burned-out helper' phenomenon 'in which an intense desire to help becomes an exhausted day-to-day coping with persons in difficulty that leads to discouragement regarding the helping endeavour itself'. Whenever they deal with groups of clients or with institutions counsellors need to think through their responsibility for themselves as people. Burned-out or 'whisky counsellors', to use another Graham Greene allusion, or those in process of nervous breakdowns through having neglected their personal needs, are hardly in positions to offer professional services.

A fifth issue is the degree to which counsellors use a conceptual framework and language conducive to client responsibility assumption. An important part of counselling is that of helping clients develop a conceptual framework that is functional rather then counter-productive when thinking about their concerns. Three approaches that pay much attention to establishing and communicating in a common conceptual framework and language are Ellis' rational-emotive therapy, Berne's transactional analysis and Meichenbaum's self-instructional training. Traditional psychiatric classification seems deficient in having a conceptual framework and language that provides common ground between psychiatrists and their patients, or one conducive to patients doing things for themselves rather than having things done to them. Psychiatrists are then faced with having to use a second conceptual framework and language for communicating. This tends to have two important characteristics lacking in traditional psychiatric classification: patients can understand it, and it allows them to have some agency in overcoming their difficulties. Nonmedical theoretical positions also may be expressed in a language which does not communicate easily to laypeople. These limit their perceptions concerning their responsibility for their lives. Many if not most counsellors and therapists could be striving for a clearer and more functional communication with their clients than they have attained at present.

A sixth issue relates to how counsellors convey to clients the concepts of a model using personal responsibility as an integrating concept. Two of the main assumptions are: (a) that people are personally responsible for their lives, within the immutable parameters of their existences; and (b) change in the direction of overcoming responsibility deficits is more likely to occur if people take responsibility for the ways they perpetuate their distress. The first of these assumptions is likely to be less threatening than the second since it accords more closely with the conventional wisdom of Western cultures. Furthermore, unlike the second assumption, it does not directly confront clients with their agency in their distress. The notion that people are personally responsible for their lives can be conveyed by counsellor attitude, by the way the counsellor structures the working relationship, and by specific interventions during counselling. By counsellor attitude is meant behaving in numerous ways that assume the notion of responsibility, without necessarily spelling it out in words. Thus, counsellors can treat clients in a democratic manner and be prepared to share the process of decision making in the counselling sessions; they can avoid making clients' outcome decisions for them; and they can avoid other behaviours which create dependency, for example giving false reassurance.

A seventh issue relating to counsellor responsibility concerns 'who pays the piper' and the degree to which this person or institution overtly or subtly calls the tune. Perhaps private practice represents the most straightforward transaction so long as the client, rather than a third party, is paying (Szasz: 1962). Here counsellors are paid agents of their clients. Any form of implicit or explicit contract they arrive at is beteen the two of them. Though ideally there should be no conflict of interest between the two, there is always the risk of counsellors being influenced by financial considerations. For example, counsellors could be taking advantage of clients by charging too much, by unnecessarily prolonging the therapeutic contact, and by failing to confront clients' responsibility avoidances, or by diluting the confrontations for fear of losing clients' fees rather than for any positive reasons. There are also broader social considerations involved in private practice: for example, the desirability of working only with the wealthier sections of the community or of having private practice at all. The charge of working only with the wealthier sections of the community can be mitigated if counsellors base their fees on ability to pay. Private practice provides a service that many choose. It may not be readily available from the state. Perhaps too, where private practice exists, there is less risk of psychology becoming an instrument of the state, as it sometimes seems in Russia.

In the United States, a large part of private practice is not of a two-person, but of a three-party nature. Alongside private practice, where the client pays, there has been a growth of insured practice, where the insurer pays. The interests of clients, who may want and/or need extended treatment, of insurers, who may want the job done as quickly as possible, and of counsellors, who may see their interests as different from either, do not always coincide. There is no longer a truly two-person arrangement and counsellors may feel under pressure to compromise on professional responsibilities in order to placate insurers and so obtain further referrals.

In Britain there is little private practice. However, there is much state practice in the National Health Service. This again affects the power relationship between clients and psychologists. Since the service is free, it is nominally available to all social classes. In practice, however, there are only about 1200 clinical psychologists eligible to work in the National Health Service. Thus access to their counselling help is very restricted, and many of these scarce resources are devoted to specialty areas such as mental handicap and geriatrics. Because clients are not in a direct fee relationship with their counsellors, the power of counsellors relative to them is increased. And the fact that the state is prepared to provide only limited resources for the service, and consequently counsellors feel under pressure of numbers, also influences the nature of the service they provide. Furthermore, counsellors get their pay cheques virtually automatically. As in any bureaucracy, there may be tendencies toward complacency and operating the system for themselves rather than for clients. Additionally, clinical psychologists in the National Health Service, like their patients, risk developing responsibility skills deficits through institutionalization. For instance, they may become timid and excessively security conscious.

In a number of countries there is the state practice of counselling in schools and in further and higher education. Here again there is no direct fee relationship between counsellors and clients. This provides many of the same advantages, disadvantages and temptations as in the British National Health Service. In schools especially, the status of counsellors may be relatively low and this, in itself, makes them vulnerable to outside pressures: for example, to breach confidentiality.

An eighth issue is the degree to which counsellors are effective in taking responsibility for making good role decisions. Role decisions relate to how counsellors allocate their time between the different possible dimensions of their job (Nelson-Jones: 1982b). For instance, counsellors in institutions can counsel individuals or groups, run psychological skills training programmes, and act as consultants to change the systems which contribute to counselling problems. With the emergence of a potentially more complex role for counsellors, there is increasing need for good role decisions. Ideally counsellors should be clear both about their objectives in regard to their overall role and also about the objectives of their specific interventions.

Three aspects of role decisions are their clientele, objectives and method. The clientele for an intervention may be an individual, a couple, a family, a group, an institution or a community. The objectives may be remediation of moderate to severe psychological skills deficits, preventing deficits, or altering the balance between deficits and resources of 'normal' people. The method of an intervention may be counselling, training or consultancy. The different interventions that counsellors make within a given time period add up to a profile which reflects their definition of their professional existence, for the time being at least. Needless to say, in formulating their objectives and programmes, it is very important for counsellors to be sensitive about the expectations and wishes of any agency or institution in which they may be working.

The final issue discussed here is counsellors' responsibility for their own professional development. This may seem so obvious that it scarcely merits mention. However, a note of realism, if not pessimism, is in order because the obstacles are considerable. Some of these obstacles have already been mentioned in different contexts. They include the need to earn a living and the pressures and compromises involved in doing this in private practice, insured practice, and state hospital or institutional practice; the pressures of a heavy case load and the risks of burn-out and breakdown; the dangers on the one hand of institutionalization, for those working in state practice, or on the other hand of isolation, for those working in private practice; the constriction in the initial teaching of counsellors through the allegiances of their teachers; the tendency to associate in professional networks of like-minded people, possibly sustaining allegiance to a narrow position; the effects of professional hierarchies with preferment sometimes being more a matter of allegiance to the norms of a particular hierarchy than recognition for independent thought and effort; the fact that professional development often has financial costs (e.g. purchase of books and journals, fees and possibly living expenses for attending conferences, courses and workshops; and income forgone while studying etc.); the possibility that clients reward some less responsible counselling behaviours, resulting, for example, in the fear that becoming more challenging and not overtly nurturing all the time may cause loss of popularity and possibly of clients; lastly, any skills deficits that counsellors bring to the job (e.g. needing to distort feedback from clients to remain seeing their counselling in a favourable light). In other words, counsellors face considerable pressures *not* to develop professionally.

There are, of course, many countervailing pressures. Institutions, hierarchies, professional networks, and the demands to earn a living can exert pressures for good as well as ill. Clients can challenge as well as restrict. Counsellors' own needs for fulfilment and for competence can provide a considerable impetus to improve professional skills. Even some skills deficits may be working for as well as against counsellors. For instance, the need for client, peer and authority figure approval, although possibly biased too much toward the need for external rather than internal evaluation, may nevertheless provide stimulation toward higher standards of practice.

A continuous theme throughout this section is that whether it be in their personal lives, their counselling interviews, their relationships with whosoever is paying them, their role decisions or their professional development, counsellors are personally responsible for creating and defining their existences by their choices. Also, they are continually having to face internal and external pressures for responsibility avoidance as well as for responsibility assumption.

Chapter 7

RESPONSIVENESS: EXPERIENCING FEELINGS

This chapter focuses on responsibility assumption in the area of responsiveness or of experiencing feelings. Lower animals experience feelings, such as fear, pleasure and pain, but lack the human capacity for conscious awareness. Focusing on responsiveness involves helping people learn to value and live with their underlying animal nature so that it works for rather than against them. Though Rogers called one of his books *On Becoming a Person* (Rogers: 1961), he might have changed the title to *On Becoming an Animal*. His thesis was that the development of personhood rests on the capacity of people to become more in contact with their organismic valuing process. People are animals first and persons second. Perls also emphasized this point with his aphorism: 'Lose your mind and come to your senses' (Perls: 1973). In this chapter the major focus is on helping people respond to rather than regulate their feelings. Thus the emphasis here is more on 'loosening up' than on 'tightening up'.

Reasons for focusing on responsiveness

There are many different reasons why counsellors, clients and people in general need to pay attention to responsiveness. First, there is the human need for catharsis. Catharsis involves getting relief through purging oneself of emotions which, if allowed to persist, might interfere with fulfilment and even survival. The emotions themselves may be functional, but keeping them pent-up and unreleased risks their becoming dysfunctional. The following are three instances in which catharsis may be desirable. First, there is the case of children who have had their integrity consistently attacked by inadequate and manipulative parents. Such children may come to counselling, either when young or later, with a back-log of insufficiently expressed hatred and resentment.

Here one of the tasks of counselling may be to allow clients to experience and release this hatred prior to being able to use the emotional energy invested in it for more constructive purposes. Second, in grief work with bereaved people, one of the counsellor's tasks in the mourning process is to enable them to experience the pain of the grief rather than to deny or distort it (Worden: 1982). Experiencing pain can also be necessary when 'working through' other stressful or traumatic experiences, for example redundancy or rape. Third, in their everyday lives, people need to release emotions. They also need to develop the skills of doing this in ways that do not violate others.

Physical health is the second reason for focusing on responsiveness. Emotions that are not adequately released may be somatized. One definition of psychosomatic disorders is that they represent maladaptive physical changes in the body systems, primarily of psychological origin. Trethowan (1979) states that more recently this narrow definition 'has been widened to include all conditions in which psychiatric investigation may contribute to the aetiology, prevention and treatment of a considerable number of physical complaints'. The American Psychiatric Association uses the term 'psychophysiologic' to emphasize that the disorders are caused and maintained primarily by psychological and emotional rather than by organic factors. Disorders which may have a psychophysiologic element include: eczema, muscle cramps, tension headaches, asthma, heart attacks, hypertension, peptic ulcers, chronic gastritis, and disturbances in urination and in menstruation. There is also some interesting research emerging that suggests that emotional suppression contributes to the acquisition and maintenance of cancer (Simonton, Matthews-Simonton and Creighton: 1978).

The third reason for focusing on responsiveness involves the desirability of lifting unwanted inhibitions and repressions. As people grow up they learn, to a greater or lesser degree, that it is unsafe to acknowledge, experience and express all feelings. Consequently an editing process takes place. This may get so internalized that people remain unaware of it. An oft-quoted example is that of sexual repression in turn-of-the century Vienna. Despite the label of the permissive society, it is possible that much inhibition of genuine sensuality still exists in Western countries. Another example is what Steiner calls scripting or basic training in lovelessness (Steiner: 1974). Strokes are defined as units of recognition and children's basic training in lovelessness consists of the following injunctions: 1. don't give strokes if you have them to give; 2. don't ask for strokes when you need them; 3. don't accept strokes if you want them; 4. don't reject strokes when you don't want them; 5. don't give yourself strokes. Though Steiner may overstate, his remarks hold true for many. People who work with families observe that they place different values both on the expression of emotions and on which emotions and senses it is safe to feel and use (Laing: 1969; Satir: 1972). Thus all people learn the permissions and inhibitions of their family scripting regarding emotional responsiveness, though change is possible.

People also give themselves permissions and carry around inhibitions according to their social characteristics. Earlier the observation was made that in America and other Western countries boys and girls were differentially conditioned concerning which feelings they could acknowledge and express; also, that such pigeon-holing of emotions caused their emotional responsiveness to be considerably diminished. Perhaps experiencing feelings according to gender is now the main area of inhibition in Western cultures. As the list of feminine and masculine items in the Bem Sex-Role Inventory indicates (Bem: 1974), this inhibition pervades numerous characteristics. Other pertinent considerations for which feelings get expressed, suppressed or repressed include: ethnic origin, social class, geographical location and the norms of one's occupational group.

A further area in which people may be inhibited is that of acknowledging and expressing their higher potentials. This is the point made by Maslow (1971) when he observes that: 'Repression, denial, reaction formation and probably all the Freudian defence-mechanisms are available and are used against the highest within ourselves just as they are mobilized against the lowest within ourselves'. These higher values include truth, beauty, goodness, justice and simplicity. Though not cited in Maslow's list of higher values, they also include generosity and a sympathetic identification with the species.

A fourth reason for focusing on responsiveness is the need for existential awareness. This is a form of responsiveness to human existence. It involves acknowledging death and finitude. Also, it entails awareness of the tragic nature of human existence. Death is one of the main areas regarding which people inhibit and repress feelings. The importance of existential awareness is the sharpening of people's attitudes toward taking responsibility for their lives. Furthermore, it may allow other people to acknowledge and talk more openly about death and dying both when in health and also when dying. Death is a vital part of life. To deny and not talk about death cuts people off from a fundamental area of their own and other people's experience.

A fifth reason for focusing on responsiveness is to facilitate awareness of wishes, wants and inner motivation. People's feelings form the basis of exploratory behaviour and of judging its outcomes according to whether it contributes to their needs for survival and fulfilment. The wish precedes the act. Often apathy and lack of feeling are defences against the anxiety attached to acting. Humans need be aware of personal needs and take their emotional responses to life seriously. Sometimes these emotional responses are more in the form of fragments than fully developed feelings. Counsellors need to be sensitive to these feeling fragments in clients and help them come more into conscious awareness. They may represent wishes and wants based on clients' own motivating drives rather than on what others think they should be feeling. Sometimes these wishes and wants may incline individuals to refrain from acting. For example, workaholics may get glimpses of feeling fragments indicating that they are heading for emotional overload. These fragments also indicate their body's need for recreation. The need for identity is a sixth reason for focusing on responsiveness. People's feelings, their unique valuing of what goes on in their lives, form the basis of a healthy sense of continuity and sameness. Identity means that people are centred in their unique capacity for responsiveness. Despite this, they still have to negotiate a set of self-conceptions with others. Nevertheless, people with a responsible and responsive sense of identity are likely to have the following characteristics. Their capacity for responsiveness allows them flexibly to take into account the realities of emerging situations. Their sense of identity is sufficiently strong for them to integrate valuable new or altered self-conceptions at the same time as maintaining the core of their personhood. They are always in process of identity formation, yet this making and remaking of themselves is a process of renewal that is in accord with rather than violates the core of their being. Furthermore, when they deviate from being authentic, they are capable of heeding their feelings of anxiety and guilt and thus returning to behaviours more consistent with their underlying sense of self.

Interventions for responsiveness

This section reviews various interventions for engendering responsiveness and also for maintaining it. Though the section is broken down into counselling, training and self-therapy interventions, these areas overlap. Additionally, though many interventions are suggested, this implies neither that all are equally important nor that all are desirable for all clients. Counsellors, trainers and people working on their own development need to develop the skills of appropriate judgement. They need to know which interventions to apply to others or themselves as well as when and how.

Counselling interventions
Personal responsibility counselling and therapy views the effective counsellor

as possessing a repertoire of skills. The application of these skills is tailored to the needs of individual or groups of clients. Some of these skills, for example empathic responding, are central to the counselling process. Other skills are much more the preserve of specific clients and problems. Though all counsellors need some central skills, other skills may be more relevant to different client populations. Consequently counsellors vary according to which skills they possess.

Empathic responding   Perhaps empathic responding is better thought of as the capacity of the counsellor to create an empathic emotional climate. Empathic responding consists of both receiver and sender subskills. The *receiver* subskills consist of accurately listening to the verbal, vocal and bodily communications of clients. In other words it means not only understanding their literal content, but also the 'framing' messages contained in their communications. At a more sophisticated level it involves understanding the ways in which clients block communicating. A remark attributed to the American psychiatrist Harry Stack Sullivan was that about ninety percent of human communication was specifically designed not to communicate. The *sender* subskills consist of communicating understanding of clients' utterances in a language attuned to their needs and at a depth that takes into account their state of readiness to acknowledge threatening material. Furthermore, empathic responding involves checking out the accuracy of responses.

The main kind of empathic response is the reflection or mirroring response. This can reflect the literal content of what clients have been saying, reflection of content, or what clients feel, reflection of feeling, or a mixture of the two, reflection of content and feeling. Counsellors who are working to 'loosen up' their clients are likely to use reflections that focus on feelings. This diminishes the possibility of colluding with clients in staying distant from their feelings.

The emotional climate of counselling is important. Though good responses to individual utterances can be helpful, it is the feeling clients obtain that counsellors are safe, caring and trustworthy people who understand them that counts. Rogers, with whose name the concept of empathy is most associated, is very against it being viewed as a 'nondirective technique'. He stresses the quality of the human encounter involved in an empathic *way of being* or an empathic *attitude*. He also talks of the 'gentle and sensitive companionship of an empathic stance' which needs to be accompanied by genuineness and caring (Rogers: 1975).

There are many reasons why an empathic climate is conducive to engendering responsiveness. First, it gives clients permission to feel and be themselves. Frequently clients have been brought up in environments where their feelings were valid according to the extent with which they fitted other people's convenience. Instead of being allowed to experience their range of feelings, they were allowed to experience them only selectively. Second, an empathic climate gives clients the opportunity to identify and label feelings. Thus feelings and feeling fragments become more accessible. Third, an empathic emotional climate helps clients explore and delve deeper into understanding their feelings.

Fourth, by creating an empathic climate, counsellors become secure bases from which clients can engage in exploratory behaviour. Such behaviour allows them to generate new and different feelings. Counsellors can also provide empathic understanding as clients explore their feelings and reactions to their new experiences. Fifth, responsiveness may be engendered by the empathic climate of counsellors who have special insights into the problems of specific groups, for instance the bereaved. They may facilitate even those clients who find difficulty in verbalizing their underlying feelings.

In addition to empathic responding there are many other interventions that counsellors may use for engendering responsiveness. However, it is important that they are used within the context of relationships in which clients feel understood. Furthermore, some of these interventions are likely to require the consent of clients. Again it is stressed that counsellors need to develop skills of judgement concerning whether, when and how to use interventions.

Providing a rationale for acknowledging feelings   The first part of this chapter was an attempt to get counsellors to take their clients' feelings seriously. Counsellors can discuss with clients the importance of taking feelings seriously. The overall message is that of learning to take responsibility for acknowledging and appropriately expressing feelings. This may be illustrated for individual clients with specific instances of the ways in which their not allowing themselves to experience feelings may contribute to their problems.

Focusing on feelings questions   Focusing on feelings questions are designed to elicit how clients feel about themselves, others, the counselling relationship, and events and situations in their lives. Counsellors need to be sensitive to the danger of getting clients talking about feelings in distant ways rather than experiencing them. Another danger of this use of questions is that clients may respond to the counsellor rather than to themselves. However, if skilfully used, focusing on feelings can give clients useful practice at learning to listen to and become more aware of their feelings. Below are some questions focusing on clients' feelings. Note that all the questions are either open-ended or tentative or both open-ended and tentative. After all, clients should, but not always will, know their own feelings better than anyone else. Focusing on feelings questions include: 'How do you feel about that?'; 'I'm wondering what the emotional impact of that is on you?'; 'How do you experience that?'; 'Would you care to describe your feelings?'; 'You seem to be feeling . . .?'; 'I'm hearing that you're feeling . . .?'; and 'You seem to have conflicting feelings . . . . is that true?'

Increasing existential awareness   There are a number of counsellor interventions specifically focused on increasing clients' existential awareness, some involving getting clients to use their imaginations. Mention has already been made of Frankl's stress on the importance of making people aware of their finiteness; also, of his categorical imperative of logotherapy: 'So live as if you were living already for the second time and as if you had acted the first time as wrongly as you are about to act now!' (Frankl: 1959). Frankl is essentially challenging people to acknowledge that they are responsible for their choices and for the outcomes of these choices on their own and on other people's lives; furthermore, to make them aware that second chances are not always possible. Another way in which clients are sometimes invited to use their imaginations is by getting them to write out their obituaries. If rightly timed, this can help increase awareness of a sense of responsibility for their lives. If wrongly timed and clients are not really involved, this may just be a wasteful gimmick. Other approaches to heightening people's awareness of life by increasing their awareness of death include: exploration of significant life events as milestones in a finite life-span; focusing on people's experiences of death and dying; and interaction with the dying. In regard to the latter, Yalom has used both observation of a terminal cancer group by his everyday clients and having a person with terminal cancer as a member of a regular psychotherapy group (Yalom: 1980).

Exploring feelings of anxiety and guilt   One way of viewing anxiety and guilt is that, on the whole, they are negative emotions that hinder rather than help individuals. Another way is that they signal that individuals may be less responsive to their true needs than desirable. May (1953) observes that conscience is generally conceived as the negative voice of tradition speaking within people. However, he redefines it and writes: 'Conscience, rather, is one's capacity to tap one's own deeper levels of insight, ethical sensitivity and awareness, in which tradition and immediate experience are not opposed to each other but interrelated.' The violation of conscience is likely to lead to feelings of anxiety and guilt. In reality, both meanings of conscience are possible. Anxiety and guilt may be either signals to discard or redefine dysfunctional rules or signals that functional rules are being violated and hence people are acting against their own best interests. The fact that anxiety and guilt can have this second function means that counsellors need to help clients experience and evaluate the true meaning of their feelings of guilt rather than automatically assume that all feelings of guilt are bad.

Focusing awareness   Gestalt therapy views itself as an experiential rather than a verbal therapy. It demands that clients experience themselves as fully as possible in the here-and-now both to understand their present manipulations and to reexperience the unfinished business of past problems and traumas. Perls writes: 'The basic sentence with which we ask our patients to begin therapy, and which we retain throughout its course – not only in words, but in spirit – is the simple phrase: "Now I am aware". (Perls: 1973). Clients are asked to become aware of their body language, their breathing, their voice quality and their emotions as much as of any pressing thoughts. This awareness technique, sometimes called focal awareness, is a concentration technique. Clients learn to experience and be responsive to each now and each need, and to be aware of how their feelings and behaviours in one area are related to feelings and behaviours in other areas. Perls aimed to make people aware not only of the fact that they were interrupting their contact with themselves and the world, but also of what they were interrupting and how they were doing it. Independent of the label of gestalt therapy, getting clients to focus on every verbal, vocal and bodily aspect of their experiencing can be a useful way of heightening their self-understanding and responsiveness.

Sensate focus   Lack of sexual responsiveness may take different forms and have multiple causes. Often it is part of a broader pattern of inadequate communication. Many clients, however, may be functioning moderately well in other areas of their life and need specific assistance in acknowledging and exploring their sexuality. This may be independent of having a more specific sexual dysfunction.

Masters and Johnson (Masters and Johnson: 1970) developed the technique of sensate focus to help couples to think and feel sensuously. Sensate focus acknowledges the importance of touch in stimulating and experiencing sexual responsiveness. Partners are asked to time their periods of sensate focus for when they feel a natural sense of warmth and compatibility. They should continue for so long as it is pleasurable. Both partners should be unclothed with a minimum of physical fatigue and tension. Avoiding specifically sexual stimulation, including genitals and breasts, the 'giving' partner is instructed to 'trace, massage, or fondle the 'getting' partner with the intention of giving sensate pleasure and discovering the receiving partner's individual levels of sensate focus' (Masters and Johnson: 1970). The rules of sensate focus for receiving partners are that they have to protect 'pleasuring' partners from causing discomfort or initiation, and there is no requirement on them, verbally or nonverbally, to comment on their experiencing, unless such expression is completely spontaneous. Giving partners are committed not only to giving pleasure, but also to acknowledging their sensations in giving pleasure, exploring another's body by touch, and receiving pleasurable reactions. After a reasonable time, partners exchange roles. Sensate focus tends to give couples time, space and permission to respond sensually without feeling that they have to perform intercourse. Kaplan observes that, though most couples experience positive reactions to sensate focus, some people experience very little reaction and others negative reactions (Kaplan: 1974). She indicates that these negative reactions may be indicative of deeper inhibitions concerning sexual responsiveness and makes suggestions for treating them.

Consciousness raising   Here the focus is on consciousness raising as a means of improving people's capacity for responsiveness. In Western countries there are few people who do not need to become more in tune with their feelings. However, consciousness raising tends to be used in terms of raising the level of awareness of specific subgroups of the population: women, men, gays, various ethnic groups, and so on. Such consciousness raising is relevant to responsiveness in two main ways. First, it aims to rid these groups of negative feelings, for example low self-esteem and overdependency in women. Second, it can aim to make subgroups more able to respond to the range of feelings that are inherent in the human condition; for example, women can be more prepared to acknowledge and express feelings of ambition and assertion whereas men can demonstrate more nurturance, vulnerability and affection.

Providing a rationale for focusing on feelings was mentioned earlier in this list of counselling interventions. Consciousness raising is more specific in that it provides a rationale and gives permission for focusing on feelings problematic to different subgroups. It may also involve other interventions like counsellor self-disclosure and focusing on feelings questions that are specifically geared to feelings and emotions concerning which consciousness may need to be raised. Groups are a popular format for consciousness raising. However, if these groups are unethically or poorly led, one set of restrictive norms may be substituted for another.

Challenging inauthenticity   Counsellors may use their here-and-now experiencing as a guide to whether clients communicate what they really think and feel. Here, instead of using empathy to allow clients' feelings to unfold, counsellors step outside their current awareness to respond in ways that challenge it. Challenging is sometimes called confrontation (Carkhuff: 1969a). Another way of viewing challenging is that it entails reflecting and/or focusing on discrepancies in thoughts, feelings and actions. The *how* of confrontations or challenges is an extremely important element along with their *what* or verbal content. Challenges can vary on such dimensions as: when they take place; whether they are gentle or forceful; whether they are brief or persistent; and the extent to which they deviate from the client's current frame of reference. Counsellors need beware that, though a good challenge may accelerate the process, premature or clumsy challenges, especially with vulnerable clients, may retard to cause clients to terminate counselling.

Below are a couple of examples of challenges focused on the authenticity of a client's response.

Challenging where verbal and vocal communication is discrepant with bodily communication:

Cl. You know I asked her to go out with me and she said that she was busy and then when I suggested another time she said perhaps it was best if we left it.

Co. You seem disappointed that she did not accept your invitation. I caught a note of pain in your voice and yet you were smiling as you were telling me of the incident.

Challenging where a response is projected onto others:

Cl. Judy and Joan seem to feel pretty angry with the way we are being taught.

Co. I'm wondering whether focusing on Judy and Joan's anger is a way of protecting yourself from acknowledging that you too feel angry with your teachers and are capable of angry feelings.

Challenges concerning authenticity can go both ways. In fact responsive clients are more likely than those more emotionally remote to challenge counsellors whose words and actions seem discrepant with underlying feelings. Here the challenge to counsellors is also the internal one of not responding defensively.

Counsellor self-disclosure   The ability of counsellors to be real in their relationships is very important for engendering client responsiveness. Rogers uses terms like congruence and genuineness (Rogers: 1957; 1975). The existential psychologists use terms like presence and authenticity (May: 1958; Bugental: 1981). May quotes Binswanger's phrase about relating to the client as 'one existence communicating with another' (May: 1958). Bugental (1978) views presence as consisting of an intake side called accessibility and an output side called expressiveness. Accessibility means 'having the intention to allow what happens in a situation to matter, to have an effect on one'; while expressiveness arises from 'the intent to let oneself be known by the other in a situation, to make available some of the contents of one's subjective awareness without distortion or disguise'. Counsellors who are present in their relationships are alive and devoting themselves to understanding, experiencing and releasing the sense of being of clients. Such counsellors model responsiveness, thus providing the opportunity for clients to engage in observational learning.

Counsellor self-disclosure is one aspect of counsellor responsiveness. In this context self-disclosure means intentional disclosure of self-referent information. Three kinds of counsellor self-disclosure that may facilitate client responsiveness are; sharing experiences; sharing feelings; and being assertive. Possibly counsellors may have had similar concerns or experience to their clients. It may be helpful to share these. Also, at times counsellors may consider it appropriate to share their feelings. These feelings may be about clients as people; what clients are currently saying or doing or avoiding saying or doing; and the counselling relationship. Additionally, there may be occasions in counselling when the emotional climate is improved by counsellors being firm and setting limits. Such occasions include: standing up to aggressive clients; not allowing counselling time to be persistently wasted; and ending sessions on time. There are obvious dangers in inappropriate counsellor self-disclosure: for example, burdening clients with problems; seeming weak and unstable; and dominating the interview. However, if well done, counsellor self-disclosure can be a good way of personalizing counselling and creating a freer and more human atmosphere. Some guidelines for appropriate counsellor self-disclosure are: communicate clearly and directly; be relevant; be nonpossessive; allow clients to accept or reject the relevance to them of your disclosures; be relatively brief; and do not do it too often.

Role-play methods   There are many variations in the use of dramatic or role-play methods that can be used in individual counselling. These role-play methods tend not to be ends in themselves but ways of allowing clients expression of feelings and catharsis which in turn may generate further self-exploration. Thus role-plays may be followed by counsellors using empathic responding to help clients explore the meaning of the feelings released, or by counsellors focusing on specific aspects of clients' thinking, or by a mixture of the two.

Role-play methods can focus either on clients' relationships with various parts of themselves or on their relationships with other people. For instance, clients can get in touch with their difficulties in making decisions by playing a dialogue between the part of themselves that is in favour of a course of action and the part that is against it. As each part is played clients may switch from one chair to another. Alternatively, clients may close their eyes and verbalize an imagined dialogue.

Role-play methods can be a powerful way of releasing and exploring the emotions invested in various kinds of personal relationships, be they past, present or future. Again clients may play both parts of a relationship either with eyes closed in imagination or by switching chairs as they play each part, or the counsellor may play one of the parts in the relationship, for example, a parent, spouse, boyfriend or girlfriend. Indeed the counsellor may switch roles and be the client as the client plays the other person in the relationship. This is known as role-reversal. Additionally, the counsellor may mirror both verbal and nonverbal aspects of the client's behaviour in an enactment. Nowadays it is also possible to video-record and play back the enactment. Conceivably this is more useful when using role-play as part of social skills training than when using it as an intervention for generating responsiveness.

Role-play methods are also used in group counselling. Sometimes, as in gestalt therapy, this is more a variation of individual counselling conducted in the presence of other group members. At other times, role-plays may involve a number of the group members. Such role-plays may be used either on an *ad hoc* basis as counsellors see fit or as part of ongoing psychodrama groups. Moreno defined psychodrama as 'the science which explores the "truth" by dramatic methods. It deals with inter-personal relations and private worlds' (Moreno: 1953). In psychodrama, some portion of the group setting is designated as a stage, though this may move around in the course of a session. There are four main participants: the subject or protagonist; the counsellor or director; the other players or auxiliary egos; and the group or audience. The auxiliary egos are members of the group who play various roles required by the protagonist's drama. The audience to the enactments may, where appropriate, make comments or share their experiences. The director not only directs the enactment, but also acts as counsellor in helping the protagonist release and handle the material generated in the enactment. Also, the director helps other group members do likewise. Members can take turns as protagonist or they may volunteer when they wish to work on an area. Since extremely strong feelings can be generated in psychodrama groups it is recommended that members be adequately screened prior to entry, and that they have access to sufficient support during and possibly after the life of the group. Another word of warning about psychodrama groups is that a few intense emotional experiences are unlikely in themselves to help clients become significantly more responsive in their everyday lives.

Relaxation methods   For many, learning to be more responsive entails learning to become more relaxed. Though relaxation methods are not a substitute for self-understanding, they can nevertheless be helpful for people who suffer either from problems of generalized tension or from anxiety in relation to specific events, for example an impending public speaking engagement. Relaxation methods may be used on their own or in conjunction with other procedures. The pioneer of relaxation training was Edmund Jacobson who saw what he termed neuromuscular hypertension' as a condition marked by reflex phenomena of hyperexcitation and hyperirritation' (Jacobson: 1938). He was aware that symptoms of hypertension were very common and not restricted to the severely disturbed. His term 'progressive relaxation' refers to the progressive cultivation of the relaxation response by tensing and relaxing the various muscle groupings of the body. The behaviourists in particular use progressive muscular relaxation as part of their repertoire of skills. This may at first entail training clients in tensing and relaxing in turn all major muscle groupings of the body. When the full muscular relaxation procedures have been learned and the client is able to attain deep relaxation, briefer muscular relaxation procedures may be introduced. These briefer procedures involve tensing and relaxing in turn composite muscle groupings, for instance seven or four composite groupings as contrasted with the sixteen separate groupings for the full treatment. Indeed, one variation is to tense and relax all muscle groupings together (Bernstein and Borkovec: 1973). Mental relaxation may be used after going through a muscular relaxation procedure. Such relaxation usually involves imagining a peaceful scene, such as 'lying in a meadow on a nice warm summer's day, feeling a gentle breeze and watching the clouds go by against a blue sky'. Counsellors can find out from their clients which scenes they find most conducive to relaxation.

Relaxation methods are used to handle inappropriate responsiveness – that is situations in which the anxiety and tension is debilitating rather than facilitating. Systematic desensitization is a technique that involves use of relaxation where clients suffer from specific rather than generalized feelings of anxiety. This consists of three main elements: first, training in progressive muscular relaxation; second, the construction of one or more lists or hierarchies of situations or scenes around a particular theme ranging from the least to the most anxiety evoking (for example, on a fear of examinations hierarchy, 'thinking about exams while revising at my desk three months before the exams' is the least anxiety-evoking scene, while the most anxiety-evoking scene is 'having to leave the exam room due to panic'); third, presentation by counsellors to clients' imaginations of progressively more anxiety-evoking scenes from their hierarchies, the assumption here being that presentation of scenes when clients are relaxed inhibits the anxiety attached to them and this reduction of anxiety is transferred into real life (Wolpe: 1958; 1973). Increasingly counsellors using systematic desensitization also train clients to alter their thinking and 'manage' their anxiety by means of self-instructional statements, both as scenes are presented and in real life. As well as using muscular and mental relaxation methods, counsellors need to be sensitive to whether their clients are blocking responsiveness through not having a sufficiently relaxed life-style. Straightforward precautions like proper holidays, leaving adequate time for meals, not taking on excessive commitments, and having regular time set aside for recreation may be important relaxation goals. Additionally, many people find that they are unable to be adequately responsive to themselves if they do not find time and ways of being responsive to nature. This may range from going for walks in parks, to playing golf, to getting right away into the wilderness.

Encouraging action   The role of empathic responding in enabling clients to feel that counsellors are secure bases from which to engage in exploratory behaviour and in personal experiments has already been mentioned. Counsellor interventions focused directly on encouraging action and on changing behaviour can also be helpful in engendering client responsiveness. Counsellors can collaborate with their clients in setting goals and making plans to attain them. For example, there is a limit to which a college student can explore his emotional and sexual responsiveness to women by talking inside counselling and fantasizing outside. Here the counsellor and client may draw up a list of subgoals in increasing order of difficulty. These subgoals might include: asking a woman out for coffee; taking a woman out to dinner; holding hands; talking more intimately about himself, etc. Just being an interested listener as the client reports back on progress may be sufficient, but some clients may also benefit from the more obvious dispensation of counsellor reward through such comments as 'good' and 'well done' as each subgoal is attained. Many of the thinking-focused interventions discussed in the next chapter are relevant to encouraging action.

Frustrating the client   Clients need to express what they think and feel not only inside but also outside counselling. Responsiveness inside counselling is of little use if feelings get inhibited or 'coming out sideways', possibly in aggression, outside counselling. Although many counsellors would not feel happy applying the technique, Perls' use of frustration was useful in getting some clients to stand up for themselves and communicate directly. Clients were placed in the 'hot seat' one at a time and Perls would almost mercilessly expose what he considered to be their every verbal, vocal and bodily way of manipulating the environment rather than relying on their own resources. Perls saw himself as focusing on the *how* rather than the *why* of their lack of contact with their senses and hence of their responsibility avoidance (Perls: 1973). In as much as the development of inner strength requires challenge, Perls was providing inside counselling the kind of assertion experience that might stand clients in good stead outside. Perhaps if he had talked more about his frustration technique as a means of teaching clients to assert themselves and less about it as a way of helping them confront the phobic impasse, it might have gained wider acceptance. Unfortunately, Perls' 'skilful frustration' approach was intuitive and lacked systematic development and presentation.

Use of aids   There is room for inventiveness in releasing clients' emotions. Counsellors often use aids in allowing children to express and work through emotions. For instance, access to a child's inner world may be facilitated by the use of conversations between either glove puppets or 'play people' purchased from toyshops. Children may need the distance provided by such aids to be able to reveal themselves. Also, photographs may be useful in helping clients reveal their feelings. For instance, Ryan and Walker (1983) advocate the compilation of life story books, including photos, to enable children in care to talk about their past, present and future in the presence of an empathic adult. Such an activity may not only help children gain more of a sense of identity but also increase their sense of worth. They observe: 'At the back of the mind of nearly all children in care is the thought that they are worthless and unlovable . . . If they have been abandoned, neglected or injured by their parents or family, they will be convinced that they brought it on themselves'. Drama, games, art, music and dance may each have a role in helping different people become more emotionally responsive.

Experiential encounter groups   A number of writers on counselling and therapy groups have observed the shift from social distance to increased intimacy as the life of the group progresses (Rogers: 1970; Mintz: 1971; Yalom: 1975). Another theme is that members shift from positions of avoidance of experiencing and working on problems to a fuller awareness and sharing of feelings; and to an increased willingness to work actively on problems. Though groups can be very threatening and destructive, there are a number of ways in which they may engender responsiveness. Here, in particular, the focus is on experiential interactive encounter groups of from five to ten members with one or two facilitators. First, these groups provide a sheltered atmosphere where clients can practise at acknowledging and sharing their feelings with peers rather than just with 'paid-up' counsellors. Second, counsellors can act as participant-observers and help members identify how they block their emotional responsiveness. Groups generate much here-and-now material that is unlikely to be directly available in individual counselling. Third, not only counsellors but also other group members can facilitate the release and experiencing of emotions. One way in which other group members can do this is by modelling emotional expressiveness. Another way is by engaging each other in emotionally tinged interactions, though counsellors need beware the vulnerabilities of individual members. Still another way is by demonstrating their healing potential for each other. Much empathy may be demonstrated by group members and not just by counsellors. A concept known as 'cohesiveness' defines the more successful counselling groups. Cohesiveness means both that group members find participation in the group attractive and that they develop a high investment in helping each other. Fourth, such groups may lessen members' feelings of isolation and tendencies toward self-denigration. They learn that other people have problems too. Fifth, some clients work harder and better in groups since they enjoy the companionship and opportunity for intimacy provided. Sometimes groups are regarded as 'second chance families' that provide emotional experiences that correct or remedy deficiencies in earlier relationships. There is also a trend toward working with families so that family styles or denying and distorting emotions can be ameliorated. This is hopefully before the emotional responsiveness of younger members gets too damaged.

Concluding comments   A number of different counsellor interventions for engendering responsiveness have been listed. This is not to advocate a 'shot-gun' approach. However, helping clients take responsibility for their emotional responsiveness is much more complex than anything that can be approached by a single counselling intervention. This reiterates the point that a number of the established counselling approaches are not necessarily wrong but rather are insufficiently comprehensive. As such they lay claim to more therapeutic power than they possess. Counsellors need to assess clients in terms of both whether the area of responsiveness should be an important focus of counselling and how they manifest their difficulties. The ultimate aim of focusing on responsiveness is to get people's emotions working as they were meant by nature to work – namely, in the interests of their survival and fulfilment – and, furthermore, to help them take responsibility for ensuring that, to the best of their abilities, this continues after counselling.

Training interventions

In training interventions counsellors adopt a mainly didactic role in working with groups of people. A distinction can be made between the roles of counsellors as facilitators and as educators, though they are interrelated. The predominantly facilitator role characterizes counselling interventions. The educator role characterizes training interventions. On the surface training people to experience their feelings may seem a contradiction in terms since feelings are meant to be spontaneous rather than produced on demand. Nevertheless, training interventions may have value both in increasing awareness and in imparting skills. Many of the counselling interventions already discussed can have their balance altered so that they become more didactic and thus become training interventions. Indeed, relaxation methods might be seen as more didactic than facilitative. Below are some possibilities for training groups of people to become more emotionally responsive.

Awareness exercises   Writers like Schutz (1967) and Perls and his colleagues (Perls, Hefferline and Goodman: 1951; Levistky and Perls: 1970) have suggested a number of exercises for making people more aware of their body and feelings. Perls' awareness technique described earlier is one exercise that can be performed in a training group or workshop. Schutz has an exercise called 'Alone time' in which each person is assigned a thirty-minute period in which they must be alone and reflect on the events they have experienced. They are to focus on themselves, their feelings and their relations to others, and to use fantasy where appropriate. He reports that many people say that they have never used their time alone in this way. It affords an opportunity for consolidating experience.

Some exercises focus on nonverbal as well as verbal responses. In Levitsky and Perls' exaggeration technique, people are asked progressively and repeatedly to exaggerate their behaviour. An example is exaggerating an arm gesture. Another exercise emphasizing nonverbal behaviour is that of physical doubling (Schutz: 1967). Here the trainer asks participants to imitate the body posture of another person and to see how it feels. One of the purposes of this exercise is to help people not only to become more aware of their own feelings, but to better understand others' emotions. This is helped by the pairs sharing and discussing their feelings. Doubling may also involve imitating or mirroring other aspects of people (and having people mirror you) such as their words, inflections, facial expressions and laughter, plus, possibly, what they think and feel. Again these exercises get participants to exchange feelings about what they have done.

A criticism of the use of exercises is that they are superficial gimmicks that do not really get people experiencing and exploring their feelings, and that they meet more the trainers' needs to direct and control others than the participants' needs to experience and become more in touch with their emotions. One of the great risks of working in the area of responsiveness is that people talk about their feelings, or go through the motions of emoting, without really engaging in authentic experiencing. To avoid such risks, the use of exercises focusing on responsiveness calls for a high degree of skill and sensitivity on the part of the trainers.

Co-counselling Counsellors can train groups or networks of people in the skills of counselling each other. At its simplest, this involves training people to give psychological space to the 'client' as he or she recounts feelings and thoughts. Then, after a mutually agreed upon period of time, the partners reverse roles and the listener becomes the 'client'. Sometimes this co-counselling just involves ensuring that listeners are silent during their partners' turns as 'client'. Some trainers encourage partners to sit opposite each other, hold hands and maintain eye contact as they co-counsel. At a more sophisticated level, co-counselling may involve teaching people the skills or empathic responding. A major aim of co-counselling training is to help participants stay more in touch with feelings through helping each other.

Focused training programmes Training programmes relevant to emotional responsiveness may be focused on developmental tasks, such as integrating sexuality and preparing for death, on transitions, such as adjusting to redundancy, and on shared individual tasks, such as coping with blindness. Often these programmes will also be focused on skills other than emotional responsiveness: for example, redundant people need skills in planning alternative activity and not just in handling emotions. Furthermore, focused training programmes can have a prophylactic aim: for instance, sex education programmes can help prevent rather than follow lack of sexual responsiveness and sexual dysfunction. Programmes to help people cope with redundancy can also be in advance of the actual event. In dealing with redundancy some of the most difficult feelings for people to handle are those generated by the threat of redundancy. Virtually every significant area of life can be prepared for by an appropriate training programme identifying and helping people to anticipate and experience the emotions involved in them.

Yalom (1980) observes that several death-awareness workshops have been reported that employ structured exercises designed to provide people with an encounter with their own deaths. Sometimes these programmes are targeted at groups, for instance nurses, who have to handle the anxieties generated by continuous contact with the dying and their relatives. In one single eight-hour workshop for eight people, the following exercises were included: members completed a death-anxiety questionnaire and discussed anxiety-provoking items; in a state of deep muscle relaxation, they were encouraged to fantasize in great detail their comfortable deaths; again in a state of muscle relaxation, they were asked to fantasize their terminal illnesses, inability to communicate, and funerals (Whelan and Warren: 1977).

Death education programmes are likely to have at least three objectives, be they implicit or explicit. First, increasing existential awareness. Second, helping people prepare for and handle the emotions attached to their own dying and deaths. Third, helping people deal with the emotions attached to other people's dying and deaths.

Focusing on thinking   Often people's emotional responsiveness is blocked, inhibited or distorted by the way they are thinking about themselves, other people and their environments. For instance, gender-related behaviour, where it goes beyond biological differences, illustrates this point. In such instances, training programmes that have a focus on helping people to think more realistically can be valuable in helping them to acknowledge a fuller range of feelings. Since this is a topic of the next chapter it is not developed here.

Self-therapy interventions

A common question across each of the four mediating goals of personal responsibility counselling and therapy is that of what people can do for themselves both to become and to stay more effective. Taking responsibility for one's emotional responsiveness can be done on one's own, in pairs or as part of groups. Self-therapy is defined as becoming and staying personally responsible predominantly without the help of a counsellor. This does not preclude the use of counsellors where people feel their own resources are insufficient. However, the assumption is that such support is not needed on a regular basis.

Inner empathy   Individuals need to develop the skills of listening to themselves. This entails acknowledging that feelings are important and require to be taken seriously. Furthermore, it is likely to entail arranging enough time and psychological space to be able to listen deeply to oneself, especially where issues of importance are concerned. For some, this may involve taking a look at their life-style to review whether they are sufficiently treating themselves as persons with feelings and limitations rather than just as machines. For many, it will mean learning to identify the danger signals of when they are ignoring emotions or in danger of inappropriately expressing them. Individuals who develop the skill of inner empathy are likely to experience and explore many of the areas and feelings that they might cover if working with skilled counsellors. For example, they are likely to become more sensitively attuned to their wishes and wants, to be able to identify and discard dysfunctional inhibitions, and to acknowledge and understand feelings of anxiety and guilt. Furthermore, they may wish to explore their emotional responsiveness by engaging in personal experiments in which they try out new behaviours. Meeting different kinds of people or engaging in new kinds of activities can all be viewed as personal experiments. The object of the experiments is to find out more about what brings fulfilment. To achieve this they need to listen accurately to feedback from their feelings.

Co-counselling   It is important that people in their personal relations acknowledge their feelings and express them appropriately. Relationships tend to be conducted in terms of psychological contracts of varying degrees of explicitness. Where possible, individuals should choose significant relationships with people who allow contracts where partners both express their own and listen to each other's feelings. Listening and encouraging each other to discuss and share feelings can be done either informally or more formally. The latter may mean the introduction of co-counselling. This can take place either when there are problems to be sorted out or when partners request it. Additionally, partners may decide to set time aside for co-counselling on a regular basis. Co-counselling need not be restricted to partners in existing relationships. Some may seek out either a congenial person or a congenial network and experience, explore and discharge their emotions within these contexts.

Support networks   Individuals can take responsibility for developing support networks for themselves. These may be especially useful in helping them experience, explore and handle feelings in transitions and crises. Individuals' support networks may consist of their intimate relationships, their family unit, their friends, and other people to whom they may feel able to entrust confidences, for example priests or doctors. Isolation may make it much more difficult for people to handle the emotions generated by personal setbacks. Even knowing that they have supportive people to whom they can turn in times of need may make crises and setbacks much more bearable.

Peer self-help groups Depending upon where they live, individuals may have all sorts of peer self-help groups available. Sometimes these groups operate with professional counsellors, psychologists or psychiatrists in the background, but this is not always the case. The range of peer self-help groups is large and they include: women's groups; men's groups; gay groups; groups for various categories of disabled people, for example those with multiple sclerosis; groups for various categories of parents, for example of the mentally handicapped or of the disabled; and groups for the bereaved, to mention but some. Often the purpose of these groups is to offer mutual support by giving people a chance to share feelings and experiences. Sometimes, for instance with women's or gay groups, political change may also be an aim.

Not all peer self-help groups are targeted on specific populations. For example, Mowrer's integrity groups are meant to be part of the lifestyle of people in general (Mowrer: 1964; Mowrer, Vattano *et al*.: 1975). Also, experiential encounter groups may be run on a leaderless basis or with rotating facilitators. Obviously peer self-help groups have risks as well as advantages – members may be allowed to wallow in self-pity or to exhibit only a restricted range of feelings. Nevertheless, people find self-help groups valuable. However, they should take care before joining them, and not remain in groups that are more destructive than constructive.

Counselling and helping others One way in which people sometimes attempt to understand and experience their feelings is by offering themselves as counsellors and helpers. The motivation of many who enter the helping professions is bound up with their need to overcome feelings of pain and rejection, be it in relation to their upbringing or to specific traumatic life events. Often people who have had emotionally tough lives have been helped by their difficulties to acquire sensitivity and insight to others' needs. The risk, of course, is that emotional deprivations result in narrowing as well as expanding perceptions. For instance, marital counsellors who have had or are having unhappy marriages, may project their own difficulties and answers onto clients rather than see them as separate individuals. This makes it desirable that counsellors and helpers have in large measure worked through their feelings in regard to their life's difficulties prior to rather than when counselling and helping. Having said that, counselling and helping others can also be a valuable way of learning to understand and experience one's own feelings more fully.

Chapter 8

REALISM: THINKING, LANGUAGE AND INNER SPEECH

Though it is necessary to take responsibility for experiencing feelings, it can also be important to regulate them. An important mediating goal in the process of personal responsibility is that of realism or the capacity to assume responsibility for thinking, language and inner speech. Thinking can be seen as consisting of many different activities including: memory, reasoning, generation of ideas, fantasizing, imagination, anticipation, reflection, evaluation, judgement and self-protective processes. One of the main methods of thinking is that of inner speech or of holding an internal conversation or dialogue with oneself. Using inner speech effectively involves paying attention to use of language.

Reasons for focusing on realism

Among the many reasons why it is important for counsellors, clients and people in general to develop the skills resources of realism are the following. First and foremost it increases people's capacity for choice. Focusing on people's thinking can affect both the quantity and accuracy of information available for choosing and also how well it gets used.

An important area of choice concerns flexible regulation of feelings. Virtually any negative emotion can be seen as having a cognitive element. By learning to think more effectively, people can be helped and help themselves to have more flexible control over the negative feelings – for instance, anger, spite, envy, self-pity and anxiety – that do so much to blight lives. Additionally, as they become more successful at controlling negative emotions, they are likely to start acting in more effective ways and hence generating positive emotions. Learning to regulate negative feelings is an important way in which taking responsibility for one's thinking can lead to more effective action. A significant side-effect of the regulation of negative feelings is that people may get more in touch with their wishes and wants. They may have more energy and motivation for acting. Focusing on people's thinking can also help them to formulate wishes and wants into clearly stated goals, which further increases the likelihood of effective action, and it can help them decide and plan the various steps that lead to attaining goals.

Focusing on thinking may increase choice by lessening people's tendencies to self-protective thinking. Humans like to maintain a degree of consistency in their view of themselves, especially where deviation from this view has had heavy psychological costs in childhood. Skilled counsellors can help people acknowledge not only aspects of themselves that previously were perceived as threatening, but also the defensive processes involved. Empathy is not the only approach in overcoming clients' denials and distortions. There is a role for interventions focused more directly on the ways in which people hinder their rational with irrational thought processes.

A major reason for focusing on thinking is to help people to define themselves rather than to be defined by others, be they significant people from their pasts or people in their current environments. Most therapies explore the parental and cultural residue that people carry around from childhood to see whether these inner rules are working for rather than against the individual's survival and fulfilment. A result may be a lifting of repressions and inhibitions as people get more in touch with their animal natures.

The ways in which people think about themselves, others and the world can help and/or interfere with the ways in which they communicate. In Chapter 5 mention was made that people create personifications of themselves and others. These personifications are mental constructions of varying degrees of accuracy. An important aspect of them is that they tend to be held as reality rather than as potentially fallible aggregates of thoughts and evaluations. Virtually all reasons given so far for focusing on thinking are relevant for improving people's capacity to communicate directly and honestly. For example, my self-protective thought processes entail a definition not only of me but of you and both these false perceptions are likely to interfere with our communication. My lack of ability to regulate negative emotions may mean that differences and conflicts get escalated rather than resolved. My tendencies toward self-devaluation may mean that my wants and wishes never get adequately verbalized to the detriment of our long-term relationship, especially if I then start blaming you for not knowing what I want.

One of the most important areas of choice in people's lives relates to decisions about shifting the balance in various psychological skills more in the direction of resources than deficits. Of particular importance for change is the realization that this is more likely to occur if people take responsibility for the ways in which they perpetuate their distress. An increased awareness, both that one is contributing to perpetuating one's distress and how, is an indication of change in itself and also a prerequisite for further change. The person-centred approach may be neither sufficient for some nor sufficiently expeditious for others in laying the basis for change. Incorporating a more direct focus on thinking, but doing this with sensitivity and flexibility, increases the likelihood of change.

Personal responsibility counselling and therapy heavily emphasizes not only what counsellors can do for clients, but also what clients and people in general can do for themselves. Focusing on thinking is a useful approach to self-therapy. An important aspect of counselling is transmitting a conceptual and linguistic framework within which clients and others can view themselves, their problems, other people and their environments. This framework needs to be expressed with simplicity and clarity. Furthermore, it needs a richness and realism in its concepts to give counsellors, clients and people the tools with which they can work on their problems. Self-therapy involves people learning and being able to think through choices, problems and issues in their own lives without relying heavily on counsellors. A focus on thinking helps counsellors lay the groundwork with clients for self-therapy. It also gives lay people insights that they can apply to themselves.

Interventions for realism

Counselling interventions

Though their timing and manner need skilful handling, counselling interventions focused on helping clients think more realistically can be important in helping them toward responsibility assumption. A focus on thinking does not preclude a prior or current focus on responsiveness. A focus on thinking alone, without taking into account clients' capacities for experiencing and understanding their feelings, risks superficiality. Additionally, focusing on thinking does not mean that counsellors prevent clients from assuming their share of responsibility during counselling. There is a difference between helping people as they learn to fish and always doing their fishing for them.

Clumsy counsellor interventions focused on thinking distance clients from feelings by being too intellectual and impersonal. Clients can be further distanced from both feelings and thoughts if counsellors keep projecting their own thinking difficulties onto them. Also, counselling interventions in this area may not only be influencing *how* clients think but also *what* they think. This too may have its dangers. Furthermore, focusing on their thinking difficulties without taking into account their state of readiness may lead to considerable client resistances, even to the extent of terminating counselling.

Tact and judgement are necessary. Each intervention must be judged on its merits in relation to the needs of particular clients when discussing particular content at particular stages of counselling. In counselling, as contrasted with training, focusing on thinking interventions needs to be tailored to individuals. Below are some of the main ways in which counsellors may intervene to help their clients think more realistically.

Focusing on attributing responsibility. In the previous chapter mention was made of some interventions for heightening existential awareness. However, it is possible to acknowledge responsibility for authorship of life and at the same time to lack the skills resource of accurately attributing responsibility on a daily basis. A combination of existential awareness and the ability to attribute responsibility accurately is needed. Helping clients explore and experience feelings can lay the groundwork for the absence of defensiveness required to attribute responsibility accurately. Furthermore, skilled counsellors convey by attitude and body language that clients are people of worth who are ultimately responsible for their own lives and choices. Here are some more specific interventions that counsellors use.

First, counsellors may *present a rationale for accurately attributing responsibility*. On the one hand this can be a rationale for the whole process of counselling, namely that counselling aims to help people to take effective responsibility for their lives. A prerequisite for this is that they learn to attribute responsibility accurately for their own, other people's and the environment's behavior. It can be emphasized that accurately attributing responsibility entails being able to assign cause realistically not just for one's life as a whole (existential awareness) but within various areas of life, for instance feelings, thoughts, personal relationships and occupation. Furthermore, unless people get some insight into the ways that they are blocking their own happiness and fulfilment, namely the attribution that they contribute to perpetuating their distress, then there is little motivation for change.

Additionally, counsellors can present a rationale for focusing on accurately attributing responsibility in particular problem areas. A client's marital difficulties could be a case in point. Here the focus of the rationale might be the attributions relevant to the disturbed relationship. It could be pointed out that in such relationships, the 'blame-game' is often played by both partners in ways that perpetuate rather than solve difficulties. This is because the 'blame-game' freezes partners into positions in which it is hard to take constructive initiatives because the double attribution is made that the other is responsible for the difficulty and therefore also responsible for getting the relationship out of the difficulty. Instead, what is needed is a set of attributions that makes it possible for partners to act in the best interests of themselves and their relationships. This can be a matter of identifying inaccurate attributions, such as the double attribution above, and reformulating them into more functional attributions: for instance, 'I am responsible for my own survival and fulfilment and hence, where possible, for altering my thinking, feeling and behaviour to achieve a more mutually enhancing relationship'. Though the above may seem simplistic at first, by working with specific situations over a period of time this rationale may make increasing sense, an observation to be shared with clients.

The second counsellor intervention concerns *focusing on accurately attributing responsibility in specific situations* in clients' lives. For instance, in a marital relationship, specific situations in which there is resentment and lack of constructive communication, could be explored. Such situations might concern finances, relating to children or in-laws, and sex. Here specific attributions that interfere with goal attainment are identified and reformulated. Counsellors and clients work together since reformulations must be owned by clients if they are to change their behaviour. Counsellors may also support clients as they try out new behaviours based on revised attributions of responsibility and help them handle their thoughts and feelings about the feedback they are getting. When exploring the accuracy of clients' attributions in specific situations, counsellors deploy many skills including: empathic responding; helping clients to be clear and specific; using questions; and, where necessary, challenging evasions.

The third counsellor intervention entails *focusing on the language of accurately attributing responsibility*. Much of this centres on using words and phrases acknowledging choice. For example, 'I lack self-discipline' implies a permanent characteristic justifying inaction. On the other hand, 'I *choose* to lack self-discipline' allows some possibility for action. Extending this example, 'I am afraid that I may be a failure because of my lack of self-discipline and emotionality' could be reformulated to 'I *choose* to feel that I may *choose* to be a failure because of my *choosing* to lack self-discipline and *choosing* to be emotional'. Another example is 'I've got to go to a meeting tonight' wich could be reformulated 'I *choose* to go to a meeting tonight'. People may lose much of their freedom and spontaneity because they have learned habits of thinking and language which minimize their sense of being active instigators in their own lives. Sometimes, of course, it is convenient to attribute responsibility externally. A simple example is that of a child who says 'It just broke' rather than 'I broke it'

Though communication is the focus of the next chapter, people can minimize their sense of their own identity by not using the language of accurate attribution in their relations with others. Gordon (1970) makes a distinction between 'I' messages and 'You' messages with the former, unlike the latter owning the individual's thoughts and feelings. For example, a 'You' message is that of telling a child 'You're a pest', whereas an 'I' message in the same situation might be 'I'm tired and want to read the paper, but I would like to play with you later'. Butler claims that many women have difficulty in communicating their thoughts and feelings in 'I' messages rather than 'You' messages (Butler: 1981). For instance, they avoid taking responsibility for their feelings and desires by using 'You' questions rather than 'I' statements. 'Don't you like this piece of pottery?' may be an indirect way of saying 'I like this piece'. Also they tend to engage in 'You did' blaming rather than clearly communicating their needs with 'I want' statements.

In Chapter 2 mention was made that Yalom asserts that therapists can help clients to acquire insights that apply leverage to their wills. Four principle insights are: 'Only I can change the world I have created'; 'There is no danger in change'; 'To get what I really want, I must change'; and 'I have the power to change'. Yalom is helping their motivation for change by teaching clients the language and inner speech of accurately attributing responsibility. The clear assumption is that they must learn to take responsibility for perpetuating their distress and hence for changing.

A fourth counsellor intervention is *focusing on excessively self-attributing responsibility*. Beck and his colleagues (1979) use terms like 'reattribution' and 'de-responsibilitizing' for such interventions. Here the focus is on identifying and challenging clients' areas of excessive self-blame. Beck *et al.* observe: 'A common cognitive pattern in depression involves incorrectly assigning the blame or responsibility for adverse events to oneself. Depressed patients are particularly prone to self-blame resulting from the negative consequences of events beyond their control as well as those relative to their actions and judgements'. Counsellors collaborate with clients in reviewing the logic of attributions. For instance, by examining whether a business failure was really all the individual's own fault, through such matters as lack of ability and effort, or whether there were other factors, for example a general decline in orders in the industry in question, etc. Even the concept of 'own fault' needs reviewing since it may lead to self-derogation rather than learning from experience. Also, counsellors need be sensitive to whether clients apply double-standards in which they judge their own behaviour much more harshly than others' similar behaviour. If so, this observation might be shared and explored.

A fifth counsellor intervention is that of *focusing on accurately attributing responsibility in proposed courses of action*. It is one thing to misattribute responsibility for past behaviour and another to change one's behaviour in ways that still misattribute. This is similar to Glasser's emphasis on getting clients to develop and share their plans for more responsible behaviour (Glasser: 1965). Relevant questions are 'How is this new behaviour going to help you?' and 'How is this new behaviour going to help you cope when your old behaviour was unsuccessful?'

Personal responsibility counselling and therapy seeks a paradigm shift in people's ability to assume effective responsibility for their lives. Everything that the counsellor does should be geared to this objective. Though a direct focus on accurately attributing responsibility can be very helpful, there are many different ways in which people avoid or do not possess the skills resources to assume responsibility. Therefore, while effective assumption of personal responsibility is the overall objective, a direct focus on realistic or accurate attribution is only one of the ways of achieving this objective.

Focusing on internal rules and standards. Counsellors can help their clients take responsibility for their internal rules and standards. For some this may require the preliminary work of a facilitative nurturing relationship to diminish their feelings of threat to the point where they can review their inner rule book with some objectivity. In chapter 5 the suggestion was made that Ellis' ABC framework, where A is the activating event, B the individual's beliefs about the activating event, and C the consequences of the activating event, might be reconceptualized into an ATC framework. Here A would remain the activating event, T would be the individual's thoughts about the activating event, and C the choices the individual makes as a result of A and C. A possible set of choices that people can make entails regulation of their feelings. This involves reformulating unrealistic thoughts that contribute to negative emotions. Here it is possible to see the ATC framework as an ATF framework, where A is the event, T represents thoughts and F feelings.

Internal rules consist of two elements: the underlying rule and the self-verbalizations or inner speech that represent the underlying rule in specific situations. For instance, a young man may have an underlying rule that approval is necessary from everyone that he meets. The relevant inner speech in a situation may be: 'I am sure that she is not going to like me if she really gets to know me. I get tense and uneasy and this makes me no good with women'. Thus in the ATF framework T consists of two parts: T(ir) relating to internal rules and T(is) relating to the inner speech derived from internal rules.

Counsellor interventions in working with clients who have unrealistic inner rules may range from helping explore them as and when they occur in counselling to more systematic approaches. A systematic approach is likely to consist of three elements: (a) presenting a rationale for focusing on internal rules; (b) identifying unrealistic internal rules and harmful inner speech; and (c) formulating realistic internal rules and helpful inner speech.

Part of the presentation of a rationale may focus on the relationship between thinking and feeling, possible using the ATF framework. Also, the need for people to define themselves by subscribing to rules that have meaning for them rather than for significant others in their past or present lives. Counsellors can discuss how to identify ineffective rules and know the characteristics of effective inner rules and speech. Some of the main charcteristics of *ineffective inner rules and speech* include: *over generalization*, or making rules for all situations rather than allowing flexibility for specific situations; *perfectionism*, making unrealistic demands on self, others and the environment; *rating oneself as a person* and not just one's characteristics – for instance the previous hypothetical client could be thinking that because he was so good with women therefore he was no good as a person; *exaggeration*, seeing situations in extreme ways and often as potential catastrophes; *ignoring positives* in situations or about oneself; and *generation of negative or false emotions*, including anxiety, hostility and depression.

Some of the main characteristics of *effective inner rules and speech include:* being *based on the individual's own needs* and values; *flexibility* or, where appropriate, being amenable to change; a *functional rating of specific characteristics* according to whether they are useful for survival and fulfilment rather than globally rating oneself as a person; *realism about one's resources*, including acknowledging positive aspects; having *an emphasis on coping* with situations to the best of one's ability rather than being perfectionist in relation to them; and *being conducive to minimizing negative emotions* and to engendering positive emotions.

Counsellors and clients work together to identify unrealistic internal rules and harmful inner speech. Some counsellors, Ellis for example, look for central erroneous or irrational beliefs. Others, for instance Beck, pay more attention to differences in clients' thought patterns. Negative feelings are clues to unrealistic thoughts. Clients are encouraged to explore thoughts and thought fragments preceding and accompanying negative feelings. This can be done both in counselling and as a homework exercise of say fifteen minutes a day. Some counsellors use a flip-chart to visually reflect back clients' thinking. Others cassette record sessions and have clients play back the cassettes outside counselling. The purposes of this are to help clients identify their own characteristic patterns of ineffective thinking as well as to give them added opportunity to hear what counsellors tell them about effective thinking.

Unrealistic internal rules and harmful inner speech need to be corrected and reformulated into realistic rules and helpful speech. For instance, the hypothetical client could revise the rule that approval is necessary from everyone that he meets to one that says that, though it might be pleasant to obtain universal approval, it is unrealistic and unnecessary in all instances. The reformulated inner speech might be, 'Now calm down, I can't be expected to please everyone. Even if she doesn't like me there are others who may. Also, I don't have to dislike myself as a person. I can only do my best and there is no point in worrying beyond that.' Alongside the reformulated inner speech the individual may engage in behaviours more task oriented toward success with women and less motivated by the need to ward off the catastrophe of rejection. Beck and Greenberg (1974) have a 'double column' technique whereby clients can practise identifying and reformulating their unrealistic rules and speech. If anything it focuses more on inner speech than on rules. Clients write down their unreasonable automatic thoughts in one column and then their answers to the automatic thoughts opposite these. An example of an automatic thought is, 'John has not called. He doesn't love me.' A corrective answer is, 'He is very busy and thinks I am doing better than last week – so he doesn't need to worry about me.' Clients can write out more than one way of correcting their erroneous inner speech. This can be made into a 'triple column' technique by writing down in the first column situations eliciting unpleasant feelings (Beck: 1976)

Clients who are focusing on changing their internal rules and inner speech have gone some way to assuming responsibility for regulating feelings and behaviour. Changing rules and speech involves self-attribution of responsibility for thoughts, feelings and behaviour. The capacity to reflect upon faulty internal rules and inner speech is an integral part of self-therapy.

Focusing on meaning and on alternatives.   Sometimes clients are in a state of 'stuckness' about the meaning either of the whole or of part of their lives. Counsellors can help clients focus on issues of meaning and purpose. Good empathic responding can be important in allowing them to listen to themselves and find their own meanings. Exploring and challenging internal rules and standards also helps identify what has meaning for them rather than for others. Indeed the process of counselling involves helping clients to discover their own meanings and directionalities. Clients are likely to need to go at their own pace.

For some, this cannot and should not be hurried. This is particularly likely when clients seek to clarify and crystallize their life's purposes. Earlier the observation was made that issues of meaning are becoming more common as counselling problems. Counsellors can acknowledge the legitimacy of clients wishing to explore such issues, including their occupational and spiritual dimensions. This alone may allow clients the psychological space to begin working on the issues *with* someone, rather than going round in circles on their own. Counsellors can help clients both clarify areas of choice and also explore and alter some of the resistances blocking presence of and restricting freedom of choice. Often the problem of meaning is that of attaining greater involvement with others and in activity. In such instances, issues of meaning may best be approached indirectly. A sense of meaning and fulfilment will be a by-product of greater relatedness and rewarding activity. On occasion, counsellors may have to refer clients to others better able to deal with specific issues of meaning and choice: for instance, to an occupational counsellor or a religious counsellor, so long as the latter respects people's freedom to explore their spiritual selves.

In many instances, clients may gain from counsellors actively facilitating their exploring alternative meanings and ways of perceiving situations. As well as empathic responding, ways in which counsellors may help 'loosen' their clients' thinking include:

Use of questions focused on generating and exploring alternatives: for example 'What are the options?', 'Is there any other interpretation to put on the matter?', and 'Is that the only solution?'

Suggesting alternative explanations and meanings to clients: for instance Frankl's suggestion to the heartbroken doctor that he had saved his wife much suffering by outliving her (Frankl: 1959)

Getting clients to 'brainstorm', which involves generating as many alternatives as possible, regardless of their quality, in a relatively brief time.

Use of role play, for example to gain insight into another person's viewpoint or to try the 'feel' of a new role for themselves.

Encouraging clients to verbalize internal dialogues in which they explore and evaluate different ways of looking at situations or decisions.

Focusing on anticipating risk and gain. Counsellors can aid clients to take responsibility for how they look at the future. Past circumstances in clients' lives often colour their views of the future, making them more fearful of acting to meet needs than might reasonably be considered necessary. Furthermore, many clients' sense of competence is lower than their actual competence might warrant. Sense of competence and anticipating risk and gain are closely related in that people who do not 'own' their competence are more likely to emphasize the risks of acting than those who do. Though possibly clients are more pessimistic than optimistic in relation to their underlying abilities, there are some whose optimism leads to impulsiveness. Thus counsellors need to help clients look at the future accurately.

The counselling relationship helps many clients look at the future more realistically because it both affirms their sense of worth and also provides the opportunity to explore and talk over specific situations. Additionally, as clients acquire more realistic internal rules, they are likely to fear the future less.

Counsellors can work with clients to explore not just why they avoid acting (exploring risk) but also, and perhaps more important, what the benefits of acting in particular situations might be (exploring gain). An underlying question in exploring gain is 'What do you enjoy/want?'. A relevant question in exploring risk is 'What are you afraid of which is blocking you from getting what you enjoy/want?'. Clients can be afraid of handling the consequences of success as well as of failure. As an initial step either a mental or written double column technique is helpful in which clients specify what they perceive as the gains and risks of certain courses of action. A subsequent step is for the counsellor to help clients assess the realism of these perceptions. A further step, based on more realistic anticipations, is to explore appropriate ways of acting in situations.

Counsellors may also focus on altering their clients' anticipations by helping them experience success. Often this is done by means of 'successive approximation' whereby clients are encouraged to perform increasingly difficult tasks. An example Beck (1976) gives of what he terms 'graded task assignment', or sometimes 'success therapy', is that of a depessed housewife who initially might be encouraged just to boil an egg. Then with a series of graded steps, decided by counsellor and client in consultation, she builds up to preparing an entire meal. Imagery can also be used to help clients alter their anticipations. They can be set homework assignments in which step-by-step they imagine themselves coping with or succeeding at tasks.

Focusing on task-oriented inner speech An important way in which clients can alter their anticipations entails learning to take responsibility for their inner speech. At its simplest this may entail teaching them to instruct themselves with statements like 'calm down', 'slow down', and 'take it easy' whenever they start feeling tense. Also, they can tell themselves 'Now start breathing slowly and regularly' as a contribution to altering both their physiological reactions and thinking. Focusing on such areas as realistic attribution and on altering unrealistic internal rules can also involve clients in paying attention to inner speech. Here the emphasis is on using inner speech to counteract the effects of stress and anxiety in relation to specific tasks. In the work reported by Meichenbaum (1977; 1983), 'self-instruction' tasks have included controlling examination anxiety, impulsive behaviour and anger.

The emphasis in using task-oriented inner speech is on *coping* with stressful situations. For instance, counsellors can work with students suffering from examination anxiety in formulating coping statements for before, during and after their examinations. The sort of coping statements that students might use to lessen negative anticipations and increase their sense of control *before* an examination are: 'Keep calm and just think about how you can relax yourself in the situation'; 'Now just keep your head, since all you have to do is to cope as best as you can'.

The sort of coping statement students might instruct themselves in *during* an examination is: 'O.K. I acknowledge I'm feeling anxious. This is the signal for me to use my coping skills. Now slow down, calm down and take a few deep breaths. All I have to do is to take one step at a time and just work as best I can. Now that's better . . . already some of the tension is starting to drain away. I'm becoming more confident that I can think through and cope with this situation.'

The idea here is that clients, instead of eroding their confidence by 'catastrophizing', learn to regulate their emotions by taking themselves through self-instructional sequences: Sometimes these are accompanied by physically oriented techniques such as regulating breathing and/or tensing and relaxing various muscle groupings.

The sort of coping statements that students could instruct themselves in *after* an examination are: 'Now that wasn't so bad after all. I'm pleased that I coped with the situation and it is a good sign for future exams'; 'I'm getting better at keeping my anxiety manageable now I've learned to instruct myself with coping statements'.

Clients have often had much experience in instructing themselves negatively. They probably need much practice at reversing this tendency. As with many areas of realistic thinking, some may benefit from hearing, and possibly seeing, a model using the self-instructional skills. Counsellors can make up homework cassettes for clients on which they 'coach' them in instructing themselves with relevant coping statements. Additionally, clients can do homework involving 'imagined rehearsal' in which they take themselves through the before, during and after self-instructions for real-life situations.

Focusing on self-protective thinking   Though it can be a very difficult area, counsellors can help clients relinquish some of the ways in which self-protective thinking contributes to their avoiding responsibility. 'Defence mechanisms', 'defences' and 'security operations' are other terms used for the ways in which clients 'operate' on incoming information in order to reduce anxiety by maintaining consistency in the ways in which they view themselves, others and the world.

As clients feel less threatened in counselling and more confident outside, many self-protective ways of thinking may 'melt' away. The person-centred approach in particular advocates such an indirect approach, based on empathic responding, to helping clients release their need for denials and distortions. Nevertheless, within the safety of a good relationship, counsellors may focus more directly on clients' self-protective thought habits.

The following are some self-protective ways of thinking. All of them involve diminishing awareness to make life more psychologically comfortable.

Distortion. People create personifications of themselves and of each other. Distortion is used here to incorporate all the ways in which people 'operate' on incoming information so as to maintain their picture of themselves. Frequently it can involve focusing on negative and ignoring positive feedback.

Rationalization. Rationalizations are ways of excusing behaviour that causes anxiety. Though plausible, they almost invariably involve some denial of responsibility. They tend to differ from excuses in that individuals do not have full insight into what they are doing: in short, they are deceiving themselves as well as others.

Denial. Denial involves totally warding off from conscious awareness something regarded as too frightening or threatening: for instance, the fact that one is dying, or some socially undesirable aspect of oneself, viz. hypocrisy.

Avoidance. Avoidance is a common manifestation of denial, for example by remaining unaware that one is avoiding a difficult person or situation.

Defences against the good. Blocking off or diluting both the awareness of and also the manifestation of positive qualities such as generosity and concern for others.

Introjection and projection. Whereas with introjection the person internalizes something which is external, with projection the person externalizes something which is internal. People tend to project onto others aspects of themselves that they do not find particularly likable.

Misattribution. All the various ways in which people attribute cause so as to protect themselves from taking full personal responsibility for their lives: for example, blaming others needlessly.

Manipulation of feedback. Here the individual operates on the experience of others by presenting a false picture of self. This presentation of a false self differs from deliberate lying since people lack awareness of how they are manipulating he environment to control others' reactions to them.

The defining game. Creating personifications of others which sustain false elements of one's own personification. Trying to control their behaviour by putting overt and/or subtle emotional pressure on them to define themselves in ways that collude with one's own self-definition.

There are a number of ways in which counsellors can help clients to assume responsibility for lessening self-protective thinking. The importance of an empathic emotional climate has already been mentioned. Indeed empathic responding may allow clients the insight into the fact that they use self-protective ways of thought as well as into specific instances of this. Another approach is that of challenging or pointing out to clients their use of self-protective thinking on an *ad hoc* basis. For example, counsellors, who feel that clients describe their own feelings when attributing them to others, can share this perception. Sometimes these challenges, as in the case of Perls, are forceful.

In as much as people frequently have the illusions of greater autonomy, rationality and consistency than they actually possess, it can come as an unwelcome surprise if counsellors suggest that aspects of their thinking may be derivative, irrational and inconsistent. Furthermore, it may be hard for clients to admit that that may be damaging and diminishing others through defining them falsely. However, attainment of personal responsibility entails an awareness of these possibilities and a commitment to guarding against them. Counselling interventions in the area of self-protective thinking need to be carefully considered in light of clients' levels of self-awareness, vulnerability and threat.

With more self-aware clients, instead of approaching self-protective thinking simply on an *ad hoc* basis, counsellors may focus on it in a more sustained way. Two possible interventions here are:

Presenting a rationale for focusing on self-protective thinking. This might be along the lines that all people in varying degrees have vestiges of childish ways of handling reality that have now become habits which interfere with their own and others' fulfilment. These self-protective ways of thinking reflect their lack of cognitive development when as children they needed to protect themselves against a stronger and sometimes frightening world. People continue using these habits of thought to operate on information to protect their views of themselves. They are skills deficits that can have extremely serious consequences for self and others. Unfortunately, the greater people's deficits in this area, the less likelihood is there that they perceive them.

Identifying and trying to counteract self-protective thought habits. Counsellors can explain to clients some of the main self-protective thought habits. Together they may explore clients' self-protective thought patterns. Some of this might be done as homework. Not only characteristic patterns but also situations that elicit them can fruitfully be identified. Clients sensitized in advance to situations eliciting defensive thinking are in reasonable positions to counteract such tendencies.

Focusing on problem-solving and planning   A personally responsible way of thinking entails taking a problem-solving approach to life. A possible distinction between decision-making and problem-solving is that the former is a largely rational process whereas the latter encompasses feelings, actions and guarding against irrational thought processes. Problem-solving consists of six somewhat overlapping stages.

Orientation. This refers to the extent to which people possess a problem-solving approach to life. It includes restraining tendencies toward impulsiveness.

Analysis. Analysis of a problem includes trying to answer the questions 'What am *I* doing that is contributing to the problem remaining unresolved?' and 'What, if anything, can *I* be doing to solve the problem?' In other words, individuals analyse themselves as part of any problems they have.

Decision-making. This entails considering options and deciding *where* to proceed.

Planning. The decision-making stage focuses on goals. The planning stage focuses on the means to attaining goals or on *how* to proceed. Plans are step-by-step approaches to changing both *inner events*, for example thoughts and feelings, and *outer events* or actions.

Action. This involves implementing plans. It is not always easy in the planning phase to identify all the difficulties that can occur in the action stage. Task-oriented inner speech may be helpful when faced with difficulties.

Evaluation. Plans and actions need to be evaluated in light of feedback and, if necessary, altered or even discarded.

Counsellors may improve clients' problem-solving skills either in a relatively unfocused way or by systematically helping them work through problematic situations. Glasser's reality therapy represents an attempt at a systematic approach. Many different counsellor skills are involved in facilitating clients' problem-solving behaviour. One such skill is that of providing a rationale for the importance of a problem-solving orientation. In addition to empathic responding, counsellor skills for the analysis and decision-making stages are mainly those of focusing on realistic thinking: for example, exploring internal rules and attributions and, where appropriate, challenging unrealistic thinking. A counsellor skill for the planning stage is encouraging clarity and specificity so that clients systematically set out their proposed courses of action, both inner and outer. Possible skills for the action stage include empathic responding and encouraging performance through appropriate use of counsellor-offered rewards, for example, praise and interest. Counsellor skills during the evaluation stage include exploring self-protective thinking when clients have difficulty fully acknowledging the feedback they get, and where necessary, assisting clients in making revised plans.

Providing access to information   In Chapter 5 mention was made that absence of adequate information is a factor contributing to the acquisition and perpetuation of responsibility skills deficits. Counsellors can help clients by: providing them with information; releasing clients inhibitions about obtaining information; and helping them develop information-seeking skills.

Counsellors in various settings require different kinds of information. For example, information needs of marital counsellors include knowledge, either in their heads or readily available, of: divorce laws and procedures; legal assistance schemes; social security benefits; where clients can get specialized help for sexual dysfunctions; support groups for single parents; and availability of conciliation services. Occupational counselling is perhaps the prime example of an area where counsellors need either to possess information or to be familiar with its sources.

In providing information, counsellors require sensitivity to whether they are helping or eroding their clients' self-help skills. Often it may be better to point clients in the direction of information than 'spoon-feed' them. Indeed sometimes counsellors help clients develop plans for the systematic collection of information. By doing so, they encourage development of information-seeking skills.

The giving, seeking and receiving of information is frequently an emotionally tinged process. For instance, skilled counsellors may sense their clients' interests in educational or occupational areas as well as their self-doubts. Here the counsellor's role is likely to include both exploring clients' resistances as well as facilitating the collection of accurate information. Counsellors must also acknowledge that the information clients receive may not always be that which they wish to hear. Consequently, it is important that they pay attention to their clients' thoughts and feelings on receiving the information.

Consciousness raising   Though much of counselling is consciousness raising, here it refers to deliberate interventions by counsellors to make clients aware of specific aspects of their situations in life. As such, it is a form of providing information. It tends also to involve exploring clients' resistances to acknowledging and acting on the information. In the previous chapter consciousness raising was mentioned as a series of interventions for helping subgroups, for instance women and gays, respond to the range of *feelings* inherent in the human condition. Some of these interventions help people *think* about themselves and their relation to environmental pressures *more realistically*. The risk of interventions labelled 'consciousness raising' is not only restricting responsiveness, but also restricting realism. The use of the label does not guarantee the desired raising of consciousness.

Training interventions

The gap between counselling and training interventions becomes narrow when it comes to focusing on realism. This is because a didactic element, in which concepts are taught, tends to be necessary for both. The objective of training in realism is to help people think more effectively so that they may become better therapists to themselves. It assumes that many people's problems have less to do with severe disturbance and more to do with unexamined habits and erroneous thoughts, language and inner speech. Consequently, virtually everyone might benefit from learning to think more realistically. However, a number of people will be unready or unwilling for the work involved in such training and thus it is not a universal remedy.

Training programmes in realistic thinking can focus either on single skills, for example task-oriented inner speech, or on a number of different skills. Such broader programmes should not be regarded as 'cure-alls', but as introductions to helping people take responsibility for their thinking. A brief programme of, say, six to eight two-hour sessions may provide a basic training in a single skill, but allows insufficient coverage for a number of skills.

Counsellors who run training programmes in realistic thinking can use a number of different interventions, including the following.

Presentation of a rationale   Presentation of a rationale involves explaining the reasons why a focus on realistic thinking is important. Its objective is to help trainees become more receptive to the training programme. Earlier a number of reasons were provided for focusing on realism. Counsellors can draw from this list to tailor-make an easily comprehensible rationale. Presenting a rationale for realistic thinking may also lay the groundwork for later use of the skills.

Presentation of concepts Whereas presentation of a rationale is an attempt to influence trainees' attitudes favourably, presentation of concepts is aimed at increasing their knowledge. Many of the concepts that might be included, singly or in combination, in realistic thinking training programmes were described earlier. They include: accurately attributing responsibility; realistic internal rules and standards; accurately anticipating risk and gain; task-oriented inner speech; identifying and discarding self-protective thinking; problem-solving and planning; effective information-seeking; and consciousness raising.

Methods of presenting concepts include lectures and lecturettes. Whereas lectures may be cumbersome and encourage passivity on the part of the training group, well presented lecturettes may help to get points across. Audio-visual aid can be used for presenting concepts, for example a black-board or flip-chart. Written aids, like books and handouts, may also be useful.

Presentation of skills It is important in realistic thinking training that, though trainers may start by discussing concepts, fairly soon they present them as skills. This involves a step-by-step breakdown of skills. For example, the composite skill of realistic internal rules and standards involves the subskills of becoming aware of negative emotions and of identifying dysfunctional thoughts and inner speech. This is prior to building up the subskills of realistic rules and inner speech. Demonstration is important. Trainers can demonstrate by modelling the skills themselves, by working with the thinking difficulties of individual members in front of the rest of the group, and by presenting audio and video-cassettes. Use of a flip-chart can assist in highlighting specific examples of harmful and helpful thinking.

Facilitating self-assessment Trainers can facilitate their trainees' attempts at self-assessment in numerous ways. Clear presentation of both concepts and skills provides a good start to trainee self-assessment. Trainees, especially if they possess basic counselling skills, may work in pairs or subgroups to facilitate each others' self-assessment. Later on, as trainees practise the skills in front of each other, they can be encouraged to review critically other people's feedback and incorporate what they find valuable into their self-assessments. Brief questionnaires, to be filled out between sessions, provide another method of self-assessment. Trainees sometimes benefit from sharing these out-of-group self-assessments during actual training sessions. They may also receive feedback on how they are perceived in the skills areas in question. Self-assessment plays an important part in the acquisition and maintenance of any realistic thinking skill. Trainees can be encouraged to assess themselves at the start of, during, at the end of, and after training.

Encouraging skills practice   Some of the disadvantages of having large groups of trainees can be minimized if trainers are creative about subdividing. For instance, trainees can be encouraged to explore the ways in which they avoid attributing responsibility accurately as a pairs exercise, or with two people counselling each other and the third acting as observer, or in a subgroup of four which divides into twos and then meets together for plenary sessions and so on. Ideal settings for skills training have facilities for subgroups to meet in privacy.

Encouraging homework   Good homework exercises encourage skills practice. Trainees do not necessarily have to conduct homework on their own. They may prefer to work in subgroups. Initially homework is likely to focus on self-assessment. A second step in homework is practising the skill in relatively safe settings, such as with another trainee. Sooner or later trainees have to start using the skills in their outside lives and thus a third step is practice in real-life settings. In most instances there will not be a natural progression through the three steps presented here. For instance, trainees who start identifying their faulty internal rules in their self-assessments may soon try to be more realistic in their lives.

Facilitating group discussion   In realistic thinking training, trainers must decide how much group discussion to allow and in what areas. Whole group and/or subgroup discussions can be useful for trainees who wish to talk about and explore concepts from their lecturettes and skills practice. However, trainees may also wish to talk about their current concerns and stresses in ways that seem unrelated to the thinking skills they are being taught. Trainers have to judge how much of this second kind of discussion to allow. Some trainees may be so involved in their concerns that, if unchecked, they might badly hamper attaining training objectives. On the other hand, trainers require sensitivity to trainees' vulnerabilities and crises. Additionally, a personal issue may start by being seemingly unrelated to the purposes of training, yet develop into a here-and-now example of the possibilities of using realistic thinking skills. A too didactic emphasis can freeze trainees into not bringing up these difficult areas in their lives where they most need to think realistically. Since realistic thinking training has experiential as well as intellectual objectives, counselling skills like empathic responding, creating a safe emotional climate, and challenging attempts to avoid responsibility are all necessary.

Self-therapy interventions

Focusing on thinking more realistically is the cornerstone of self-therapy. It entails admitting first that one may have faulty thinking habits and second that the price of realism is constant vigilance. It is easy to backslide into bad habits especially when stressed.

Inner empathy   It may seem surprising to start with inner empathy in a section on regulating one's thinking. However, here inner empathy is meant in two senses. The first sense is that of the previous chapter: namely, learning to listen to one's feelings and feeling fragments. Especially if these feelings are both negative and persistent, they are often clues that one's thinking may be less realistic than desirable. The second sense involves developing a sensitivity to one's underlying thoughts, thought fragments and internal rules. Furthermore, it entails developing a sensitivity to one's inner speech. The old adage 'know thyself' might be viewed as consisting of two subrules: 'Know thy own feelings' and 'Know thy own thoughts, language and inner speech'. Inner empathy in both senses is likely to entail the need to give oneself sufficient psychological space to get in touch with thoughts and feelings.

Focusing on specific areas   Individuals may have different areas of their thinking upon which they need to focus. For example, people wishing to regulate depressive feelings may need to focus on the internal rules and inner speech contributing to the depression. This might either be done on an *ad hoc* basis or with a more systematic approach in which they set aside some time each day to monitor and correct erroneous internal rules and inner speech. One option is to use a homework sheet with four headings: feeling; context in which the feeling occurred; unrealistic rules and inner speech; and more realistic rules and inner speech. The same approach could be taken to other negative feelings such as anger and jealousy. In reviewing anticipating accurately, people can use a 'double column' technique to explore the gains and risks of action. In reviewing personal relationship difficulties instead of mulling over 'the problem', people can acknowledge their involvement in it by asking themselves 'What am I contributing to the problem and how could I be seeing it differently?' As with much of self-therapy, individuals engage in these activities anyway, but they could do so in better and more effective ways.

Situation analysis and problem-solving Problems frequently involve more than one area of unrealistic thinking. Earlier a six-stage approach to problem-solving was outlined: orientation; analysis; decision-making; planning; action; and evaluation. Sometimes it may pay people to take the time to analyse problems in some detail.

The kinds of questions that people might ask themselves as they work on problems include:

What am I contributing to the situation?

How is my behaviour helping me?

How realistic am I being:
in attributing responsibility?
regarding my internal rules and inner speech?
regarding anticipating risk and gain?
in looking at alternative explanations?
in avoiding self-protective thinking?

What are the other parameters in the situation, viz. other people's needs and vulnerabilities?

What are my objectives in the situation?

What are the options open to me?

How do I assess the options?

How do I develop the steps of a plan?

What is my commitment to the plan?

What are gains to me and others in carrying out the plan?

How can others help me with my plan?

How do I monitor and evaluate my plan?

The above is a long list. Nevertheless, most of these questions are likely to be relevant to major problems in people's lives. Not being able to find solutions to some of these problems, for example a relationship with a marital partner or boss, may be extremely costly both emotionally and financially. Therefore, the time and effort involved in trying to think realistically is well spent.

Co-counselling Co-counselling can be expanded so that partners not only work on their feelings, but also on their thinking, language and inner speech. This requires additional skills both for 'counsellors' and 'clients'. The issue of how directive 'counsellors' should be is relevant. Obtrusive interventions may retard rather than accelerate exploring thinking. So long as 'clients' possess some insight regarding the realism of their thinking, there is much to be said for 'counsellors' remaining in a primarily empathic role. Nevertheless, good co-counselling partners may usefully challenge, highlight thinking errors, and discuss options for more effective thinking.

Peer self-help groups A complaint sometimes heard about counselling groups is that, though individuals ventilate their feelings, they are not helped to handle them constructively. At worst, they may wallow in self-pity and other negative feelings rather than use such feelings as the catalyst for trying to alter dysfunctional thoughts. Especially if some members already possess knowledge and skills in the area of realistic thinking, peer self-help groups can have a focus that includes both thoughts and feelings. For example, a women's or a men's group can explore and try to alter the thoughts which contribute to women and men realizing only part of their potential. A group of executives with stress problems can explore and try to alter the types of thinking that are part of their stress pattern. People coming up to retirement can examine their assumptions so as to improve both their transition to and their actual retirement.

People with severe illness can explore their beliefs in the area of the illness as well as their beliefs about death. For instance, Simonton and his colleagues (1978) consider that negative expectancies contribute to the effects of cancer and positive expectancies enchance the chance of getting well. Negative expectancies include: 'Cancer is synonymous with death'; 'Cancer is something that strikes from without and there is no hope of controlling it'; and 'Medical treatment is drastic and ineffective and frequently has many negative side effects'. Positive expectancies include: 'Cancer is a disease that may or may not be fatal'; 'The body's own defenses are the mortal enemy of cancer, however it is caused'; and 'Medical treatment can be an important ally, "a friend in need", in support of the body's defenses'. These and other beliefs can be explored in cancer self-help groups. Two final examples are that bereavement self-help groups can explore thoughts contributing to the bereaved's feelings of guilt, anger and helplessness. Also, parents of mentally handicapped children can explore the extent to which they are disparaging themselves unnecessarily because of their rules about how they should be thinking, feeling and behaving in their predicament (Hannam: 1975). Self-help groups can have skilled counsellors or therapists in the background, both as resources for the group process and also as a 'safety-net' for those requiring individual consultations.

Chapter 9

RELATEDNESS: SELF-DEFINITION AND COMMUNICATION

A Hungarian proverb states: 'Tell the truth, and you will get your head bashed in'. Though the goal of taking responsibility for the way one relates to others may seem obvious, its achievement, as the proverb implies, can be anything but easy. Relating to others involves the psychological skills of responsiveness and of realism. Thus some overlap with the preceding two chapters is inevitable. Nevertheless, assuming responsibility for one's relationships also involves some different interventions from those already mentioned.

Reasons for focusing on relatedness

Personal responsibility counselling and therapy assumes that, within the parameters of their lives, people are responsible for creating and defining their existences. One of the main ways in which people create and define themselves is in relating to others. However, relating to others is based on the adequacy of one's relationship with oneself. Thus the greater capacity people have for experiencing feelings and for thinking effectively, the more likely they are to be able to engage in satisfying relationships. Personal responsibility entails the courage to define oneself and not to collude in other people's false definitions of oneself. Though this is similar to the behavioural concept of assertion, it is also different. For example, personal responsibility involves paying more attention to self-protective thinking. Also, it does not assume that the self is something which is already known and only has to be asserted. Rather, self-exploration and getting in touch with one's real wants and wishes can be both a difficult task and also an integral part of creating oneself. In Chapter 1 mention was made that, if anything, personal responsibility works from 'inside to outside'. Put another way, inner assertion or the capacity to face fears and experience feelings is often the precursor to external assertion involving defining oneself to others. Involvements with others are qualitative as well as quantitative. Thus it is possible to be lonely in a sea of acquaintances and to feel involved having the secure base of one close relationship. Focusing on relatedness cannot guarantee that people will find the quality of relationships that they desire. Indeed they may become even more conscious of their existential isolation. Nevertheless, such a focus can increase the possibilities for finding and achieving more fulfilling personal relationships. Also, it can decrease the need for people to anaesthetize their loneliness with excessive alcohol, drugs, conformity to peer group pressures and promiscuous sex. Additionally, the feeling of enhancement that people obtain from good relationships can then counteract tendencies toward overt and subtle aggression.

Another consideration is that failure to relate satisfactorily to others can contribute to physical as well as psychological pain. Psychosomatic symptoms, such as ulcers, insomnia, headaches and tension, are frequently partly caused either by people's inability to relate well to others and/or by others' difficulties in relating well to them. Additionally, poor past and current relationships may contribute to proneness to heart attacks and possibly also to proneness to cancer. Thus people's communication difficulties may be not only psychologically painful, but also potentially fatal.

Improving people's capacity for intimacy is important. As mentioned previously, people create personifications of themselves and of each other. These personifications can interfere with intimacy, which entails the ability to know and be known by each other as you really are rather than in terms of presentations of self which conceal rather than reveal (Goffman: 1959). Intimacy is not an either/or matter. The better able people are both to understand and disclose themselves and to create the conditions whereby others can disclose themselves in a climate of understanding, the more likely they are to attain it. Intimacy involves the capacity to share and be attuned to each other's thoughts, feelings and emotions, including those which are likely to be more threatening to express and reveal in other contexts and relationships. This entails being able to acknowledge and reveal both vulnerabilities and strengths. Intimacy is most likely to occur in relationships where both partners are reasonably successful in taking responsibility for their own thoughts, feelings and actions. In other words, it is the interdependence of two separate, equal and developing persons, rather than a relationship in which one or both partners may be creating and colluding in unnecessary dependency. Though intimacy does not necessarily entail an erotic relationship, in many instances effective sharing of sexuality is likely to be an important element. Here it is important that partners be prepared jointly to take responsibility for the quality of their own and their partner's sexual experiencing (Brown and Faulder: 1977).

Much of what has been written above about intimacy applies to the capacity for friendship, though often friendship has a task orientation, for example, playing tennis, as well as a person orientation. Most people seem to require a circle of friends beyond a core intimate relationship and this is more likely to be achieved if they can communicate adequately. These friendships provide a network in which people can feel affirmed and supported as well as express different parts of themselves and gain a wider variety of stimulation than by just relating to a single partner.

The psychological skills of relatedness are also important in work settings. Unfortunately people do not leave their skills deficits at home, but also take them to work. Consequently many work settings are characterized by personal animosity, egotism, dishonesty, and opportunism at the expense of others. Focusing on the way people listen, talk and resolve conflicts can be helpful in increasing their ability to cooperate with others and others willingness to cooperate with them.

Though clients frequently are or have been victims, they often possess characteristics which damage or diminish others. There can be a circularity in the process since when Person A frustrates Person B's needs, Person B may in turn frustrate Person A's needs and the whole process may escalate. Thus one way of taking personal responsibility is to avoid unnecessarily damaging others. The first step is to acknowledge one's capacity to have negative as well as positive impacts on others.

There are numerous ways in which people block each other's strivings for fulfilment, ranging from the obvious to the much more subtle. Steiner (1981) lists a number of 'power plays' designed to control others in one's own rather than their interests. These include varying kinds of intimidation, lies and omissions of truth, and passive-aggression. Berne's *Games People Play* (Berne: 1964) provides descriptions of dishonest series of interpersonal transactions which, unless corrected, damage both parties. Also, Milgram's studies show that willingness to damage others may be increased in situations of obedience to authority (Milgram: 1974).

People usually are aware when they are creating happiness, but frequently remain unaware when they are hurting and restricting others. Two of the main ways in which people damage each other are by being poor listeners and by not disclosing themselves openly. Through poor listening, they do not truly understand others nor make them feel understood. By incomplete or dishonest disclosure, others find it difficult to understand and communicate with them. Diminishing others is frequently built into everyday communication and is not just a matter of overt or even subtle hostility.

A further point is that it is possible to damage innocent others by colluding with those who have or are creating the difficulties. In hierarchies, people frequently consciously or unconsciously collude in their superior's false definitions of colleagues. This may both suit their competitive position and also avoid the risk of their boss's disapproval.

Since communication difficulties are widespread, it is impossible to avoid being damaged in some measure by others both when growing up and also in adult life. Nevertheless, it is possible to take responsibility for minimizing the chances of this happening. For example, not engaging in needless aggression is one way of avoiding retaliation. Developing the skills of conflict resolution may prevent potentially destructive differences from escalating. Being prepared to communicate one's wants and wishes clearly may help avoid misunderstandings. Knowing how to assert oneself to avoid being deprived of rights and how to set limits on others' negative behaviours can also be important. Additionally, just as people can collude with an aggressor in damaging or diminishing others, they can also collude in damaging and diminishing themselves. One way of doing this is to accept another person's false definition of a situation in a way that is advantageous to them and damaging to you, though you may not realize it at the time.

So far the major thrust the reasons for focusing on self-definition and communication has been concerned with relationships between equals, for example marital partners and friends. When it comes to child-rearing, good communication between parents can be critical. This greatly lessens the chances of children being brought up in broken or emotionally disrupted homes. If parents are not at ease with each other this is likely to lower their self-esteem which in turn may negatively affect the way they relate to their children: for example, being easily irritated with them, viewing them as 'soldiers' in their marital war, or making emotional demands upon them to fill the vacuum left by a poor marriage. Though it still has a long way to go, there is a growing interest in preventive work with prospective and actual parents so that they communicate better with their children. This may reduce the risk of their later becoming purveyors of avoidable psychological distress to their own children.

The term 'social empathy' is used here to refer to a broader identification than that required to meet people's need for intimacy. It is possible that at the higher levels of personal responsibility the identification with the community and species may be so strong that self-interest and social interest are synonymous. Adler used the term *Gemeinschafsegefühl* – social feeling or social interest – to describe the individual's innate potentiality to develop a 'deep sense of his fellowship in humanity' (Adler: 1927; Ansbacher and Ansbacher: 1956). This referred both to people's capacity for identification with those in their immediate community and to a striving for an ideal human community. Social feeling or interest was something that had to be consciously developed. Responsibility for developing social empathy can be assumed or avoided. Though the early development of such empathy relies on such people as teachers and parents, ultimately individuals are responsible for its development. It is hard to see how social empathy can be highly developed without being expressed in some form of social commitment. Furthermore, since much aggression on the wider scene represents a continuation and projection of unresolved inner difficulties, social empathy is not just a matter of developing positive but of containing negative qualities.

Interventions focused on relatedness

Counselling interventions

Just as virtually all counselling problems involve difficulties in experiencing feelings and in thinking, most also manifest themselves in difficulties in taking effective responsibility in communicating with others. This tends not to be helped by the illusion many possess that their manner of communicating is entirely natural and represents an integral part of what they call 'I' or 'me'.

Human communication consists of a continuous series of choices by both parties in an interaction. These choices refer to the sending and receiving of verbal, vocal and bodily communication. In general, people tend to be unaware of the range of available choices. As a consequence, they often remain stuck in unproductive and self-destructive patterns of relating. Furthermore, since these choices take place in contexts which have implicit and explicit rules of behaviour, there is frequently social pressure to restrict alternative ways of behaviour.

Below are a variety of counselling interventions pertinent in helping people with self-definition and communication difficulties.

Empathic responding   Empathic responding is relevant in a number of ways to helping clients with their relationship difficulties. Some clients need a nurturing counselling relationship characterized by empathy prior to being able to acknowledge their own relationship skills deficits and resources. Also, counsellor empathy may provide them with a secure base for testing out new behaviours.

Many clients have latent relationship skills and, given the support provided by empathic responding, are freed to use these resources where previously they had experienced 'stuckness'. However, other clients may need to acquire relationship skills before they can implement them. Frequently, clients need a mixture of the two.

Presenting a rationale for personal responsibility in relationships
Though the timing of the intervention needs to be sensitively judged, clients can be introduced to the idea that people in relationships are ultimately responsible for their own thoughts, feelings and actions. In other words, the choices that clients make about how they relate to others are acts of self-creation and of self-definition. Clients' choices and behaviour in relationships influence how they think and feel about themselves, how others think and feel about them, and the feedback they receive from others. This feedback influences how they think and feel about themselves.

Clients may need help in removing psychological barriers that impede choice. Additionally, they can be helped to an awareness that their choices relate both to the ways in which they receive information and to the ways in which they send it. Specific areas of choices relevant to particular clients may be used to illustrate the presentation of a rationale. For example, clients in a conflict might be shown how by choosing to attribute blame to others they have also chosen to absolve themselves of any responsibility for acting to make their own lives more fulfilled. A related example is that of irritable clients who could be shown that they have the possibility for different behaviour if prepared to choose to think differently and, possibly, also to develop better relationship skills. A further example is that of parents, frustrated in relationships with their children, who may be helped to make the choices involved in good listening. Depending on the needs of particular clients, the presentation of a rationale for personal responsibility in relationships can stress some of the reasons for focusing on relatednesses mentioned earlier.

Focusing on thoughts and inner speech impeding self-definition   Butler (1981) calls putting a pejorative tag on one's own assertive impulses or actions 'negative self labelling'. Though Butler refers to women, men also inhibit themselves by placing negative labels on their attempts at self-definition. Amongst possible negative self-labels are: 'uninteresting', 'immature', 'egotistical', 'selfish', 'demanding', 'pushy' and 'self-centred'. Counsellors can help clients explore the realism of their rules and inner speech concerning defining themselves to other people. Often clients will have a double standard in which they anticipate others will evaluate their disclosures more negatively than they would evaluate others' disclosures (Nelson-Jones and Dryden: 1979; Nelson-Jones and Coxhead: 1980). If so, this can be discussed. Additionally, clients may make the perfectionist demand of never allowing themselves to make mistakes, since these are catastrophes. Counsellors can help clients see that their attempts at fuller disclosure and self-definition are personal experiments in which they learn how to be more authentic. The feedback from such personal experiments is information which may or may not be useful rather than right or wrong.

Counsellors can help alter clients' expectations concerning the risks of concealing less of themselves. For example, in general people anticipate that disclosing characteristics that they value negatively is more risky than disclosing characteristics valued positively. However, in building relationships this anticipation is frequently inaccurate. Disclosure of negatively valued characteristics can have *positive* consequences and disclosure of positively valued characteristics *negative* consequences (Nelson-Jones and Strong: 1976). Additionally, counsellors can help their clients explore the possible gains of revealing more of themselves in appropriate circumstances. These possible gains include: greater intimacy and friendship; self-definition rather than being defined by others; standing up for oneself; greater self-knowledge and self-acceptance; and a feeling of greater confidence and control over one's life. Furthermore, counsellors can help clients face their unrealistic fears and inner speech concerning rejection and their capacity to withstand it.

Inner speech can also be used to enhance self-definition. Butler (1981) talks of the need to go from self-criticism to self-support in her assertion training for women. Self-definition can be stressful. Intimate disclosures may need to be approached in graded steps (Altman and Haythorn: 1965). Inner speech can help clients have the courage to be known before, during and after their disclosures.

Possible inner speech *before* disclosing includes: 'It's my life not theirs. I am responsible for defining myself'; 'I may have a better relationship if I am honest about my thoughts and feelings'; 'What is important is that I am prepared to experiment with letting other people know me better'.

Possible inner speech *during* disclosing includes: 'Now calm down and say what you think and feel gently and firmly'. 'There is no perfect way of saying this, but I feel it is better said than left unsaid'; 'Feelings of vulnerability are O.K. I know that I can handle them'.

Possible inner speech *after* disclosing includes: 'I'm really pleased that I'm starting to have the courage to be myself'; 'That wasn't as bad as I thought it was going to be. What was I so afraid of?'; 'Just because they may feel like rejecting me, there is no reason why I should reject myself'.

Focusing on vocal and bodily communication impeding self-definition
Some clients may be helped if counsellors pay attention to their vocal and bodily communication. Perls, in particular, was sensitive to how clients manipulated others' impressions by their use of vocal and bodily communication: for instance, seeming helpless little boys or girls rather than owning their strengths. The word manipulation has a negative connotation. Perhaps it is better to emphasize that people need to learn to take responsibility not only for *what* they say but *how* they say it. Vocal and bodily communication should match verbal communication.

Frequently people lack accurate awareness of their vocal and bodily communication. For instance, self-disclosure may be weakened by inadequate eye contact, an unexpressive face, lack of gesture, slouched posture, and a timid tone of voice. Counsellors may need to use their own experiencing of clients to confront them with how they block direct communication. After clients obtain some awareness of their difficulties, they may still need coaching to overcome them. For many clients, inadequate vocal and bodily communication indicates deeper difficulties. Consequently just focusing on outer skills is a superficial approach to inner problems and deficits.

Focusing on minimizing colluding in others' false definitions   Much human communication is a contest in which people jockey to impose their definitions on others. Since unacknowledged responsibility deficits are common, clients need beware of allowing themselves to be defined to their own disadvantage. Sometimes other people's control moves or power plays are obvious. However, on many occasions they can be subtle and devious. Assuming responsibility for self-definition also means avoiding colluding in others' false definitions.

Counsellors can help clients develop the skills of minimizing colluding in others' false definitions. An important skill is that of a realistic awareness of other people's control moves and of one's own vulnerabilities in regard to them. Already it has been mentioned that people who actively define themselves are less vulnerable to internalizing other people's definitions. Some clients may find it difficult to acknowledge that others, for instance their parents, may have mixed motivations in their relationships with them. Furthermore that parents may be getting other people, for instance friends and siblings, to collude in identifying them negatively. Clients may get sucked into self-fulfilling prophecies whereby, resenting the false definitions, they react aggressively thus seeming to justify them. Here counsellors can facilitate their clients in obtaining a clearer awareness of the dynamics of their relationships. This includes understanding how their own attributions and rules may be leaving them vulnerable. Furthermore, counsellors can help clients to behave appropriately.

There are numerous ways in which people attempt to control other people's definitions of themselves and their behaviour. Prominent among these is withdrawal either of love or of approval, which enlists their fear of rejection. Intimidation can be physical, such as a 'Fist in the face', or psychological, such as attempting to induce guilt and insecurity. A common way in which people operate on the self-definitions of others is to define themselves as victims and others as aggressors. In reality, it may be the other way round or a mixture of the two. This passive-aggressive stance, which represents attacking under the guise of defence, can be very damaging to the self-esteem of those who do not identify the manoeuvre. The real victims of such attacks need beware that they then do not fall into the trap of becoming persecutors. This again relinquishes their power to defend themselves.

Being aware of others' attempts to operate on your self-definition is the first step in being able to handle their control moves. There are many possible responses including: (a) submission or at least tacitly acquiescing in the defintion; (b) escalation or raising the emotional temperature by counter-attacking; (c) quietly yet firmly persisting in your own definition of yourself, which may also include working on your own tendencies to acquiescence or escalation; (d) identifying any unmet needs in the other person which may be contributing to their defining you negatively and, if appropriate, trying to meet their needs; (e) attempting to engage in a discussion with the other person about what is going on in the relationship; and (f) getting out of the relationship.Clients may also need to develop the skills of identifying and, if necessary, resisting peer group pressure. Furthermore, if they fall into any subgroups like women, men, gays, ethnic minorities, the disabled, etc. they may need help in identifying subtle subgroup pressures encouraging them to define themselves in negative and/or restricting ways; and in developing the confidence to resist these pressures.

Focusing on minimizing damage to others   Personal responsibility in relationships entails minimizing the psychological damage one does to others. This is not just because hate tends to beget hate. Earlier mention was made that two of the main ways in which people damage each other are by being poor listeners and by not disclosing themselves openly. Consequently counsellors who help clients send and receive information better help them toward less destructive and more mutually enhancing relationships. Some suggestions have already been made, whereby counsellors can facilitate clients' self-disclosure.

Here are some suggestions for how counsellors can help clients develop listening skills. First, by responding to clients empathically, counsellors model good listening skills and, hopefully, increase clients' self-esteem. Second, by exploring clients' self-protective processes, for example their misattributions in relationships, counsellors can help free them to start listening to their partners again. Third, counsellors can confront clients with the fact that, like most people, they need to develop good listening skills. This may both shake them from their fantasies that they are already good listeners and make them more receptive to developing skills. Fourth, counsellors may need to teach clients the rudiments of good listening, for instance the difference between internal and external frames of reference and the 'dos and don'ts of effective listening (Nelson-Jones: 1983). Fifth, it may be suggested to clients that they enter a counselling group, assuming it emphasizes communication skills, and/or participate in a structured life skills training programme focused on effective listening.

Helping clients handle their anger effectively is important for minimizing their chances of being in relationships characterized by reciprocity of negative and displeasing behaviours (Margolin: 1981). Anger can be expressed verbally, by rejection, ridicule, disparagement and other forms of negative evaluation. It is also expressed vocally and bodily, by shouting, tut-tutting, turning away, finger-shaking, physical violence and other threatening behaviour. Hops observes: 'Some individuals have nonverbal responses that are obvious put-downs but they simply act as if they were unaware that they are behaving like that' (Hops: 1976). Part of the treatment of marital problems he describes involves identifying aversive behaviours, illustrating the effect they are having on the partner, and rewarding reductions in the frequency of such behaviours. Video feedback is used as part of this procedure.

The causes of anger are many and varied. They can include low self-esteem, poor physical health, excessive stress and lack of recreational outlets. Also, anger in itself is not necessarily a destructive emotion. For instance, it can signal problem areas on which to work. Also, it may release negative feelings that block more positive ones. Thus, taking responsibility for anger does not mean trying to eliminate it altogether rather than controlling and channelling it.

Counsellors who, by means of a nurturing relationship, help their clients to feel more secure are, almost by definition, helping them to be less threatened and anger-prone. Helping people take responsibility for their anger can focus both on their definitions of persons or situations as threatening and hence justifying anger and on developing skills to handle threats. Clients may need to acknowledge their aggressive feelings prior to being able to work on them. To some, the self-conception that 'I have angry and aggressive feelings' is threatening. Furthermore, if denied, it increases the likelihood that difficulties in relationships will be attributed to others.

Anger and resentment are almost invariably in relation to rules. Clients can explore whether they are making unrealistic demands on themselves, others and the environment which leave them vulnerable to anger and self-pity. A further contributor to anger can be the feeling of powerlessness arising from the attribution 'Things aren't going well and it's all his/her fault'. By attributing the cause of negative feelings entirely outside, people make it difficult to acknowledge their power to act in situations. Thus they increase their feelings of vulnerability and threat.

Clients' definitions of people and situations as threatening are related to their sense of being able to handle the threat. There are a number of approaches to increasing clients' skills in handling threatening situations. Sometimes different approaches are applied in isolation (Moon and Eisler: 1983), but this need not be the case. Meichenbaum's stress inoculation training can be applied to coping with anger-evoking situations (Meichenbaum: 1983). The following are examples of coping inner speech which clients could be trained to use before, during and after the stressful situation: preparing for anger, 'Remember, stick to the issues and don't take things personally'; confronting anger, 'There's no point in getting mad. Concentrate on what has to be done'; coping with angry feelings, 'My anger is a signal telling me what I need to do: it's problem-solving time'; reflection when the conflict is unresolved, 'Relax. It's a lot better than getting angry'; and reflection when the conflict is resolved, 'My pride can get me into trouble, but I'm getting better at stopping myself getting into trouble'.

Though Meichenbaum's approach may reduce anger-inducing thoughts, some clients gain from assistance on how to behave in stressful situations. For instance, they might acquire skills of being assertive in anger-evoking situations. Additionally, they might be trained to take a problem-solving approach to their anger (Goldfried and Davison: 1976; Moon and Eisler: 1983). Clients could be taught that anger is a normal part of life and that effective coping is possible. They could then be instructed to resist the urge to act impulsively when faced with anger-evoking situations. Clients could monitor and record situations in which they were angry. Counsellors could then help them to: define their anger problems precisely, generate alternative solutions, and choose the 'best' one. The role of counsellors in helping clients generate alternative solutions includes informing them of ways of coping with anger, for instance training in inner speech and in assertion.

A distinction is sometimes made between anger and resentment. This is based on anger being a short-term emotion relative to resentment which 'is a long-term restressing process' (Simonton *et al.*: 1978). Counselling approaches to clients with continuing resentments include: facilitating catharsis; focusing on thinking errors contributing to the resentments; getting clients to imagine themselves behaving positively to those whom they resent; and helping them to be assertive. Some clients inhibit the requests they make of others behind their resentment. This can lead to 'You' messages, such as 'You don't love me', rather than 'I' messages, such as 'I would really appreciate your love and attention'. 'You' messages, with their implication of blame, are more likely to perpetuate situations creating resentment than 'I' messages, which clearly state wants and wishes. Counsellors can help clients identify and appropriately express the requests behind the resentments. Furthermore, they may help clients release resentments and learn to forgive the fallible human beings who have harmed them, not least since resentment, expressed or unexpressed, is destructive of self as well as of others.

Focusing on resolving conflicts Counsellors can help clients assume responsibility for being more effective at resolving conflicts. Virtually everything that was said about minimizing damage to others applies here: for instance, good listening, controlling and channelling anger, and avoiding 'You' messages. There are a number of areas on which counsellors and clients may focus:

Reducing negative communication. Negative communications occur frequently in certain relationships. They include: outbursts of anger, complaints, criticisms, negative mindreading (attributing unflattering thoughts, feelings, and motives to the other), sidetracking or introducing irrelevancies, and negatively affected disagreement (Bornstein *et al.*: 1983). Negative communications can also be part of people's behaviour when attempting to solve problems. This risks escalating the difficulties. Counsellors can help clients target such behaviour and understand its effect on others. Furthermore, they can work with clients to develop alternative strategies, both for their behaviour and inner speech.

Increasing helpful communication. Good listening and honest yet unaggressive disclosure helps resolve conflicts. Using video feedback, partners can be shown their behaviour in problem-solving sessions and encouraged to identify the responses of the other that they find helpful. This may lead to training partners in making helpful responses (Margolin and Weiss: 1978).

Increasing positive behaviours. Distressed relationships compared to happy ones show a lack of reciprocity of pleasing behaviours (Margolin: 1981). Clients can be helped to identify and increase behaviours regarded positively by their partner (Jacobson: 1979).

Problem-solving. Clients may need to learn to take a problem-solving approach to their difficulties. A stage approach to problem-solving was provided in Chapter 8. Problem-solving involves setting aside a period of time when both partners are reasonably fresh and can avoid other distractions. Furthermore, sometimes partners may need to adhere to 'fair fight rules' (Lieberman and Hardie: 1981). These might include: no yelling; no physical violence; being able to say 'I want' without incurring disapproval; and neither fighting in bed nor in front of the children, etc. Such rules or contracts vary from couple to couple.

Butler's concept of 'muscle' is relevant to assuming responsibility for resolving conflicts. She writes: 'As I am using the term, muscle essentially means strength . . . I pesonally prefer to begin my assertions at the lowest level of muscle . . . If the first level of muscle does not suffice, I am perfectly willing to move on to a higher level' (Butler: 1981). Conflicts are best resolved with the minimum use of force. This does not preclude taking a firm stand.

Focusing on social empathy   Some clients may wish to explore their relationships with those not in their immediate environments and with the human species. Some of these clients have a religious orientation. Viewing personal responsibility as encompassing responsibility for the well-being and survival of the species is likely to be a by-product of being a fulfilled person, with or without counselling. Nevertheless, counselling sessions may also have the development of social empathy as their focus. For instance, some clients may benefit from empathic responding as they search themselves more deeply to discover their values in relation to their fellow human beings.

Szasz cynically observes: 'Men are rewarded or punished not for what they do, but rather for how their acts are defined. This is why men are more interested in better justifying themselves than in better behaving themselves' (Szasz: 1973). Counsellors can go beyond empathic understanding to help those who are more interested in better behaving themselves. They can explore thoughts and inner speech which may contribute to clients resisting social feeling and actions. These thoughts include: fear of being seen as different from others; of being soft; of being taken advantage of; of imposing oneself on others; and of being a do-gooder. The tendency toward privatism or just looking after oneself may be justified with the notion that, because individuals cannot solve all the world's problems, they cannot make a positive contribution to any. For some clients, confronting their finitude may accelerate appreciation of fundamental human values. As well as helping clients to understand and clarify thoughts and feelings, counsellors can explore with them actions by which they can develop and demonstrate social empathy. As Fromm observes: 'Insight separated from practice remains ineffective' (Fromm: 1976). One of the main ways in which counsellors can help clients attain greater social empathy is to model it themselves.

Group counselling Counsellors can help both couples and families assume greater responsibility for their communication with each other. Counsellors' roles can include: being resources who remain outside power struggles as 'official observers' (Satir: 1967, 1972); providing feedback on how people communicate; facilitating clients' exploration of their manner of relating, possibly using video feedback; exploring the implicit and explicit rules and assumptions that govern their interactions; and helping partners or family members build up the skills resources of good communication, such as becoming better at listening, disclosing and resolving conflicts. Counselling a couple or family does not preclude time spent with individual partners or family members.

Group counselling, with from five to ten members, has potential advantages over individual counselling when working with clients' self-definition and communication difficulties. For instance, counsellors observes the difficulties. Also members get practice at personal relations. In Chapter 7 some ways were indicated in which experiential encounter groups could release members' experiencing of feelings. Acknowledging feelings in front of other members can be an important part of relating to them. Often members make valuable comments on the way other members 'come across' to them. Sometimes counsellors may reflect such comments to emphasize their importance. On other occasions counsellors may provide direct feedback to clients on how they relate in the group. Such feedback can cover the following skill areas: amount of disclosure, manner of expressing feelings, directness of communication, vocal and bodily communication, listening and resolving conflicts.

Yalom sees group therapy as a particularly rich arena for observing distorted patterns of relating (Yalom: 1980). Such patterns tend to incorporate unrealistic thinking language and inner speech. Consequently, the thinking underlying members' manner of relating can also be fruitfully explored. The role of counsellors in groups focused on relatedness is to help members become aware that they are responsible for their thoughts, feelings and actions in relationships. Also to aid them in becoming more effective senders and receivers of information.

Training interventions

There are many possibilities for training people in structured programmes to become better communicators. These programmes aim to help people make better choices in relationships. Frequently social behaviour is the result of unexamined habits. People need to become more aware of how these habits may interfere with their own and others' fulfilment and be shown alternative behaviours. Then they may change without prolonged counselling. This assumes an initial minimum level of self-awareness and of ability to experience feelings. There have been many books written about training people in relationship skills (e.g. Gordon: 1970; Egan: 1977; Guerney: 1977). Sometimes these books focus mainly on overt behaviour (Wilkinson and Canter: 1982). On other occasions they focus on both thinking and behaviour (Butler: 1981). Relationship training within a personal responsibility framework requires focusing not only on thoughts and actions but also on feelings. In this sense it is a three-dimensional approach (thoughts, feelings and actions), rather than a two-dimensional (thoughts and actions), or a one-dimensional (actions alone) approach.

A central part of any relationship skills training programme is learning to use the skills afterwards. These programmes can focus either on specific skills, such as listening, or on a number of skills (for instance, by taking a broad approach to responsibility for thoughts, feelings and actions in relationships). The interventions tend to be the same as for realistic thinking training programmes. These interventions include: presentation of a rationale, presentation of concepts, presentation of skills, facilitating self-assessment, encouraging skills practice, encouraging homework, and facilitating group discussion.

Below are suggestions for the content of training programmes in some central skills of relatedness. Each programme is best tailor-made to the needs of the particular training groups.

Training in listening   Training people in effective listening entails helping them become aware that they are responsible for its quality. Good listening is not something that just happens. In everyday life, pocket therapists are very boring. However, there is much to be said for teaching people basic listening skills as in counsellor training. Elsewhere, a programme for training people in the skills of empathic responding is described in some detail (Nelson-Jones: 1983). Elements of a training programme for responsible listening include:

Presenting a rationale for responsibility in relationships.

Increasing trainees' awareness of blocks to their listening.

Helping trainees distinguish when they are responding to others from their own rather than the other person's frame of reference.

Increasing awareness of vocal and bodily communication.

Increasing knowledge of specific ways of avoiding low empathy. Developing the sender and receiver skills of accurate empathy. Integrating the use of empathic responding skills and of being a psychologically 'safe' person into trainees' everyday lives.

Training in self-definition Training in self-definition entails helping people become more aware that the breadth, depth and direction of their disclosures reflects choices concerning what to conceal and to reveal. Disclosures are not a 'natural' part of what they call 'I' or 'me'. The term self-definition is used in preference to self-disclosure because it emphasizes more creating a self than revealing a self that already exists.

Training in self-definition can focus on responsiveness. For instance, counsellors can help trainees develop inner empathy. However, a large part of training is likely to focus on thoughts and inner speech impeding self-definition. This may entail focusing on: internal rules and standards; accurately attributing responsibility in relationships; anticipating risk and gain; and on task-oriented inner speech.

Training in self-definition also focuses on actual behaviour: on how people avoid responsibility for defining themselves clearly in their vocal, bodily and verbal communication; on how they can assume responsibility; and on how they can avoid colluding in others' false definitions of them. Butler (1981) sees assertiveness in terms of self-definition and states, 'assertiveness can be more broadly defined as the continuing statement "This is who I am."'. To her, assertiveness encompasses self-definition in at least four areas: expressing negative feelings, expressing positive feelings, setting limits on others' behaviour and taking initiatives. Though her book is aimed at women, her message is that people need to learn to assert themselves independent of gender stereotypes.

Training in assertion can be an important focus of self-definition training. Albeit with much overlap with assertion, self-disclosure is another focus of self-definition training. People may need training in how to be a self to another person by means of their disclosures. These disclosures can be much broader (e.g. work, sex) than the four assertiveness areas listed by Butler. The following are some specific self-disclosure skills which might be included in a self-definition training programme.

Positive and negative self-disclosure. This relates to the ability to reveal positive and negative information and feelings about oneself rather than just positive and negative feelings about others.

Development of relationships. Altman and Haythorn (1965) suggest that people generally disclose more information on both breadth and depth dimensions as relationships advance from strangers to casual acquaintances to close friends. Some trainees, even partners in established marriages may need training in how to develop the range and intimacy of their relationships.

Sending 'I' messages. 'I' messages involve people acknowledging their thoughts and feelings as their own rather than focusing on the other person by means of 'You' messages.

Specificity. Specificity means communicating clearly and specifically rather than in vague and abstract terms.

Immediacy. Immediacy relates to the capacity of people to respond immediately to their experiencing of a relationship and to disclose what otherwise might be left unsaid. It is 'you-me' talk regarding the 'there-and-now'.

Handling feedback. Trainees may need to develop both overt skills of handling feedback after their disclosures and covert skills of dealing with their emotions concerning the feedback.

Vocal and bodily communication. Trainees may be helped both to become more aware of their vocal and bodily communication and where necessary, to make it match their verbal communications.

Training in regulating negative feelings   Some people may benefit from a training programme specifically focused on helping them handle their anger and aggression. As mentioned earlier, anger of itself can serve positive functions. If continuously bottled up it may emerge in 'heavy' outbursts, or 'come out sideways' as in gossiping, or be somatized, for example, ulcers. Depending upon the needs of the participants, a training programme for taking responsibility for anger in relationships might include the following:

Assessment. This means helping people become more aware of their anger on a number of dimensions: such as frequency; intensity; the sorts of things that act as triggers; what they are thinking when they become angry; how they behave when they are angry; any contextual considerations, e.g. fatigue, redundancy; the consequences for themselves; and the consequences for others.

Regulating the thoughts and inner speech contributing to anger. Here trainees are helped to reformulate unrealistic into realistic standards. Additionally, anger-producing misattributions are identified and reformulated. Trainees may also be taught appropriate inner speech to make the anger-evoking situations less stressful.

Eliminating aggressive behaviours. Trainees can be helped to eliminate verbal, vocal and bodily behaviours which go beyond assertion and risk escalating conflicts since they are uncalled for 'put-downs' of others.

Developing the skills of assertion. Often anger reflects people's feelings of powerlessness in being able to handle situations appropriately. They can develop the requisite skills for handling specific situations and people assertively. This entails focusing on inner speech as well as on behaviour.

Developing the skills of 'mending fences'. This entails helping trainees to become more aware of when they have been aggressive or 'gone over the top'. They can develop the skills of repairing relationships, including both how they think about their behaviour and also how they act toward others.

Developing the skills of self-regard. This part of the programme is geared to those who strive too hard and expect too much not only of others but of themselves. These people can acknowledge the legitimacy of their own needs and be encouraged to lead more balanced lives. This in itself is likely to reduce their proneness to aggression.

Releasing resentments through forgiveness. Some trainees may be holding on to past hurts in ways that lower their self-esteem. The realism of holding on to past hurts in the present can be explored. Trainees may be helped to understand other people's vulnerabilities, and that they must learn to assume responsibility for avoiding being the emotional victims of their own resentments. Some trainees may need assistance in ventilating their resentments before they can release them.

Training in resolving conflicts In relationships conflicts are less likely if partners behave in ways that please rather than displease. However, given the virtual inevitability of differences, and hence of conflict, in long-standing relationships, counsellors can help trainees mitigate the harm and increase the likelihood of positive outcomes. In general, the better partners are at listening to and at revealing themselves to each other, the better the prospects for their being able to resolve their conflicts. They have more accurate information rather than relating to each other on the basis of fantasy and incomplete disclosure.

Training in resolving conflicts may contain training in the skills of listening, self-definition and regulating negative feelings. Training in regulating negative feelings does not necessitate the presence of others. However, training in resolving conflicts is best conducted in programmes containing both partners. Thus conflict-resolution skills are learned using real issues. Audio-visual aids may highlight how partners behave when trying to resolve conflicts. Both helpful and harmful communications can be identified by the partners themselves, other trainees or by counsellors. Partners can be encouraged to increase helpful and to reduce harmful communications. Additionally, they can be helped to identify thoughts and inner speech contributing to conflicts.

Training in taking responsibility for resolving, or at least containing conflicts entails encouraging partners to take a problem-solving approach to divisive issues in relationships. This increases the likelihood of focusing on issues rather than on people. Individuals may be trained to explore their roles in sustaining conflicts along the lines of the situation analysis and problem-solving section of the previous chapter. Also, they may be trained in the skills of working *together* to resolve conflicts.

Two approaches to problem solving involving both partners are Gordon's 'no-loss' approach (Gordon: 1970) and the Main-Roark consensus method (Main and Roark: 1975). Gordon's method, claimed not to involve coercive power, has six separate steps: (a) identifying and defining the conflict; (b) generating possible alternative solutions; (c) evaluating the alternative solutions; (d) deciding on the best acceptable solution; (e) working out ways of implementing the solution; and (f) following up to evaluate how it worked. With the Main-Roark method both parties involved: (a) describe the situation as they see it; (b) describe how they feel about the conflict and what personal meaning it has for them; (c) describe a desired situation to reduce the conflict; (d) determine what changes are necessary to achieve that situation; and (e) outline an agenda or plan of action to reach that situation. Both methods involve negotiation. The final outcome is hopefully an agreement or 'contract' to which both parties feel they can subscribe without resentment.

Personal relations training   Frequently the emphasis in social skills training is on helping people develop skills of initiating contact and of handling specific stressful situations appropriately. The focus in personal relations training is not only on helping people initiate relationships, but also on helping them nurture and sustain relationships on a day-to-day basis. Personal relations training involves offering trainees composite programmes aimed at the central skills of relating to others. For instance an introductory programme might cover, albeit briefly, the four skills areas mentioned so far: listening, self-definition, regulating negative feelings and resolving conflicts. The main focus in personal relations training is partner and family relationships, though not necessarily so. After taking an initial overview course, trainees could take further courses in specific areas of deficit. While many would not admit the need for this kind of training, at least as applied to themselves, the high incidence of divorce indicates a need for developmental and preventive training in personal relations.

Training in personal relations can be geared to specific clienteles. This assumes that groups, such as women and gays, have particular areas requiring emphasis. For example, programmes for women may emphasize overcoming the effects of gender conditioning, while gay groups may focus on helping gays take effective responsibility for defining themselves to others. Much training in personal relations can be on a preventive basis. Two ways of achieving this are parent training and training people when they are young. For example, Resnick and her colleagues combined both parents and their infants in their fathering classes (Resnick et al.: 1978). The first part of each class was devoted to imparting knowledge and skills regarding infant development. Fathers were taught how to communicate with their infants and to facilitate their sensory-motor, cognitive and affective development. The second part of each class was a sharing and discussion period focused on the impact of fatherhood. Another preventive programme was Gordon's *Parent Effectiveness Training* (Gordon: 1970). He attempted to train parents in the skills of active listening, sending 'I' messages, and resolving conflicts in 'no-lose' ways.

Personal relations training programmes need to help participants assume an attitude of responsibility for maximizing their fulfilment in relationships. Furthermore, to become more effective in assuming the responsibility, participants need to develop the skills of regulating their thoughts, feelings and actions in relationships.

Self-therapy interventions

Even for people who have access to counselling or to personal relations training, the issue ultimately comes down to what can they do for themselves to relate better. Below are some suggestions.

Inner empathy   In personal relations there are always at least three relationships involved: the joint relationship and each partner's relationship with themselves. Partners need to give themselves time and space to listen to their own experiencing in relationships. In Chapter 7 mention was made that people who develop the skills of inner empathy are likely to become more sensitively attuned to their wishes and wants, to be able to identify and discard dysfunctional inhibitions, and to acknowledge and understand feelings of anxiety and guilt. Additionally, people who develop inner empathy are more likely to own their feelings. Inner empathy is a process which requires constant attention both because of one's own self-protective tendencies and because of pressures from others to ignore one's feelings.

Partners can help each other develop inner empathy by being safe people with whom each can reveal and discover themselves. The quality of listening in relationships affects the extent to which each person experiences their true feelings. Some partners may wish to set aside time on a regular basis for co-counselling.

Self-definition Whereas inner empathy tends to be a private process, self-definition includes defining oneself to others. Individuals can become aware of the thoughts, inner speech, and verbal and bodily communications by which they block defining themselves openly to others. Furthermore, they can gain awareness of when they are colluding in other people's false definitions and power plays. Self-definition requires courage. People must learn to take responsibility for the choices by which they become known or fail to be known. This involves paying attention not just to what is revealed but also to how it is revealed.

Regulating negative feelings Regulating aggressive feelings is one of the ways in which people can take responsibility for lessening the chances of negative reciprocity in relationships. Individuals can become adept at understanding the thoughts, inner speech and environmental pressures that contribute to their negative feelings. Furthermore, they can become sensitive to behaviours which are likely to be regarded as 'put-downs' by others. The attribution that 'I am responsible for my feelings in a relationship' can be a great incentive to working on altering negative feelings.

Effective listening It cannot be stressed too strongly that individuals must learn to assume responsibility for adequate listening to others. Effective listening is a *discipline* which entails giving time and attention to others while not allowing extraneous thoughts and feelings to intervene. Rather than have the self-statement 'I am a good listener', it is preferable to have the self-statement 'Listening is something that requires constant attention not just to the other person, but also to elements of myself that may interfere with the process'.

Resolving conflicts Each partner needs to take responsibility for resolving conflicts. However, someone has to make the first move. Partners may need to persist in working on issues without necessarily getting much cooperation from others. Suggestions have already been made for problem solving and resolving conflicts. Implementing these methods can be difficult even with, and probably more so without, the support of counsellors. Nevertheless, partners who wish to sustain relationships have a responsibility to themselves for realistic attempts at resolving differences. Additionally, they need to recognize their limits in this regard.

Co-counselling   Earlier, co-counselling was mentioned as a way of helping partners listen to each other and to themselves. However, co-counselling can also be useful when the people involved are not in a close relationship, but come together just for their sessions. Co-counselling can help people focus on assuming more responsibility for their thoughts, feelings and behaviours in relationships. There is a risk that other partners in relationships will not be happy with intimate details being discussed with third parties. This is less of a risk if both partners become part of the same co-counselling network. However, in some instances, the risks outweigh the gains.

Peer self-help groups   There are numerous peer self-help groups that get together both to meet relatedness needs and to improve skills. If conducted within a personal responsibility framework, they assume that each member needs to learn responsibility for their thoughts, feelings and actions in their relationships inside and outside the group. Peer self-help groups tend to be homogeneous rather than heterogeneous in composition: they may be women's groups, men's groups, disabled people's groups, student groups, single people's groups, couple's groups, etc. Peer self-help groups and co-counselling networks are not readily available for most people. Consequently, the major emphasis in self-therapy must be on what people can do for themselves in their everyday relationships independent of outside help.

Support networks   Most individuals already have some kind of support network of family, friends and trusted people in the community. Those deficient in such networks can make a conscious attempt to spend the time and effort necessary to build them up. These support networks are partly to help meet everyday relatedness needs, but also to provide assistance when existing relationships get into difficulty or crisis. People need to be discriminating in whom they choose to turn to when discussing relationship problems. Ideally people in support networks can provide a framework and emotional climate whereby individuals feel free to explore their own contribution to perpetuating relationship difficulties. Thus a support network can act as a stimulus for assuming responsibility rather than for collusion in avoiding responsibility.

Chapter 10

REWARDING ACTIVITY: MEANING IN OCCUPATION

Approaches to counselling and therapy are far more ready to emphasize personal relationships than rewarding activity. For example, Freud, Rogers, Perls, Berne and Ellis say little about people's occupational lives. However, theorists like Super (1957) and Holland (1973) focus mainly on career development and choice. They have little to say about the other mediating goals of personal responsibility. Such division between occupational and nonoccupational theory is regrettable. Here great emphasis is placed on people learning to take responsibility for their occupational fulfilment. This incorporates choice of activities, performance during them, and handling stress, transitions and setbacks.

Some relevant terms now get reviewed rather than precisely defined. Rewarding activity is used in the broad sense of that which occupies time and brings fulfilment. Super (1980) takes a life-span life-space approach to occupation when he identifies nine major roles (child, student, 'leisurite', citizen, worker, spouse, homemaker, parent and pensioner) that people play in their lifetime in four principal theatres (home, community, school and workplace). Various roles interact and get combined during each life stage. In this chapter the emphasis is on occupying time other than in personal relations.

Warr (1983) writes: 'In general terms "work" may be defined as as activity directed to goals beyond the enjoyment of the activity itself'. Work invariably has connotations of effort, be it either short-term or sustained. It mostly does not occupy free or discretionary time. Instead work tends to be perceived as time that people spend maintaining themselves (housework, etc.) or the hours they sell to other people for money (jobs, etc.). Leisure is regarded as free or discretionary time in which people can exercise choice. Though its main connotation is recreation, leisure may also involve effort. Employment is paid work. Unemployment has been defined as 'The condition of being without some socially acceptable means of earning a living' (Garraty: 1978). To be unemployed does not necessarily mean to be without work.

Though personal responsibility counselling and therapy focuses mainly on the individual, many issues of occupational fulfilment require either organizational or social changes to be satisfactorily resolved. Though individuals contribute to such changes, frequently their occupational lives also entail coming to terms with environmental limitations.

Reasons for focusing on rewarding activity

The reasons why counsellors, clients and people in general need to focus on rewarding activity include the following. Possibly the major reason is that people need to give meaning to their lives. The existential psychologists heavily emphasize the need for meaning, the opposite of which is meaninglessness, sometimes called the 'existential vacuum' (Frankl: 1959). One approach to meaning is intellectual, namely through philosophy and religion; another is in personal relations; still another, albeit related to the previous two, is through occupation. Occupations possessing meaning entail activities of importance, significance and concern to individuals. Meaninglessness is a state of despair. It is characterized by boredom, apathy and the feeling that both oneself and the world are a void.

Unemployment penetrates right to the heart of people's need for meaning. Some gain from (Warr: 1983) and others have little difficulty coping with unemployment (Roberts, Duggan and Noble: 1982). However, many suffer negative psychological and physical consequences (Hayes and Nutman: 1981: Jahoda: 1982; Stafford: 1982; Warr: 1983). There are numerous reasons why unemployment affects people negatively: loss of income, loss of status, feelings of rejection and self-rejection; alienation from the wider society; family difficulties, etc. A major reason is that unemployment can take meaning out of people's lives. Many do not find it easy to replenish what they have lost, even if their previous employment was unsatisfactory. Retirement can also frustrate people's need for meaning. Some are better at coping with it than others.

Occupations provide people with opportunities for creating and defining themselves. Occupational development is sometimes seen as the implementation of self-concepts (Super: 1957). However, occupational self-concepts are created as well as implemented. Furthermore, these self-concepts may involve choosing to be how others want you rather than as you really are. Just as parents may need children to relate to them in ways that sustain parental personifications so they may need children to engage in activities that fulfil parental needs.

Occupational self-definition involves both *directional* and *performance* choices. Not only *what* to do but *how* to do it. Some performance choices entail enriching what may be already good employment. Other performance choices relate to handling employment difficulties: for example, interpersonal conflict, difficulties with authority, over and under promotion, pressure for results, and excessive hours and overload. Occupational self-definition also includes performance and directional choices regarding leisure.

Rewarding activity and physical health are connected. First, people's bodies and brains may be strengthened by appropriate, and stay underdeveloped or be weakened by inappropriate, use. Second, people's physical health and sense of well being may be improved if they take physical exercise. Simonton *et al.* (1978) observe that 'regular physical exercise is one of the best tools for appropriately channelling the physiological effects of stress, and may also stimulate the body's natural defenses to do battle with malignancy'. Third, just as rewarding activity enhances, unrewarding activity may debilitate physical health. People have an optimal level of stimulation at which they feel most comfortable. At this level they experience what Selye (1974) terms 'stress without distress'. Beneath this level they feel insufficiently stimulated and bored; above, they may experience physiological and psychological distress. Bodily reactions include hypertension, proneness to heart attacks and ulcers. The weakest parts of different people's bodies are most adversely affected by stress. The amount of stress people feel is both a matter of external pressures and of how they interact with them. For instance, Friedman and Rosenman (1974) noted that those whom they labelled type A individuals were more prone to heart attacks than type B individuals. Type A individuals, unlike type B, were competitive, achievement-oriented, had a great sense of time urgency and were prone to get angry.

By assuming more responsibility for their occupational lives, people are also assuming responsibility for participating in improving and maintaining their physical health. In part this will be a by-product of keeping mentally and physically active. Sometimes it may involve a conscious effort to engage in regular exercise. Also, it may entail improved efficiency at coping with occupational stress.

Activities frequently involve others. In them people meet needs for relatedness and belonging. Lowered activity often leads to less social contact. For example, unemployment may contribute to isolation in a number of ways. First, individuals lose regular contact with workmates who, however difficult, were at least a source of human contact. Second, they may also lose some of the secondary contacts that resulted from regular contact with workmates. Third, they may become depressed, wishing to withdrawn physically from previous social contacts. Fourth, less income may either curtail or impede social activities. Fifth, unemployed people's lessened self-esteem may contribute to difficulties with marital partners and children, thus further isolating them. Retired people are also vulnerable to isolation on leaving their jobs (Hayes and Nutman: 1981). On the other hand, some people isolate themselves by too much activity: ambitious executives who ignore family and friends or shy people who use work as a defence against social contact.

The notion of paying attention to transitions was introduced in Chapter 6. Counsellors can help people during a number of occupational transitions: for example, from school to work, and from employment to unemployment or retirement. Transitions are periods of heightened stress. Holmes and his colleagues developed a Social Readjustment Rating Scale (SRRS) indicating the amount of coping behaviour required by 43 life events (Holmes and Rahe: 1967). Death of a spouse ranked first and was assigned a mean required coping behaviour value of 100. Occupational transitions included: fired at work, rank 8, mean value 47; retirement, rank 10, mean value 45; business readjustment, rank 15, mean value 39; change to different line of work, rank 18, mean value 36; change in responsibilities at work, rank 22, mean value 29; change in work hours or conditions, rank 31, mean value 20; and change in recreation, rank 34, mean value 19.

The transition to unemployment can be extremely stressful. Hayes and Nutman (1981) suggest three broad stages. First, 'shock and immobilization, followed by a phase characterized by renewed hope, optimism, and a tendency to minimize or deny that there has been a change'. Second, depression and withdrawal. Third, the internalization of a new identity which, for those continuing to be unemployed, can entail a move from pessimism to fatalism. Transitions involve people's thoughts, feelings, actions, health and social relationships. Their potential impact, both good and ill, should not be underestimated.

People's sense of competence relates to their thoughts and feelings about being able to interact competently with their environments. The converse of a sense of competence is a sense of incompetence, and this can have devastating effects upon self-esteem. People unable to feel competent in some of their major activities are very vulnerable. To some extent a sense of incompetence is socially conditioned. For instance, unemployed people are more likely to feel incompetent in societies viewing unemployment negatively than in those more tolerant.

Tendencies to feel incompetent also result from negative events in people's pasts. However, they may represent a realistic appraisal of lack of ability. Frequently senses of and actual competence differ, with both under- and overestimations possible. A reason for counsellors focusing on people's occupational lives is to help them both feel and be competent in areas which are of importance to them. For instance, exam-anxious students may need to *feel* more competent as an antecedent to *being* more competent during their exams.

Generation of income is a major reason why most people work. Jahoda, writing of the differences in unemployment in the 1980s as compared with the 1930s, talks about the change 'from absolute physical deprivation to relative deprivation for large numbers of the unemployed' (Jahoda: 1982). Though there is more welfare provision in the 1980s, Warr observes that in Britain studies of unemployed working class men suggested that about two-thirds of them had a household income which was half or less of their income when employed. Furthermore, worries about money strongly predicted unemployed people's overall distress scores (Warr: 1983).

Lack of an adequate income can lead to all sorts of secondary difficulties including: a change of status within the family; not being able to provide as much for family members as they or you may want; having less choice and variety in one's life; and being vulnerable to further 'hard knocks' when having to raise money or sell assets. Additionally, the future may seem very insecure. Indeed, money worries can trigger off a more fundamental existential anxiety about the physical survival of oneself and one's family.

Loss of income can also contribute to a sense that people have little control over what happens in their lives, and, for the young unemployed, it may prolong dependency on parents when they are physically and psychologically ready for independence. Counselling may help some unemployed clients back into the workforce. It may help others make difficult choices regarding how to handle their lessened income more effectively, including exploring fears and anxieties about their finances. Even employed and relatively well-off clients can have financial worries.

Interventions for rewarding activity

The area of rewarding activity is wide. It encompasses such topics as career choice, job enrichment, emotional factors affecting performance, effects of stress, gender-role conflicts, physical health, psychological well-being, viz. combating depression through activity, and use of leisure. Consequently, in suggesting interventions, each topic is not covered in detail. Rather, sufficient interventions are mentioned to indicate a comprehensive approach.

Counselling interventions
Below are a range of counselling interventions that can be used both to coun-

teract tendencies to responsibility avoidance and to facilitate responsibility assumption in the area of rewarding activity.

Empathic responding Empathic responding has numerous uses in occupational counselling. First, some clients may be so out of touch with their feelings that to commence a rational approach to choosing a career or job would be superficial. Initially, they need a nurturing relationship focused on helping them acknowledge, experience and express feelings. Such people require more of a sense of self prior to making decisions. Second, empathic responding helps create relationships with clients, lets them feel understood and facilitates their occupational self-exploration. This applies to all categories of clients: for instance, school leavers choosing a career, women seeking a balance between activity inside and outside the home, and unemployed people rebuilding their occupational lives. Third, empathic responding provides a secure base from which people can engage in personal experiments to test out aspects of their occupational selves. One way of looking at the use of empathy in occupational counselling is that an empathic emotional climate should be present at virtually all times. However, empathy alone is frequently insufficient.

Focusing on attributing responsibility Some clients may gain from counsellors providing a rationale for their assuming greater responsibility in finding meaning in occupation. Part of such a rationale may be that the search for meaning is likely to be an active process, namely that they are being challenged and questioned by life, rather than a passive process in which meaning is automatically provided. A number of the points made earlier in this chapter might be included in the rationale: for example, that humans are meaning-seeking beings; that people define themselves through choice of activities; and that rewarding activity is related to physical health and psychological well-being.

The presentation of a rationale for focusing on rewarding activity can be interwoven with increasing clients' existential awareness. Choice of activity takes place within a finite life-span. Each individual is responsible for his or her own survival and fulfilment during this limited period. How people spend their time is comprised of a series of choices. As long as they live, nobody can evade what Frankl terms the mandate to choose among possibilities (Frankl: 1959).

Counsellors may help clients assess the realism of how they attribute responsibility in specific situations. As mentioned earlier, Weiner and Kukla (1970) produced evidence showing that individuals who are high and those who are low in achievement motivation differentially attribute the causes of success and failure. High achievement oriented individuals are more likely to attribute suc cess to effort and failure to lack of proper effort. Low achievement oriented individuals are less likely to ascribe their failure to lack of effort and more likely to attribute it to a deficiency in ability. Counsellors working with either group should endeavour to help them *accurately* attribute responsibility for success and failure. Work relationships are another area where accurately attributing responsibility is important. It is tempting to play the 'blame-game' with superiors, subordinates or peers in ways that perpetuate rather than resolve difficulties.

Focusing on accurately attributing responsibility can also be important when working with unemployed people. For example, excessively attributing responsibility to oneself may contribute to depression. Unemployment may reflect bad luck and adverse market conditions rather than personal inadequacy. However, the depressive feelings of the unemployed are likely to have many contributing factors other than attributional ones (Feather and Barber: 1983).

Failure to attribute responsibility accurately may freeze some unemployed people into resigned fatalism even when they might succeed given persistence in seeking employment. Inaccurate attributions may lead to a sense of helplessness not justified by circumstances. Unhappily sometimes circumstances also justify pessimism. Nevertheless, the attribution still needs to be made that people are responsible for maximizing their occupational fulfilment even when unemployed.

Focusing on internal rules and standards   There are many opportunities in people's occupational lives for faulty internal rules and harmful inner speech. Counsellors may create safe atmospheres in which clients can cut through social conditioning and tendencies to reindoctrinate themselves with other people's standards. However, sometimes counsellors also need to help clients clearly identify internal rules acting as significant barriers to fulfilment. Below are a number of rules that cause people difficulty.

Achievement
> 'High status occupations are always better than low status occupations.' 'Making money is the highest good.'
> 'I must always be seen to be successful.'

Performance
> 'I must get on with everyone in my workplace.'
> 'I cannot accept myself making mistakes even when learning a new task.'
> 'Because something has gone wrong in the past it will go wrong in the future.'

Gender
> 'A woman's place is in the home.'

'Women should not aspire to high professional achievement.'
'Primary school teaching and nursing are not good jobs for men.'

Unemployment

'People who are unemployed are second-class citizens.'
'People who feel depressed after losing their jobs are weak.'
'People who are unemployed are failures.'

Leisure

'Leisure is not nearly as important as work.'
'Since leisure is recreation, people should not have to make any effort to develop leisure interests.'
'People who are not good at their leisure pursuits cannot enjoy them.'

Retirement

'Life after sixty is downhill all the way.'
'It's too late to develop new interests and relationships.'
'People are not responsible for participating in their health by staying mentally and physically active.'

Counsellors can help their clients become more realistic about their internal rules where these impede occupational fulfilment. Additionally, they may teach clients as a self-help skill how to change their inner rules and speech.

Focusing on anticipating risk and gain   Occupational decisions can be very threatening since so much of people's view of themselves is involved. Consequently clients may 'play it on the safe side' and avoid changes. Without advocating risk and changes as universal panaceas, counsellors can help clients assess more accurately both the gains and the risks attached to specific decisions, such as a mid-life career change or developing a new leisure interest.

Focusing on self-protective thinking   Occupational decision-making is not entirely rational. People are motivated by fears and anxieties as well as by needs for fulfilment. For example, a young man may have a considerable emotional investment in wanting to become a doctor and be reluctant to accept that his deeper occupational inclinations are more toward the arts. Consequently, incoming information from both external sources, for example, exam results, and internal sources, viz. his feelings, may get operated on to coincide with his occupational personification. This occupational personification may have a further layer of rigidity if it is being rewarded because it colludes with others' personifications; for instance 'If I am a really successful mother, then my son must be a doctor'. Another example is that of a young woman who is reluctant to admit her academic ability because she considers it 'unfeminine' and likely to put her in competition with men, thus risking lack of popularity. She may then find various ways of denying and distorting her ability, including not trying too hard. Work relationships are also an area for self-protective thinking. In their work as well as personal relationships, people have personifications of themselves and of others. These are at varying levels of accuracy. For instance, employers may state that they encourage independence, but remain unaware that they reward compliance and mediocrity. Also, employees when at work may ventilate resentments generated outside without awareness of this. Many find it hard to accept criticism at variance with their self-concepts. Such information may be 'operated' on by devaluing its importance, denigrating its source, and possibly counter-attacking.

Counsellors can focus on clients' self-protective processes in their occupational lives. Though empathic responding may be helpful in creating a safe emotional climate to explore self-protective thought processes, sometimes more active interventions are called for. These range from gentle explanation to firm challenges.

Focusing on meaning and on alternatives   Sometimes clients in occupational counselling are confronting the meaning of their existences at a deep level. For example, middle-aged people in secure jobs may undergo career crises because they feel their chances of leading fulfilled lives are slipping away. Unemployed and retired people, who have much unstructured time, may also be confronted with fundamental doubts and questions about the meaning of their existences. At this level, occupational counselling centres around not only specific occupational pursuits but also values and philosophies of living. The kinds of questions that clients may ask implicitly or explicitly are: 'What is the underlying purpose of my life?', 'What values should guide my occupational choices?', 'How can I find or create real meaning in my existence?', and 'What is the relationship between looking after my own needs and helping others?'. Counsellors require sensitivity to those clients needing to explore questions of value prior to examining specific occupational choices. Empathic companionship helps clients' self-exploration. Counsellors may also suggest alternative value systems but in ways that do not pressurize clients. Additionally, counsellors may disclose their own philosophies of living.

On a more mundane level, clients can be helped to generate alternatives by use of questions such as 'What are the options?' and by encouraging them to 'brainstorm'. The interest counsellors take in their decisions may loosen some clients' thinking in regard to new possibilities. Additionally, there may be outside pressures in clients' lives which, if handled sensitively, can lead to responsibility assumption rather than avoidance. For instance, unemployed clients get a series of rejection letters when seeking employment. Without counselling support, some might either give up or freeze their job-seeking activities into rigid and repetitive patterns. With counselling support, they might be more realistic in handling the rejection letters, for example by persisting in present job-seeking activities or flexibly thinking about employment alternatives or further reviewing how to occupy their time while unemployed.

Use of tests and measures   Sometimes counsellors can help clients better understand themselves by using occupational tests and measures as part of evaluating clients' interests, values, aptitudes, abilities and behaviour. Details of psychological tests are available elsewhere (Buros: 1978; Anastasi: 1982; Nelson-Jones: 1982a). However, below are a few points about client responsibility and testing. First, it is preferable if clients play a role in deciding when to test and the characteristics to be tested. This is similar to *precision* testing, tailoring tests to individuals rather than *saturation* testing, that is administering a battery of tests only some of which may have relevance for individuals (Super: 1950). The responsibility for choosing tests should also, as much as possible, be joint between counsellors and clients. Second, in presenting a rationale for using tests, counsellors can ensure that clients understand that they are only one means of gaining information about themselves. Also, that clients do not abdicate responsibility for defining themselves by unquestioning reliance on 'what the tests say'. Third, counsellors need beware of clients' responsibility avoidances when test results are reported. Since some test feedback may vary with existing self-conceptions, attention needs to be paid to clients' feelings and self-protective processes.

Fourth, sometimes clients can take responsibility for choosing, administering, scoring and understanding their own tests. An example is Holland's *Self-directed Search* (Holland: 1979). Here the counsellor's role is that of back-up resource, only to be used if clients cannot manage on their own. Fifth, counsellors may not be able to find appropriate tests for particular clients. For example, there appears no test ideally suited to people, like the retired or long-term unemployed, whose needs may fall between measures focused either on employment or on leisure. Here there is a responsibility for the helping professions to develop appropriate measures. Sixth, some measures from clinical settings may help depressed clients identify activities that are rewarding for them. Two examples are MacPhillamy and Lewinsohn's *Pleasant Events Schedule* and Cautela's *Reinforcement Survey Schedule* (MacPhillamy and Lewinsohn: 1982; Cautela: 1967). The current widespread unemployment has highlighted the fact that the occupational and emotional areas of people's lives are closely interwoven.

Facilitating information gathering   Counsellors can help clients assume responsibility for gathering appropriate information. This may consist of a number of interventions including: providing clients with the information; letting them know where to find it; and encouraging the development of information-gathering skills. Information gathering can be presented as part of learning to make occupational decisions wisely. It has a number of different functions: helping clients search for alternatives; getting a fuller understanding of particular alternatives; and helping clients effectively implement their occupational choices. There are many issues concerning client responsibility in gathering information. First, they are much more likely to use information that is available, easily comprehensible and accurate. Second, they should be helped to identify what information is appropriate for them rather than have the responsibility for this entirely taken over by counsellors Third, counsellors need to weigh up carefully the advantages and disadvantages of presenting information to clients as contrasted with giving them responsibility for gathering it. Fourth, counsellors may have to teach some clients the skills of information gathering. Fifth, counsellors need to be alert to client responsibility avoidances regarding both gathering information and also perceiving it accurately. Sixth, the most appropriate way for a client to gather certain kinds of information may be by *doing* rather than by reading or talking. This might include trying out the activity itself, trying out a simulation of the activity, and, though less direct, the opportunity to observe and interact with people regularly engaging in it. Sometimes it may be appropriate for counsellors to present information. However, the main emphasis should be on clients learning information-gathering skills. They may also need support in their initial attempts at implementing the skills.

Money counselling   A number of clients may be in distress because of real or perceived money worries. Also, some areas of rewarding activity may be closed because of shortage of money. For instance, students may be able neither to undertake courses nor to concentrate on them because of money worries. Unemployed people may also be extremely worried about meeting current financial commitments, such as education of children or loan agreements. Counsellors need to familiarize themselves with financial information relevant to their clienteles, such as scholarship, grant and loan information for students, and debt and benefit information for the unemployed, and when they cannot provide the information they should make effective referrals. Additionally, counsellors can reduce some clients' anxieties about money by helping them perceive their situation more realistically. This includes helping them acknowledge their own strengths in dealing with adversity. For instance, some unemployed clients may be greatly helped by professional support, both emotional and in terms of acquiring job-seeking skills, as they struggle to find their way back into employment.

Focusing on action planning Much of this chapter has been focused on decision *making*. Counsellors can also help clients develop the skills of making plans to *implement* decisions. Obvious as it may seem, these plans should be based on clear statements of goals. They should then contain step-by-step approaches to attaining each goal. Furthermore, attention should be paid to: fears and anxieties about implementing plans; monitoring progress; and coping with setbacks, including using task-oriented inner speech. It is often helpful if clients write an outline of their plans. Possible areas for action planning include: obtaining jobs; implementing programmes of retirement activities; and developing schedules of meaningful activities while unemployed.

Focusing on coping with transitions Transitions are best prepared for in advance. Counsellors can help clients understand the psychology of transitions. Even positive transitions, for example a better job, are likely to be stressful. Negative transitions, for example unwanted unemployment, create numerous stresses. Counsellors can prepare clients for change by helping them anticipate problems that are likely to arise. Lazarus writes of an 'anti-future shock imagery' technique: 'By taking stock of the most probable changes that are likely to occur, and by encouraging the client to *visualize* himself or herself coping with these changes, you facilitate the client's acceptance of the inevitable' (Lazarus: 1981).

Whether counsellors are preparing clients for or working with them during transitions, there is much to be said for a problem-solving approach. Such an approach might include: reviewing clients' orientation to change; analyses of problems and of clients' coping capacities and support networks (Brammer and Abrego: 1981); making decisions based on these analyses; action planning; and evaluation. A problem-solving approach takes into account clients' feelings and is not just focused on thoughts and actions.

Focusing on managing stress Counsellors can help clients to handle 'distress' or excessive stress in their occupational lives, interventions for handling stress should be tailor-made. They include the following:

Focusing on internal rules and standards. Helping clients to identify unrealistic standards which contribute to their being 'driven, striven' individuals. Replacing such standards with more realistic reformulations.

Focusing on clients' recreational outlets. Exploring the extent to which clients lead balanced lives based on their own needs rather than on others' demands. Specific recreational activities, for example golf or tennis, might be explored and plans developed for participating in them.

Focusing on problem solving. Clients can be helped to identify situations where they perpetuate their distress. An example is that of someone sustaining a poor work relationship through always waiting for the other person to make the first move to improve it. Alternative ways of handling situations can be reviewed.

Assertion training. Sometimes clients feel under stress because they are insufficiently assertive. For example, a secretary may find difficulty in limiting her boss's requests for extra work. Counsellors can use behaviour rehearsal as part of coaching their clients in appropriate responding.

Focusing on task-oriented inner speech. Essentially Meichenbaum's 'stress inoculation' technique in which clients are trained in making appropriate coping statements before, during and after stressful situations (Meichenbaum: 1977; 1983).

Relaxation training. Clients can be trained in muscular relaxation procedures and in appropriate relaxation self-talk (Bernstein and Borkovic: 1973).

Focusing on physical health. Physical unfitness makes a contribution to many people's feelings of stress. This is partly a matter of their not exercising regularly, or they may be smoking too much, drinking too heavily, overweight and taking insufficient care over their diets (e.g. eating too much animal fat). Such individuals need to explore their attitude toward taking more responsibility for their health. Additionally, counsellors should refer clients to doctors where they have physical symptoms attributable to stress. For instance, even young people may require drug treatment for hypertension.

Developing support networks. On the assumption that 'a trouble shared is a trouble halved', clients can be encouraged to make their existing support networks more understanding and effective; and also, if necessary, to develop further support networks.

Group counselling Group counselling can focus on the emotional and occupational needs of specific categories of people: for instance the unemployed, the retired, and women contemplating reentering employment. As in cohesive groups focused on personal relations, much helping is done by other group members. An important function of counsellors is creating a climate in which people can drop social masks, show vulnerabilities, and allow themselves to help and be helped by others. As well as providing each other with emotional support, group members may help each other by modelling coping skills and offering sound practical advice. Counsellor skills in occupational groups include helping members: express and experience feelings; think more realistically; develop better personal relations; and cope with any tasks providing the ostensible reason for forming the group, for example handling unemployment.

Couples counselling and family counselling are variants of group counselling. For instance, couples might work through thoughts and feelings surrounding the division of activities inside and outside the home. The unemployment of a 'breadwinner' can have numerous ramifications for family life. Consequently, group counselling can be offered to families. The objectives are two-fold. First, minimizing the unemployment's damage both on family cohesiveness and on individual fmaily members. Second, enhancing the possibility of discovering challenges in the predicament conducive to individual and family responsibility assumption.

Training interventions

There are many possibilities for structured group training programmes in the area of rewarding activity. Sometimes a number of skills training programmes are grouped together under an umbrella term like 'careers education', especially if these training programmes are conducted in school settings. A few of the many training possibilities are mentioned below.

Training in opportunity awareness The contents of training programmes in occupational opportunity awareness include: lectures and seminars; outside speakers; occupational visits; films, videos and cassettes illustrating different occupations; use of interest measures keyed to suggest and describe suitable occupations, such as the *JiiG-CAL System for Computer Assisted Career Guidance* (Closs: 1980) and Holland's *Self-directed Search* (Holland: 1979); the chance to feed data into a computer and obtain information on opportunities matched to trainee characteristics; and games and activities simulating experiences in different occupations.

Opportunity awareness training needs be geared to its audience. School-leavers, women who have raised a family, and redundant executives each have different needs. If possible, since the barriers to opportunity may be internal as well as external, opportunity awareness training should include a focus on trainees' feelings and thoughts concerning the opportunities.

Training in decision making Counsellors can train people to be more effective decision makers. On the one hand, occupational decision making can be presented as a rational process involving: (a) defining decisions; (b) generating alternatives; (c) collecting information about alternatives; (d) examining consequences of alternatives; (e) if necessary, redefining decisions; (f) making decisions; and (g) monitoring and evaluating consequences. On the other hand, occupational decision making can be presented as a process in which people need also become aware of their unrealistic or irrational thinking. Training in decision making is best timed and integrated with important decisions for the trainees. Also it may entail training in making plans to implement decisions. Models, either on cassette or live, can verbalize the inner speech of effective decision making so that trainees learn to talk similarly to themselves.

Training in job seeking   Though training in job seeking assumes opportunity awareness and decision making, here the focus is on the mechanics of obtaining jobs once decisions have been made. There are a number of skills, including the following:

Action planning. Thinking through and outlining a step-by-step approach to achieving occupational goals, including ways of overcoming any tendencies to avoidance.

Written self-presentation skills. These include skills of letter-writing to prospective employers and of drafting a curriculum vitae.

Telephone self-presentation skills. Learning to present oneself and to answer questions on the telephone.

Interview skills. Many trainees may be insufficiently aware of the impact of their verbal, vocal and bodily communications on others. Furthermore, they may go to interviews inadequately prepared and fail to get into prospective employers' frames of reference. Video recorded interview practice is valuable in providing trainees both with insight into their behaviour and with material to discuss and learn from. Additionally, attention can be paid to how trainees handle areas of vulnerability and anxiety in interviews.

Handling rejection skills. Rejection letters create stress for many clients. The outcome of this may be to curtail or distort future job seeking. Counsellors can work with trainees on thoughts and inner speech for coping with rejection letters.

Training in managing stress   Training in managing stress can have a dual focus of helping trainees take responsibility both for living in ways that reduce excessive stress and for managing specific stressful situations. Training programmes can be designed relevant to specific groups. Virtually all counselling interventions for helping clients manage stress can also be used as training interventions.

Training in handling unemployment Training in handling unemployment can focus on skills and attitudes for reentering employment. Three areas here are: promoting job-seeking skills; developing new employment-related skills; and developing positive attitudes toward employment and acceptable employment habits (Hayes and Nutman: 1981). Another focus is on training people to handle the transition to unemployment, including their feelings. Transition training may be conducted either before or during the early stages of unemployment. This leads on to training people to handle the challenges provided by lack of structured activities in their lives. An additional focus for some is training in claiming welfare entitlements and in avoiding unnecessary financial hardships. Also, some may benefit from training in learning to define themselves to others as unemployed, including handling negative reactions. A further area in unemployment training is that of learning to use existing support networks and to develop new ones.

Training in relationship skills Counsellors can run training programmes to help people assume responsibility for more effective occupational relationships. To give examples: managers and supervisors may gain from training in counselling skills; many people need to learn to become more assertive at work, though this is likely to be more of a problem for women than men (Butler: 1981); managers and others need to learn leadership skills which facilitate rather than inhibit communication with those in subordinate positions. Public speaking anxiety is a further area for structured group training.

Additionally, relationship skills training programmes can be designed to meet the needs of specific jobs. For example, police can be trained to handle their anger when insulted and provoked; doctors to communicate bad news sensitively; and welfare officers to discuss benefit claims in ways minimizing rejection.

Self-therapy interventions

People's occupational lives are shaped by numerous influences over which they have varying degrees of control. These include: genetic endowment; technological developments; prevailing economic conditions; social policies; and the contingencies of good or bad luck. Nevertheless, within these parameters, individuals can exercise some choice in finding meaning and fulfilment. Below are some suggestions.

Inner empathy   Individuals can develop skills of being closely attuned to their feelings. For instance, in making choices about jobs or leisure, it is important that people listen to the feedback, both positive and negative, they receive from feelings. If a choice of career elicits anxiety, this is valuable information for consideration prior to embarking on it. Another example is that of people whose bodies communicate in all sorts of ways – fatigue, sleeping difficulties, tension, digestive difficulties – that they are excessively stressed. Failure to heed such warnings can lead to nervous breakdowns or, possibly, to heart attacks. People with inner empathy are aware of their limits.

Realistic thinking   People can discipline themselves to think realistically about their occupational lives. For example, they can counteract tendencies not to acknowledge responsibility for occupational fulfilment. Additionally, they can discipline themselves to take a problem-solving skills approach to decisions and difficulties. Thinking realistically under conditions of occupational distress, for example being in poor work environments or unemployed, is difficult. Nevertheless, it provides the best hope of avoiding greater distress. Also, of finding paths to fulfilment.

Developing relationship skills   There are numerous ways in which people can take more responsibility for their occupational relationships. These include developing the skills resources of effective listening, assertion, regulating negative feelings and resolving conflicts. These skills were mentioned in more detail in the preceding chapter.

Participating in health   Participating in health entails both avoiding bad and engaging in good habits. Many interventions were mentioned for handling excessive stress. These are skills that people learn to apply to themselves, and an ounce of prevention may be worth far more than a pound of scure. For instance, heart attacks can kill or permanently disable. Regulating weight and diet, avoiding smoking, and taking regular physical exercise contribute to health, as does maintaining a balance between recreational and nonrecreational activities.

Co-counselling   Co-counselling provides people with psychological space to work through occupational as well as other concerns. This can be independent of employment. Alternatively, a co-counselling network may be established within an employment setting. There is frequently much distrust and alienation in organizations. A co-counselling network might help participants relate to each other as persons as well as in task-oriented ways.

Peer self-help groups   There is a role for peer group counselling, possibly with professional support in the background, to help people deal with occupational concerns. For example, self-help groups comprised of the retired or the unemployed might not only lessen members' feelings of isolation, but also help participants take more effective responsibility for facing the challenges posed by their respective situations.

Support networks   It is valuable to have trusted people with whom to talk when occupational decisions, problems, set-backs or crises arises. People can identify in advance those to whom they can turn in times of occupational difficulty. A good support network may help those under stress keep more in touch with reality and thus avoid compounding their problems.

SUMMARY OF BOOK

The concept of personal responsibility provides a useful integrating focus for psychological theory and practice relevant to people in general rather than just to the moderately or severely disturbed. As old certainties erode and people come up against different life-styles, the pressures increase for them to assume responsibility for themselves. A brief definition of personal responsibility is that it is the process of making the choices that maximize the individual's happiness and fulfilment. Such choices relate to people's developmental tasks, transitions and individual life-tasks. Humans are always choosers.

Personal responsibility is an interrelated series of psychological skills. For each skill, people can have either resources, deficits, or a mixture of the two. The processes of acquiring skills resources include personal experiments, conditioning, learning from observing others, and the availability of adequate information and opportunity. Conversely, acquiring skills deficits entails deficiencies in the above learning opportunities. Skills resources and deficits are not only acquired initially, but also perpetuated. A number of important thinking errors, with accompanying inner speech, contribute to humans sustaining their distress. These thinking errors include possessing dysfunctional internal rules and misattributing responsibility. Additionally, lack of being empathically understood and adverse conditioning and modelling can contribute to perpetuating skills deficits.

The paramount objective of personal responsibility counselling and therapy is to increase people's effective conscious control over themselves and their environments so that they may best meet the four basic needs or four Rs of psychological well-being: responsiveness; realism; relatedness; and rewarding activity. Each basic need consists of psychological skills. Illustrative skills are: for responsiveness, existential awareness and awareness of feelings; for realism, realistic internal rules and realistically attributing responsibility; for relatedness, appropriate self-disclosure and empathic listening; and for rewarding activity, identification of interests and an appropriate activity level.

The notion of personal responsibility provides a framework for counselling, life skills training and living. There is no assumption of mental illness, no concept of cure and no blaming. A shift in the balance from skills deficits to resources is more likely to occur if people learn to assume responsibility for the ways in which they perpetuate their distress, and ultimately people need to learn to be their own best therapists. Furthermore, counsellors both in their professional and private lives, are continually having to resist internal and external pressures to avoid responsibility.

The effective counsellor possesses a repertoire of skills to facilitate clients' responsibility assumption. Some of these skills, for example empathic responding, are central. Other skills are much more the preserve of specific clients and problems. Specific counselling interventions in the area of emotional responsiveness include providing a rationale for acknowledging feelings and focusing on feelings questions. Interventions for realism include both identifying and reformulating dysfunctional internal rules, and clarifying and changing misattributions of responsibility. Interventions for relatedness include both focusing on thoughts and inner speech impeding self-definition, and help with handling aggressive feelings. Interventions for rewarding activity include focusing on realistic thinking regarding specific occupational decisions and using tests.

Counsellors may run structured training programmes focused on single or groups of psychological skills in each of the four Rs. For instance, life skills training programmes for relatedness include empathic listening, self-definition, regulating negative feelings and resolving conflicts.

The need for people to live within a personally responsible framework is stressed. Self-therapy involves developing and maintaining skills resources despite inner and outer pressures to avoid responsibility. As well as having good support networks, people may help themselves and others by participating in co-counselling networks and peer self-help groups.

Postscript

A final comment on being personally responsible is taken from Goethe's *Faust*:

Yes! to this thought I hold with firm persistence;
The last result of wisdom stamps it true;
He only earns his freedom and existence;
Who daily conquers them anew.

Appendix

Toward a theory of personal responsibility counselling and therapy: a list of theoretical propositions from Chapters 4 and 5.

Assumptions

1. Human existence is a process which takes place both within existential parameters and also within a continually changing world.
2. Humans are primarily motivated by a set of biologically derived needs and fears related to survival.
3. Ultimately each individual is personally responsible for his or her survival and unique fulfilment.
4. The process of being personally responsible is a continuous struggle in face of inherent human fallibility.
5. From early in their lives humans are in a continuous process of implementing and validating their self-conceptions. These self-conceptions imply definitions of other people.
6. Humans are significantly motivated by their fears and anxieties as well as by their wants.

Acquisition

7. Humans grow up in the context of a two-way power and influence process between themselves and the environment in which they negotiate a set of self-conceptions and, with varying degrees of success, acquire a repertoire of psychological and other skills.
8. Humans are more likely to develop a personally responsible set of self-conceptions and to acquire a repertoire of psychological skills resources if they are brought up having at least one significant adult in their lives with whom they have regular contact and by whom they feel understood.
9. The processes of acquiring personally responsible self-conceptions and psychological skills resources include personal experiments, conditioning, learning

from observing others and the availability of adequate information and opportunity.
10.   The processes of acquiring personal responsibility skills deficits include lack of empathic understanding, irresponsible conditioning and modelling, and lack of adequate information and opportunity.
11.   When humans are in groups and hierarchies, they may acquire and exhibit responsibility skills deficits that may differ from those in their one-to-one personal relationships.

Perpetuation

12.   Humans' self-conceptions and psychological skills resources and deficits mediate the quantity and quality of the information that they have available for making choices.
13.   There are a number of important thinking errors, with accompanying inner speech, which contribute to humans sustaining their distress.
14.   Humans who do not have access to at least one person who is able to offer them a relationship characterized by empathic understanding are more likely than those who do to sustain responsibility skills deficits.
15.   The processes of perpetuating personal responsibility skills deficits include irresponsible conditioning and modelling and lack of adequate information and opportunity.
16.   Humans tend to be part of groups and hierarchies which may also place pressure on them to sustain responsibility skills deficits.

Change

17.   Change in the direction of overcoming responsibility skills deficits is more likely to occur if individuals learn to assume responsibility for the ways in which they perpetuate their distress.
18.   The assumption of personal responsibility is more likely to occur if approached in the context of a relationship characterized by empathic understanding.
19.   Counsellors need a repertoire of skills in addition to empathic understanding if they are going to be as effective as possible in helping clients overcome their responsibility skills deficits.
20.   Counselling and therapy should not be seen independent of living and ultimately the best form of therapy is self-therapy.

REFERENCES

Abramson, L. Y., Seligman, M. E. P. and Teasdale, J. D. (1978). Learned helplessness in humans: critique and reformulation. *Journal of Abnormal Psychology, 87*, 1, pp. 49–74.

Adler, A. (1927). *Understanding Human Nature*. New York: Premier.

Ainsworth, M. D. S., Blehar, M. C., Waters, E. and Wall, S. (1978). *Patterns of Attachment: Assessed in Strange Situations and at Home*. Hillsdale, N.J.: Lawrence Erlbaum.

Altman, I. and Haythorn, W. W. (1965). Interpersonal exchange in isolation. *Sociometry, 28*, pp. 411–426.

American Psychiatric Association (1968). *Diagnostic and Statistical Manual of Mental Disorders* (2nd edn.). Washington: American Psychiatric Association.

Anastasi A. (1982). *Psychological Testing* (5th edn.). New York: Macmillan.

Ansbacher, H. and Ansbacher, R. (1956). *The Individual Psychology of Alfred Adler*. New York: Harper Colophon.

Asch, S. E. (1956). Studies of independence and conformity. A minority of one against a unanimous majority. *Psychological Monographs, 70*, 9 (Whole No. 416)

Bandura, A. (1977a). *Social Learning Theory*. Englewood Cliffs, N.J.: Prentice Hall.

Bandura, A. (1977b). Self-efficacy: toward a unifying theory of behavioral change. *Psychological Review, 84*, 2, pp. 191–215.

Bandura, A. (1978). The self system in reciprocal determinism. *American Psychologist, 33*, 4, pp. 344–358.

Bandura, A. and Walters, R. H. (1963). *Social Learning and Personality Development*. New York: Holt, Rinehart & Winston.

Bateson, G. (1960). Minimal requirements for a theory of schizophrenia. *Archives of General Psychiatry, 2*, pp. 477–491.

Beck, A. T. (1976). *Cognitive Therapy and Emotional Disorders*. New York: International Universities Press.

Beck, A. T. and Greenberg, R. L. (1974). *Coping with Depression*. New York: Institute for Rational Living.

Beck, A. T., Rush, A. J., Shaw, B. F. and Emery, G. (1979). *Cognitive Therapy of Depression*. New York: John Willey.

Bem, S. L. (1974). The measurement of psychological androgyny. *Journal of Consulting and Clinical Psychology, 44*, pp. 155–162.

Berne, E. (1961). *Transactional Analysis in Psychotherapy*. New York: Grove Press.

Berne, E. (1964). *Games People Play*. New York: Grove Press.

Berne, E. (1972). *What Do You Say After You Say Hello?* London: Corgi Books.

Bernstein, D. A. and Borkovic, T. D. (1973). *Progressive Relaxation Training: A Manual for the Helping Professions*. Champaign, Illinois: Research Press.

Blocher, D. H. (1966). *Developmental Counseling*. New York: Ronald Press.

Bornstein, P. H., Hickey, J. S., Schulein, M. J., Fox, S. G. and Scolatti, M. J. (1983). Behavioural-communications treatment of marital interaction: negative behaviours.

Journal of Clinical Psychology, 22, pp. 41-48.

Bower, S. A. and Bower, G. H. (1976). *Asserting Your Self: A Practical Guide for Positive Change*. Reading, Mass.: Addison-Wesley.

Bowlby, J. (1979). *The Making and Breaking of Affectional Bonds*. London: Tavistock.

Brammer, L. M. and Abrego, P. J. (1981). Intervention strategies for coping with transitions. *The Counseling Psychologist*, 9, 2, pp. 19-36.

Brown, P. and Faulder, C. (1977). *Treat Yourself to Sex*. Harmondsworth: Penguin.

Bry, A. (1976). *EST - 60 Hours That Transform Your Life*. New York: Harper & Row.

Bugental, J. F. T. (1978). *Psychotherapy and Process: The Fundamentals of an Existential--Humanistic Approach*. Reading: Mass: Addison-Wesley.

Bugental, J. F. T. (1981). *The Search for Authenticity*. New York: Irvington Publishers.

Buros, O. K. (ed.) (1978). *The Eighth Mental Measurements Yearbook* Vols. 1 and 2. Highland Park, New Jersey: Gryphon Press.

Butler, P. E. (1981). *Self-assertion for Women* (new edn.). San Francisco: Harper & Row.

Carkhuff, R. R. (1969a). *Helping and Human Relations: Volume One, Selection and Training*. New York: Holt, Rinehart & Winston.

Carkhuff, R.R. (1969b). *Helping and Human Relations: Volume Two, Practice and Research*. New York: Holt, Rinehart & Winston.

Cautela, J. (1967). A Reinforcement Survey Schedule for use in therapy, training and research. *Psychological Reports*, 20, pp. 1115-1130.

Closs, S. J. (1980). *Computer Assisted Career Guidance: Manual for the JiiG-CAL System*. Sevenoaks: Hodder & Stoughton.

Coleman, J. C. (1972). *Abnormal Psychology and Modern Life* (4th edn.). Glenview, Illinois: Scott Foresman.

Coleman, J. C. (1976). *Abnormal Psychology and Modern Life* (5th edn.). Glenview, Illinois: Scott Foresman.

Dweck, C. S. (1975). The role of expectations and attributions in the alleviation of learned helplessness. *Journal of Personality and Social Psychology*, 31, pp. 674-685.

Egan, G. (1977). *You and Me: The Skills of Communicating and Relating to Others*. Monterey: Brooks/Cole.

Egan, G. (1982). *The Skilled Helper: Model, Skills and Methods for Effective Helping* (2nd edn.). Monterey, Calif.: Brooks/Cole.

Egan, G. and Cowan, M. (1979). People in Systems: *A Model for Development in the Human-Service Professions and Education*. Monterey: Brooks/Cole.

Ellis, A. (1958). Rational psychotherapy. *The Journal of General Psychology*, 59, pp. 35-49.

Ellis, A. (1962). *Reason and Emotion in Psychotherapy*. New York: Lyle Stuart.

Ellis, A. (1973a). *Humanistic Psychotherapy: The Rational-emotive Approach*. New York: Julian Press.

Ellis, A. (1973b). Rational-emotive therapy, pp. 167-206 in R. Corsini (ed.). *Current Psychotherapies*. Itasca, Illinois: Peacock.

Ellis, A. (1977a). The basic clinical theory of rational-emotive therapy, pp. 3-34 in A. Ellis and R. Grieger (eds.), *Handbook of Rational–emotive Therapy*. New York: Springer Publishing Company.

Ellis, A. (1977b). Irrational ideas (handout). New York: Institute for Rational Living.

Ellis, A. (1977c). Personality hypotheses of RET and other modes of cognitive-behaviour therapy. *The Counseling Psychologist*, 7, 1, pp. 2–42.

Ellis, A. and Harper, R. A. (1961). *A Guide to Rational Living*. Englewood Cliffs, N.J.: Prentice Hall.

Erikson, E. H. (1963). *Childhood and Society* (2nd edn.). New York: Norton.

Feather, N. T. and Barber, J. G. (1983). Depressive reactions and unemployment. *Journal of Abnormal Psychology*, 92, pp. 185–195.

Feifel, H. (1969). Death – relevant variable in psychology, pp. 58–71 in R. May (ed.), *Existential Psychology* (2nd edn.). New York: Random House.

Ferster, C. B. and Skinner, B. F. (1957). *Schedules of Reinforcement*. New York: Appleton-Century-Crofts.

Fineman, S. (1983). Counselling the unemployed – help and helplessness. *British Journal of Guidance and Counselling*, 11, pp. 1–9.

Fish, B. and Karabenick, S. A. (1971). Relationship between self-esteem and locus of control. *Psychological Reports*, 29, p. 784.

Frankl, V. E. (1959). *Man's Search for Meaning*. New York: Pocket Books.

Frankl, V. E. (1967). *Psychotherapy and Existentialism*. Harmondsworth: Penguin Books.

Frankl, V. E. (1969). *The Doctor and the Soul*. Harmondsworth: Penguin Books.

French, J. R. P. and Raven, B. (1968). The bases of social power, pp. 259–269 in Cartwright, D. and Zander, A. *Group Dynamics: Research and Theory* (3rd edn.). New York: Harper & Row.

Freud, S. (1935). *An Autobiographical Study*. London: Hogarth Press.

Freud, S. (1936). *The Problem of Anxiety*. New York: W. W. Norton.

Freud, S. (1949). *An Outline of Psychoanalysis*. New York: W. W. Norton. Original edition, 1940.

Freud, S. (1962). *Civilization and its Discontents*. New York: W. W. Norton. Original edition, 1930.

Freud, S. (1964a). *The Future of an Illusion*. New York: Anchor Books. Original edition, 1927.

Freud, S. (1964b). *The Question of Lay Analysis*. New York: Anchor Books. Original edition, 1926 (1927 Postscript).

Freud, S. (1973). *New Introductory Lectures on Psychoanalysis*. Harmondsworth: Penguin Books. Original edition, 1933 (1932).

Friedman, M. and Rosenman, R. (1974). *Type A Behaviour and Your Heart*. Greenwich, Conn.: Fawcett Publications.

Fromm, E. (1942). *The Fear of Freedom*. London: Routledge & Kegan Paul.

Fromm, E. (1956). *The Art of Loving*. New York: Bantam Books.

Fromm, E. (1976). *To Have or to Be?* London: Cape.

Garfield, S. L. (1982). Eclecticism and integration in psychotherapy. *Behavior Therapy*, 13, pp. 610-623.

Garfield, S. L. and Kurtz, R. (1974). A survey of clinical psychologists: characteristics, activities and orientations. *The Clinical Psychologist*, 28, pp. 7-10.

Garfield, S. L. and Kurtz, R. (1977). A study of eclectic views. *Journal of Consulting and Clinical Psychology*, 45, pp. 78-83.

Garraty, J. A. (1978). *Unemployment in History*. London: Harper & Row.

Ginzberg, E. (1972). Toward a theory of occupational choice: a restatement. *Vocational Guidance Quarterly*, March, pp. 169-176.

Ginzberg, E., Ginsburg, S. W. Axelrad, S. and Herma, J. L. (1951). *Occupational Choice: An Approach to a General Theory*. New York: Columbia University Press.

Glasser, W. (1965). *Reality Therapy*. New York: Harper & Row.

Glasser, W. (1969). *Schools Without Failure*. New York: Harper & Row.

Glasser, W. (1975). *The Identity Society* (rev. edn.) New York: Harper & Row.

Glasser, W. and Zunin, L. M. (1973). Reality therapy, pp. 287-315 in R. Corsini (ed.), *Current Psychotherapies* Itasca, Illinois: Peacock.

Goffman, E. (1959). *The Presentation of Self in Everyday Life*. Harmondsworth: Penguin.

Goffman, E. (1963). *Stigma: Notes on the Management of Spoiled Identity*. Harmondsworth: Penguin.

Goldfried, M. R. (1982). On the history of therapeutic integration. *Behavior Therapy*, 13, pp. 572-593.

Goldfried, M. R. and Davison, G. C. (1976). *Clinical Behavior Therapy*. New York: Holt, Rinehart & Winston.

Goldfried, M. R. and Robins, C. (1982). On the facilitation of self-efficacy. *Cognitive Therapy and Research*, 6, 4, pp. 361-380.

Gordon, T. (1970). *Parent Effectiveness Training*. New York: Wyden.

Guerney, B. G. (1977). *Relationship Enhancement*. San Francisco: Jossey-Bass.

Hall, C. S. and Lindzey, G. (1970). *Theories of Personality*. New York: John Wiley.

Hannam, C. (1975). *Parents and Mentally Handicapped Children*. Harmondsworth, Middlesex: Penguin Books.

Harris, T. A. (1967). *I'm OK - You're OK*. London: Pan Books.

Havighurst, R. (1972). *Developmental Tasks and Education* (3rd edn.). New York: David McKay.

Hayes, J. and Nutman, P. (1981). *Understanding the Unemployed*. London: Tavistock Publications.

Heider, F. (1958). *The Psychology of Interpersonal Relations*. New York: Wiley.

Heron, J. (1973). Re-evaluation counselling: personal growth through mutual aid. *British Journal of Guidance and Counselling*, 1973, 1, 2, pp. 26-36.

Holland, J. L. (1973). *Making Vocational Choices*. Englewood Cliffs, N.J.: Prentice Hall.

Holland, J. L. (1979). *Professional Manual for the Self-directed Search*. Palo Alto: Consulting Psychologists Press.

Holmes, T. H. and Rahe, R. H. (1967). The social readjustment rating scale. *Journal of Psychosomatic Research*, 11, pp. 213–218.

Hops, H. (1976). Behavioral treatment of marital problems. In W. E. Craighead, A. E. Kadzin and M. J. Mahoney (eds.), *Behavior Modification: Principles, Issues and Applications*, pp. 436–439. Boston: Houghton Miflin.

Hopson, B. and Adams, J. (1976). Towards an understanding of transition: defining some boundaries of transition dynamics. pp. 3–25 in J. Adams, J. Hayes and B. Hopson (eds.), *Transitions*, London: Martin Robertson.

Houston, G. (1982). *The Relative-sized Red Book of Gestalt*. London: The Rochester Foundation.

Jackins, H. (1965). *The Human Side of Human Beings*. Seattle: Rational Island Publishers.

Jackins, H. (1970). *Elementary Counselors Manual*. Seattle: Rational Island Publishers.

Jacobson, E. (1938). *Progressive Relaxation* (2nd edn). Chicago: University of Chicago Press.

Jacobson, N. S. (1979). Increasing positive behavior in severely distressed marital relationships: the effects of problem-solving training. *Behavior Therapy*, 10, pp. 311–326.

Jahoda, M. (1958). *Current Concepts of Positive Mental Health*. New York: Basic Books.

Jahoda, M. (1982). *Employment and Unemployment*. Cambridge: Cambridge University Press.

James, M. and Jongeward, D. (1971). *Born to Win: Transactional Analysis with Gestalt Experiments*. Reading, Mass: Addison-Wesley.

Jenkins, H. (1983). Families and family therapy – future directions. Paper presented at the British Psychological Society Counselling Psychology Section, June 10 conference in London on 'Counselling Psychology and the Family'.

Jourard, S. M. (1964). *The Transparent Self*. Princeton, N. J.: Van Nostrand.

Kaplan, H. S. (1974). *The New Sex Therapy: Active Treatment of Sexual Dysfunctions*. Harmondsworth: Penguin.

Kelly, G. A. (1955). *A Theory of Personality: The Psychology of Personal Constructs*. New York: W. W. Norton.

Kelvin, P. (1981). Work as a source of identity: the implications of unemployment. *British Journal of Guidance and Counselling*, 9, pp. 2–11.

Kennedy, E. (1977). *On Becoming a Counsellor*. Dublin: Gill & Macmillan.

Kinsey, A. C., Pomeroy, W. B. and Martin, C. E. (1948). *Sexual Behavior in the Human Male*. Philadelphia: W. B. Saunders.

Kinsey, A. C., Pomeroy, W. B., Martin, C. E. and Gebhard, P. H. (1953). *Sexual Behavior in the Human Female*. Philadelphia: W. B. Saunders.

Laing, R. D. (1969). *The Politics of the Family*. London: Tavistock Publications.

Lazarus, A. A. (1981). *The Practice of Multi-Modal Therapy*. New York: McGraw-Hill.

Levitsky, A. and Perls, F. S. (1970). The rules and games of gestalt therapy, pp. 140–149 in J. Fagan and I. L. Shepherd (eds.), *Gestalt Therapy Now*. Palo Alto, Calif.: Science and Behavior Books.

Lewis, S. and Cooper, C. L. (1983). The stress of combining occupational and parental roles: a review of the literature. *Bulletin of the British Psychological Society*, 36, pp. 341-345.

Lieberman, M. and Hardie, M. (1981). *Resolving Family and Other Conflicts*. Santa Cruz: Unity Press.

Lieberman, M., Yalom, I. D. and Miles, M. (1973). *Encounter Groups: First Facts*. New York: Basic Books.

Luria, A. (1961). *The Role of Speech in the Regulation of Normal and Abnormal Behaviors*. New York: Liveright.

MacPhillamy, D. J. and Lewinsohn, P. M. (1982). The Pleasant Events Schedule: studies on reliability, validity, and scale intercorrelation. *Journal of Consulting and Clinical Psychology*, 50, pp. 363-380.

Main, A. P. and Roark, A. E. (1975). A consensus method to reduce conflict. *Personnel and Guidance Journal*, 53, pp. 754-759.

Margolin, G. (1981). Behavior exchange in happy and unhappy marriages: a family cycle perspective. *Behavior Therapy*, 12, pp. 329-343.

Margolin, G. and Weiss, R. L. (1978). Communication training and assessment: a case of behavioral and marital enrichment. *Behavior Therapy*, 9, pp. 508-520.

Maslow, A. H. (1965). *Eupsychian Management*. Homewood, Illinois: Richard D. Irwin, Inc. and The Dorsey Press.

Maslow, A. H. (1970). *Motivation and Personality* (2nd edn.). New York: Harper & Row.

Maslow, A. H. (1971). *The Farther Reaches of Human Nature*. Harmondsworth: Penguin Books.

Masters, W. H. and Johnson, V. E. (1970). *Human Sexual Inadequacy*. London: J. A. Churchill.

May, R. (1953). *Man's Search for Himself*. New York: W. W. Norton.

May, R. (1958). Contributions of existential psychotherapy, pp. 37-91 in R. May, E. Angel and H. F. Ellenberger (eds.), *Existence*. New York: Basic Books.

May, R. (1969). The emergence of existential psychology, pp. 1-48 in R. May (ed.). *Existential Psychology* (2nd edn.). New York: Random House.

Meichenbaum, D. (1977). *Cognitive-Behavior Modification: An Integrative Approach*. New York: Plenum Press.

Meichenbaum, D. (1983). *Coping with Stress*. London: Century Publishing.

Meichenbaum, D. and Genest, M. (1981). Cognitive behavior modification: an integration of cognitive and behavioral methods, pp. 390-422 in Kanfer, F. H. and Goldstein, A. P. (eds.). *Helping People Change* (2nd edn.). New York: Pergamon.

Merton, R. K. (1968). *Social Theory and Social Structure*. New York: Free Press.

Milgram, S. (1974). *Obedience to Authority: An Experimental View*. London: Tavistock.

Miller, G. A. (1969). Psychology as a means of promoting human welfare. *American Psychologist*, 24, pp. 1063-1075.

Mintz, E. E. (1971). *Marathon Groups*. New York: Appleton-Century-Crofts.

Moon, J. R. and Eisler, R. M. (1983). Anger control: an experimental comparison of three behavioral treatments. *Behavior Therapy*, 14, pp. 493-505.

Moreno, J. L. (1953). *Who Shall Survive?* New York: Beacon House.

Mowrer, O. H. (1964). *The New Group Therapy.* Princeton: Van Nostrand.

Mowrer, O. H. (1966). *Abnormal Reactions or Actions?* Dubuque, Iowa: Wm. C. Brown.

Mowrer, O. H. (1972). Integrity groups: principles and procedures. *The Counseling Psychologist, 3,* 2, pp. 17–33.

Mowrer, O. H., Vattano, A. J. and others (1975). *Integrity Groups: The Loss and Recovery of Community.* Urbana, Illinois: Integrity Groups.

Nelson-Jones, R. (1979). Goals for counselling, psychotherapy and psychological education: responsibility as an integrating concept. *British Journal of Guidance and Counselling, 7,* 2, pp. 153–168.

Nelson-Jones, R. (1982a). *The Theory and Practice of Counselling Psychology.* Eastbourne: Holt, Rinehart & Winston.

Nelson-Jones, R. (1982b). The counsellor as decision-maker-role, treatment and responding decisions. *British Journal of Guidance and Counselling, 10,* 2, pp. 113–124.

Nelson-Jones, R. (1983). *Practical Counselling Skills.* Eastbourne: Holt, Rinehart & Winston.

Nelson-Jones, R. and Strong, S. R. (1976). Positive and negative self-disclosure, timing and personal attraction. *British Journal of Social and Clinical Psychology,* 15, pp. 323–325.

Nelson-Jones, R., and Dryden, W. (1979). Anticipated risk and gain from negative and positive self-disclosure. *British Journal of Social and Clinical Psychology,* 18, pp. 79–80.

Nelson-Jones, R. and Coxhead, P. (1980). Neuroticism, social desirability and anticipations and attributions affecting self-disclosure. *British Journal of Medical Psychology,* 53, pp. 164–180.

Novaco, R. (1977). Stress inoculation: a cognitive therapy for anger and its application to a case of depression. *Journal of Consulting and Clinical Psychology,* 45, pp. 600–608.

Patterson, C. H. (1976). Correspondence to author dated 6 January 1976.

Parloff, M. D. (1967). Goals in psychotherapy: mediating and ultimate. In A. H. Mahrer (ed.), *The Goals of Psychotherapy.* New York: Appleton-Century-Crofts.

Pavlov, I. P. (1955). *Selected Works.* Moscow: Foreign Languages Publishing House.

Perls, F. S. (1969a). *Gestalt Therapy Verbatim.* New York: Bantam Books.

Perls, F. S. (1969b). *In and Out of the Garbage Pail.* New York: Bantam Books.

Perls, F. S. (1973). *The Gestalt Approach and Eyewitness to Therapy.* New York: Bantam Books.

Perls, F. S., Hefferline, R. F. and Goodman, P. (1951). *Gestalt Therapy.* London: Souvenir Press.

Pierce, R. M. and Schauble, P. G. (1970). A note on the role of facilitative responsibility in the therapeutic relationship. *Journal of Clinical Psychology,* 26, pp. 250–252.

Rayner, C. (1982). Handout on family breakdown. London: BBC.

Resnick, J. L., Resnick, M. B., Packer, A. B. and Wilson, J. (1978). Fathering classes: a psycho/educational model. *The Counseling Psychologist, 7,* 4, pp. 56–60.

Riesman, D., Glazer, N. and Denney, R. (1950). *The Lonely Crowd.* New Haven, Conn.:

Yale University Press.

Roberts, K., Duggan, J. and Noble, M. (1982). Out of school youth in high unemployment areas: an empirical investigation. *British Journal of Guidance and Counselling*, 10, pp. 1-11.

Rogers, C. R. (1942). *Counseling and Psychotherapy: Newer Concepts in Practice.* Boston: Houghton Miflin.

Rogers, C. R. (1951). *Client-centred Therapy.* Boston: Houghton Miflin.

Rogers, C. R. (1957). The necessary and sufficient conditions of therapeutic personality change. *Journal of Consulting Psychology*, 21, pp. 95-104.

Rogers, C. R. (1959). A theory of therapy, personality, and interpersonal relationships, as developed in the client-centred framework, pp. 184-256 in S. Koch (ed.), *Psychology: A Study of Science* (Study 1, Volume 3). New York: McGraw-Hill.

Rogers, C. R. (1961). *On Becoming a Person.* Boston: Houghton Miflin.

Rogers, C. R. (1969). *Freedom to Learn.* Columbus, Ohio: Charles E. Merrill.

Rogers, C. R. (1970). *Encounter Groups.* London: Penguin.

Rogers, C. R. (1973). *Becoming Partners: Marriage and its Alternatives.* London: Constable.

Rogers, C. R. (1975). Empathic: an unappreciated way of being. *The Counseling Psychologist*, 5, 2, pp. 2-10.

Rogers, C. R. (1977). *Carl Rogers on Personal Power.* London: Constable.

Rogers, C. R. (1980). *A Way of Being.* Boston: Houghton Miflin.

Rotter, J. B. (1966). Generalized expectancies for internal versus external control of reinforcement. *Psychological Monographs: General and Applied.* 80, 1 (Whole No. 609).

Rotter, J. B. (1972). Generalized expectancies for internal versus external control of reinforcement, pp. 260-295 in Rotter, J. B., Chance, J. E. and Phares, E. L. *Applications of a Social Learning Theory of Personality.* New York: Holt, Rinehart & Winston.

Rotter, J. B. (1975). Some problems and misconceptions related to the construct of internal versus external control of reinforcement. *Journal of Consulting and Clinical Psychology*, 43, 1, pp. 56-67.

Rotter, J. B. (1978). Generalized expectancies for problem-solving and psychotherapy. *Cognitive Therapy and Research*, 2, 1, pp. 1-10.

Ryan, T. and Walker, R. (1983). *Making Life Story Books.* Privately published. Available from 146 Austhorpe Road, Leeds, LS15 8E5, England.

Rykman, R. M. and Sherman, M. F. (1973). Relationship between self- esteem and internal-external control for men and women. *Psychological Reports*, 32, p. 1106.

Sanford, R. N. (1962). Developmental status of the entering freshman. pp. 253-282 in R. N. Sanford (ed.), *The American College: A Psychological and Social Interpretation of the Higher Learning.* New York: Wiley.

Satir, V. (1967). *Conjoint Family Therapy* (rev. edn.). Palo Alto: Science and Behavior Books.

Satir, V. (1972). *Peoplemaking.* Palo Alto: Science and Behavior Books.

Schutz, W. C. (1967). *Joy.* Harmondsworth, Middlesex: Penguin Books.

Seligman, M. E. P. (1975). *Helplessness: On Depression, Development, and Death.* San Francisco: W. H. Freeman.

Seligman, M. E. P., Abramson, L. Y., Semmel, A. and Von Baeyer, C. (1979). Depressive attributional style. *Journal of Abnormal Psychology*, 88, 3, pp. 242–247.

Selye, H. (1974). *Stress Without Distress*. Sevenoaks: Hodder & Stoughton.

Simonton, O. C. Matthews-Simonton, S. and Creighton, J. L. (1978). *Getting Well Again.* London: Bantam Books.

Skinner, B. F. (1953). *Science and Human Behavior.* New York: Macmillan.

Skinner, B. F. (1971). *Beyond Freedom and Dignity.* Harmondsworth: Penguin Books.

Smail, D. J. (1978). *Psychotherapy – A Personal Approach.* London: Dent.

Spindler, G. D. (1963). Education in a transforming American culture, pp. 132–147 in G. D. Spindler (ed.), *Education and Culture: Anthropological Approaches.* New York: Holt Rinehart & Winston.

Stafford, E. M. (1982). The impact of the Youth Opportunities Programme on young people's employment prospects and psychological well-being. *British Journal of Guidance and Counselling*, 10, pp. 12–21.

Steiner, C. M. (1974). *Scripts People Live.* New York: Bantam Books.

Steiner, C. M. (1981). *The Other Side of Power.* New York: Grove Press.

Sullivan, H. S. (1953). *The Interpersonal Theory of Psychiatry.* New York: W. W. Norton.

Super, D. E. (1950). Testing and using test results in counseling. *Occupations*, 29, pp. 95–97.

Super, D. E. (1957). *The Psychology of Careers.* New York: Harper & Row.

Super, D. E. (1977). The identity crisis of counseling psychologists. *The Counseling Psychologist*, 7, 2, pp. 13–15.

Super, D. E. (1980). A life-span, life-space approach to career development. *Journal of Vocational Behaviour*, 16, pp. 282–298.

Szasz, T. S. (1962). *The Myth of Mental Illness.* London: Paladin.

Szasz, T. S. (1973). *The Second Sin.* London: Routledge & Kegan Paul.

Thoresen, C. E. and Mahoney, M. J. (1974). *Behavioral Self-Control.* New York: Holt, Rinehart & Winston.

Tillich, P. (1952). *The Courage to Be.* New Haven: Yale University Press.

Trethowan, W. H. (1979). *Psychiatry* (4th edn.). Oxford: Blackwell.

Walker, A. M., Rablen, R. A. and Rogers, C. R. (1960). Development of a scale to measure process changes in psychotherapy. *Journal of Clinical Psychology*, 16, pp. 79–85.

Warr, P. B. (1983). Work, jobs and unemployment. *Bulletin of the British Psychological Society*, 36, pp. 305–311.

Watson, J. B. (1913). Psychology as the behaviorist views it. *Psychological Review*, 20, pp. 158–177.

Watson, J. B. and Raynor, R. R. (1920). Conditioned emotional reactions. *Journal of Experimental Psychology*, 3, pp. 1–14.

Whelan, W. and Warren, W. (1977). *A Death Awareness Workshop: Theory Application and Results.* Unpublished manuscript. Reported in Yalom, I. D. (1980), *Existential*

Psychotherapy. Basic Books.

Weiner, B. and Kukla, A. (1970). An attributional analysis of achievement motivation. *Journal of Personality and Social Psychology,* 15, pp. 1-20.

Wilkinson, J. and Canter, S. (1982). *Social Skills Training Manual.* Chichester: John Wiley.

Wolpe, J. (1958). *Psychotherapy by Reciprocal Inhibition.* Stanford: Stanford University Press.

Wolpe, J. (1969). *The Practice of Behavior Therapy.* Oxford: Pergamon Press.

Wolpe, J. (1973). *The Practice of Behavior Therapy* (2nd edn.). Oxford: Pergamon Press.

Worden, J. W. (1982). *Grief Counselling and Therapy.* London: Tavistock Publications.

Working Party on Marriage Guidance (1979). *Marriage Matters.* London: HMSO.

Yalom, I. D. (1975). *The Theory and Practice of Group Psychotherapy.* New York: Basic Books.

Yalom, I. D. (1980). *Existential Psychotherapy.* New York: Basic Books.

Zuroff, D. C. (1981). Depression and attribution: some new data and a review of old data. *Cognitive Therapy and Research,* 5, 3, pp. 273-281.

Index of Names

Index of Subjects